The Baptism of Jesus the Christ

The Baptism of Jesus the Christ

Ralph Allan Smith

WIPF & STOCK · Eugene, Oregon

THE BAPTISM OF JESUS THE CHRIST

Copyright © 2010 Ralph Allan Smith. All rights reserved. Except for brief quotations in critical publications or reviews, no part of this book may be reproduced in any manner without prior written permission from the publisher. Write: Permissions, Wipf and Stock Publishers, 199 W. 8th Ave., Suite 3, Eugene, OR 97401.

Wipf & Stock
An Imprint of Wipf and Stock Publishers
199 W. 8th Ave., Suite 3
Eugene, OR 97401

www.wipfandstock.com

ISBN 13: 978-1-60899-198-3

Manufactured in the U.S.A.

Unless otherwise noted, all Scripture quotations are from the American Standard Version, Thomas Nelson and Sons, 1901. Public domain in the United States. In some cases, the author has revised this version slightly for greater accuracy.

Scripture quotations marked ESV are from The Holy Bible, English Standard Version® (ESV®), copyright © 2001 by Crossway, a publishing ministry of Good News Publishers. Used by permission. All rights reserved.

Scripture quotations marked NASB are from the New American Standard Bible®, Copyright © 1960, 1962, 1963, 1968, 1971, 1972, 1973, 1975, 1977, 1995 by The Lockman Foundation. Used by permission.

Scripture quotations marked NKJV are from the New King James Version®. Copyright © 1982 by Thomas Nelson, Inc. Used by permission. All rights reserved.

Scripture quotations marked NRSV are from the New Revised Standard Version Bible, copyright 1989, Division of Christian Education of the National Council of the Churches of Christ in the United States of America. Used by permission. All rights reserved.

Scripture quotations marked YLT are from Young's Literal Translation, Robert Young, 1898. Public domain in the United States.

*This book is dedicated to my son, Berek Qinah,
with prayer and hope that he will fulfill the meaning of his name
and be truly zealous for the right worship of the Father, the Son, and
the Holy Spirit.*

כִּי לֹא תִשְׁתַּחֲוֶה לְאֵל אַחֵר
כִּי יְהוָה קַנָּא שְׁמוֹ אֵל קַנָּא הוּא

Exodus 34:14
(Deut 4:24; 5:9; 6:15)

Contents

Acknowledgments / ix

1. Introduction / 1
2. The Messianic Dimension / 24
3. The Adamic Dimension / 61
4. The Trinitarian Dimension / 102
5. The Christian Dimension / 152

Appendix 1 / 203

Bibliography / 229

Acknowledgments

Financial debt is a crushing burden. The Bible says that the debtor is a slave to the lender. Debts of gratitude, however, are different. To owe it to friends to tell them "Thank you" relieves the strains of life. To acknowledge such debts is a joy. I am, therefore, thankful to be able to thank so many people for the help and encouragement they have given me in writing this book. The only drawback to repaying these debts is the difficulty of mentioning them all, which I have certainly failed to do below.

First, I thank God for leading me through a weird and winding path to learn from His word. I trust He will continue to guide and teach me. Even in thanking, I covetously seek for more.

Next, I must thank my wife for enduring many long days when I did nothing but write and revise. Her love, wisdom, and support is and always has been crucial to my thoughts, my writings, and my life.

I am deeply grateful to Auburn Avenue Presbyterian Church and its pastor, Steve Wilkins, for inviting me to give the Bucer Institute lectures that were the basis for this book. The whole church was gracious, and I enjoyed the visit with them very much. Duane Garner and Jerrod Richey were especially helpful and kind. I am also grateful for the generosity of Covenant Presbyterian Church in Sulphur, Louisiana, whose generous contribution made the publication of this book possible.

As in previous books, I must acknowledge my deep indebtedness to the work of James B. Jordan and Peter J. Leithart. I do not always know when I am borrowing from their insights, and I have no doubt forgotten to give them credit for ideas which I learned in their books but which have become so much a part of me I did not think to footnote them. Jordan's and Leithart's books brought about a revolution in my own theological understanding and I highly recommend them to others. Jordan first introduced me to the idea of baptism as a covenantal ceremony. Through him I was persuaded of the importance of baptism and came to believe in infant baptism and child communion. Leithart's study on baptism, *The Priesthood of the Plebs*, is the best biblical theology of baptism I have ever read and the stimulus for my Bucer Institute lectures and this essay.

Also, through the Biblical Horizons email list I became friends with men like Jeffrey Meyers, who together with Jordan and Leithart, read an earlier draft of chapter 4 on the Trinity and offered helpful advice. Another friend of mine, Steven Wedgeworth, tried to dissuade me from certain positions in chapter 4. If anything in that chapter causes a problem, it was not Steven's fault.

John Barach did the work of copy editing for me and offered numerous detailed suggestions and corrections. John's interaction was invaluable. Without his help, this book would have been much less than it is. Needless to say, the remaining faults belong to me.

In addition, I owe a special word of thanks to a young man in our church, Keiya Kanno, who made it possible for me to read and search the *Complete Works of Cornelius Van Til* CD on my spectacular MacBook Pro. This enabled me to do word searches for topics like "self-consciousness" that Van Til does not address at length in any single place and that do not necessarily appear in an index, since most of Van Til's works have very limited indices at best.

Finally, I would also like to express my gratitude to the members of the Mitaka Evangelical Church who have prayed for me while I worked on this project and tried to show understanding to a busy pastor. When I began this work, I never imagined that before it was completed I would lose two church members, two friends. Christopher D. Witmer and Shigeru Suwazono, both still in their forties, were called home to be with Christ during the months that I was working on this book. They were good husbands and good fathers. They left behind godly wives and a total of eleven children. Our little church has suffered great loss. I hope that those who read this book will remember their families in prayer.

1

Introduction

The aim of this book is to help the reader understand Christian baptism from a perspective that many evangelicals may have never considered, or at least not considered deeply. In so doing, I am not offering new insights on baptism so much as reminding my readers of a very old view that many Bible-believing Protestants have forgotten. I am referring to the view of the early Church that the baptism of Jesus by John the Baptizer is a paradigm for Christian baptism. Anglicans, Catholics, and Eastern Orthodox are more familiar with this view, though it is not universal among them either.

At the same time, I hope to put this old insight into a new light, for the early fathers did not view the whole Scripture as God's covenant word. The covenant relationship among the persons of the Trinity and the place of the covenant in God's relationship with man and the world were neither central to their theology, nor related to their view of baptism. This means that though I agree with them that the baptism of Jesus is a paradigm for Christian baptism, I am also significantly modifying the paradigm itself because I understand baptism as covenant initiation. In this work, I propose combining the ancient view of Jesus' baptism with a covenantal view of the meaning of baptism, a marriage of insights that I believe profoundly enriches our understanding of baptism.

I intend to discuss the baptism of Jesus in four dimensions, that is, four different but overlapping and interrelated perspectives. First, I will introduce the Messianic dimension of Jesus' baptism and show that John was consecrating Jesus as Messiah of Israel. Second, I will offer a discussion of the Adamic dimension of Jesus' baptism, relating Israel's Messiah to the new Adam. These first two dimensions can be described as the biblical theology of Jesus' baptism. The last two dimensions are extensions of the biblical theological analysis, but view the baptism of

Jesus more in terms of systematic theology, while maintaining exegetical roots. Thus, the third dimension is the Trinitarian dimension of the baptism of Jesus, for in the synoptic accounts, we see all three persons of the Trinity in mutual relationship. Fourth, I hope to show how all of these dimensions come together in the Christian dimension, so that we will learn to look at Jesus' baptism to understand our own.

TWO PRELIMINARY MATTERS

Before I discuss the various dimensions of Jesus' baptism, this chapter must address two preliminary matters, one historical and one exegetical. First, there was a controversy at the time of the Reformation over the understanding of the baptism of John the Baptizer. Second, one of the most highly respected New Testament scholars of our day, James D. G. Dunn, in his classic work on the baptism of the Holy Spirit,[1] includes an extended exegetical argument against the view I hold. Dunn claims that the baptism of Jesus by John and the gift of the Spirit are two distinct events. Even more, he says they are "antithetical." His exegetical arguments require consideration, for if Dunn is correct, the entire thesis of this book is in error.

Rome versus the Reformers

Controversies about baptism lie at the heart of the Reformation since they are part of the whole controversy between Rome and the Reformers about sacraments and also since they are a central issue in the concurrent debate with the Anabaptists. Within the larger debate about the sacraments, the question of John's baptism had broad significance, as Steinmetz explains in his chapter on "Calvin and the Baptism of John":

> [T]he question of the status of John's baptism was an issue of some importance in the sixteenth century. John the Baptist stands between the two testaments and a number of crucial issues intersect in him. How one views the role of John in the gospel narratives affects in important ways how one views the nature of the history of salvation, the character of the sacraments, and the validity of infant baptism.[2]

---

1. Dunn, *Baptism in the Holy Spirit*.
2. Steinmetz, *Calvin in Context*, 157.

Introduction   3

Medieval theologians discussed John's baptism and most of them apparently agreed with the opinion of Gabriel Biel that since John's baptism lacked the correct Trinitarian form it was not true baptism in the sense of the Christian sacrament. For medieval theologians, Steinmetz explains, John's baptism was "sacramental (a sign that depends for its power on the piety of the recipient) rather than a sacrament (a sign that infallibly communicates grace)."[3] Thus, disciples of John the Baptizer who believed in Christ had to be re-baptized with Christian baptism, but this was not "repeated baptism" since the recipient had only been baptized in the name of the Trinity one time.

The Reformation era debate began with Zwingli's attack on the medieval tradition. Zwingli argued that the baptism of John and Christian baptism were basically the same. Since John taught his disciples to trust in the Coming One, who was Jesus, his baptism was, in effect, baptism in the name of Christ and therefore Trinitarian. Zwingli pointed out that Peter and others had been baptized by John the Baptizer, but there is no record of them ever being re-baptized. Of course, Zwingli denied the Catholic distinction between "sacramental" and "a sacrament" and regarded all baptism as "a sign that depends for its power on the piety of the recipient" rather than "a sign that infallibly communicates grace." From the Catholic perspective, this denial was Zwingli's greatest offense.

Thus, Zwingli maintained that baptism was a sign "but only a sign":

> It should never be confused with the thing signified, as the scholastics do when they claim the waters of baptism contain or convey grace. No material or external thing can justify. Grace remains in God's power, who gives it to the faithful by an immediate and invisible act. The flesh (that is, the world of material signs and symbols) profits nothing; it is the Holy Spirit who makes one alive. To place one's confidence in external rites and ceremonies is to lapse, willy-nilly, into idolatry.[4]

Luther famously and violently disagreed with Zwingli on the efficacy of baptism. Calvin's disagreement was both less famous and less intense, but the fact is he did not follow Zwingli in his view of sacraments as mere signs. However, both Luther and he did agree that the baptism of John the Baptizer was Christian baptism. From the first to the final edition of the *Institutes*, Calvin argued that John's baptism and Christian

---

3. Ibid., 159.
4. Ibid., 160–61.

baptism were "exactly the same" because "both baptized to repentance, both to the forgiveness of sins, both into the name of Christ, from whom repentance and forgiveness of sins came."[5]

Against this position, Rome was adamant. In the Canons of the Council of Trent, Session VII, Canon One on Baptism, the Church of Rome declared:

> Canon I.—If any one saith, that the baptism of John had the same force as the baptism of Christ: let him be anathema.[6]

What is the reason for this strong denunciation? First, as the medieval theologians make clear, it has to do with the importance of baptism in the Trinitarian name, for that was certainly not done before Pentecost and the Trinitarian name is essential to distinctly Christian baptism. True baptism must include the proper form, which includes baptizing in the name of the Trinity.

Surprisingly, however, this is not argued by the article on baptism in the *Catholic Encyclopedia*, which actually concludes, "All things considered, we can safely state, therefore, that Christ most probably instituted baptism before His Passion. For in the first place, as is evident from John 3 and 4, Christ certainly conferred baptism, at least by the hands of His Disciples, before His Passion."[7] The irony here is that the baptism practiced by the disciples in John 3 and 4 seems to be much closer to the baptism of John the Baptizer than to subsequent Christian baptism, since none of the essentials of Christian baptism—the Trinitarian name (Matt 28:19–20), identification with Jesus' death and resurrection (Rom 6:1ff.), and the gift of the Spirit (cf. 1 Cor 12:13)—could possibly be present at this stage in Christ's ministry. The *Catechism of the Catholic Church* does better by suggesting that John's baptism is not yet Christian baptism, since the baptism of Jesus is placed between old covenant baptism and Christian baptism.[8] At any rate, in spite of Trent's anathema, the Roman Catholic church is not necessarily unified, either in its view of John the Baptizer's baptism in general or, more particularly, of his baptism of Jesus.

---

5. Ibid., 164.
6. Schaff, *Creeds of Christendom*, 2:122.
7. Fanning, "Baptism."
8. *Catechism of the Catholic Church*, § 1223–24.

Another reason for the strong language of Trent may be found in the decrees of the Council of Florence (1439), which specifically distinguished the sacraments of the old covenant from the new by saying that the sacraments of the old were figures of Christ, but were not causes of grace, whereas the sacraments of the new were said to contain and confer grace to worthy recipients.[9] The Council of Trent followed this language:

> Canon VI.—If any one saith, that the sacraments of the New Law do not contain the grace which they signify; or, that they do not confer that grace on those who do not place an obstacle thereunto; as though they were merely outward signs of grace or justice received through faith, and certain marks of the Christian profession, whereby believers are distinguished amongst men from unbelievers: let him be anathema.[10]

Trent, in other words, endorsed the medieval view that because John's baptism is still an old covenant sacrament, it could not possibly have the "same force" as Christian baptism. What is at stake, then, is not just what is happening in baptism, but the whole question of the relationship between the sacraments of the law of Moses and the sacraments of the new covenant. Catholicism affirmed what Leithart calls a "semi-Marcionist" sacramentology,[11] because it radically distinguished the sacraments of the old and new covenants, making the old covenant sacraments dependent on the recipient's faith but the new covenant sacraments effectual instruments for conveying grace.

It was this view of the sacraments that Zwingli denied, but he did it by denying that any sacrament conveys grace. For him they are always mere signs. By arguing that no sacrament conveys grace, Zwingli attempted to undermine the whole Catholic doctrine of the sacraments. But he was also concerned with Anabaptists. By arguing for the continuity of the old and new covenants, he sought to establish a biblical basis for infant baptism. If the old and new covenants are essentially the same and infants joined the old by circumcision, then infants should join the new by baptism.

---

9. Leithart, *Priesthood*, 16 n. 23.

10. Session VII, Canon 6 "On the Sacraments in General," in Schaff, *Creeds of Christendom*, 2:120–21.

11. Leithart, *Priesthood,* 16.

Like Zwingli, Calvin came out clearly on the side of continuity in his theology of the old and new covenants,[12] though his understanding of the nature of a sacrament differed substantially. For Calvin, although the issue of the continuity of the testaments is involved, there is another, profounder reason why the baptism of John and Christian baptism are identified.

In Calvin's theology, what was important about the baptism of John was not what his baptism was for the Jews of Jesus' day, but what his baptism meant for Christ and for the Church. In other words, by insisting that the baptism of John was wholly continuous with Christian baptism, Calvin was interested primarily in demonstrating essentially the same point I argue for in this book, that the baptism of Christ by John the Baptizer is the paradigm of Christian baptism.

> Lastly, our faith receives from baptism the advantage of its sure testimony to us that we are not only engrafted into the death and life of Christ, but so united to Christ himself that we become sharers in all his blessings. For he dedicated and sanctified baptism in his own body [Matt. 3:13] in order that he might have it in common with us as the firmest bond of the union and fellowship which he has deigned to form with us. Hence, Paul proves that we are children of God from the fact that we put on Christ in baptism [Gal. 3:26–27]. Thus we see that the fulfillment of baptism is in Christ, whom also for this reason we call the proper object of baptism. Consequently, it is not strange that the apostles are reported to have baptized in his name [Acts 8:16; 19:5], although they had also been bidden to baptize in the name of the Father and of the Spirit [Matt. 28:19]. For all the gifts of God proffered in baptism are found in Christ alone. Yet this cannot take place unless he who baptizes in Christ invokes also the names of the Father and the Spirit. For we are cleansed by his blood because our merciful Father, wishing to receive us into grace in accordance with his incomparable kindness, has set this Mediator among us to gain favor for us in his sight. But we obtain regeneration by Christ's death and resurrection only if we are sanctified by the Spirit and imbued with a new and spiritual nature. For this reason we obtain and, so to speak, clearly discern in the Father the cause, in the Son the matter, and in the Spirit the effect, of our purgation and our regeneration. So John first baptized, so later did the apostles, "with a baptism of repentance unto forgive-

---

12. According to Leithart, Calvin failed to follow through with his basic conviction (*Priesthood*, 17).

ness of sins" [Matt. 3:6; 11; Luke 3:16; John 3:23; 4:1; Acts 2:38, 41]—meaning by the word "repentance" such regeneration; and by "forgiveness of sins," cleansing.[13]

Note Calvin's language. By receiving baptism from John, Jesus "consecrated and sanctified baptism in his own body." In his commentary on the Gospels, Calvin's comments are similar:

> Hence we infer, that his intention was not at all to distinguish between his own baptism, and that which Christ taught his disciples, and which he intended should remain in perpetual obligation in his Church. He does not contrast one visible sign with another visible sign, but compares the characters of master and servant with each other, and shows what is due to the master, and what is due to the servant. It ought not to have any weight with us, that an opinion has long and extensively prevailed, that John's baptism differs from ours. We must learn to form our judgment from the matter as it stands, and not from the mistaken opinions of men. And certainly the comparison, which they imagine to have been made, would involve great absurdities. It would follow from it, that the Holy Spirit is given, in the present day, by ministers. Again, it would follow that John's baptism was a dead sign, and had no efficacy whatever. Thirdly, it would follow, that we have not the same baptism with Christ: for it is sufficiently evident, that the fellowship, which he condescends to maintain with us, was ratified by this pledge, when he consecrated baptism in his own body.
>
> We must therefore hold by what I have already said, that John merely distinguishes, in this passage, between himself and the other ministers of baptism, on the one hand, and the power of Christ, on the other, and maintains the superiority of the master over the servants. And hence we deduce the general doctrine, as to what is done in baptism by men, and what is accomplished in it by the Son of God. To men has been committed nothing more than the administration of an outward and visible sign: the reality dwells with Christ alone.
>
> Scripture does sometimes, though not in a literal sense, ascribe to men what John here declares not to belong to men, but claims exclusively for Christ. In such cases, however, the design is not to inquire, what man has separately and by himself, but merely to show, what is the effect and advantage of signs, and in what manner God makes use of them, as instruments, by his

---

13. Calvin, *Institutes*, IV.15.6.

Spirit. Here also is laid down a distinction between Christ and his ministers, that the world may not fall into the mistake, of giving to them what is justly due to him alone: for there is nothing to which they are more prone, than to adorn creatures with what has been taken from God by robbery. A careful attention to this observation will rid us of many difficulties. We know what disputes have arisen, in our own age, about the advantage and efficacy of signs, all of which may be disposed of in a single word. The ordinance of our Lord, viewed as a whole, includes himself as its Author, and the power of the Spirit, together with the figure and the minister: but where a comparison is made between our Lord and the minister, the former must have all the honor, and the latter must be reduced to nothing.[14]

In his comments on Matthew 3:13, Calvin wrote the following:

For what purpose did the Son of God wish to be baptized? This may be learned, in some measure, from his answer. We have already assigned a special reason. He received the same baptism with us, in order to assure believers, that they are ingrafted into his body, and that they are "buried with him in baptism," that they may rise to "newness of life," (Rom. vi. 4.) But the end, which he here proposes, is more *extensive: for thus it became him to fulfill all righteousness*, (verse 15.) The word *righteousness* frequently signifies, in Scripture, the observation of the law: and in that sense we may explain this passage to mean that, since Christ had voluntarily subjected himself to the law, it was necessary that he should keep it in every part. But I prefer a more simple interpretation. "Say nothing for the present," said our Lord, "about my rank: for the question before us is not, which of us deserves to be placed above the other. Let us rather consider what our calling demands, and what has been enjoined on us by God the Father." The general reason why Christ received baptism was, that he might render full obedience to the Father; and the special reason was, that he might consecrate baptism in his own body, that we might have it in common with him.[15]

In these comments, Calvin expresses his motive for considering the baptism of John to be essentially one with Christian baptism. More than anything else, he aims to assure us that the baptism of Jesus was the paradigm for Christian baptism. Jesus, Calvin says repeatedly, "consecrated

---

14. Calvin, *Harmony of the Evangelists*, 197–98.
15. Ibid., 201–2.

baptism in his own body." When we are baptized, therefore, we are not only "ingrafted into the death and life of Christ, but so united to Christ himself become sharers in all his blessings."

I am in hearty agreement with Calvin's view that Jesus' baptism is the paradigm for Christian baptism. But I also have to agree with the older Roman Catholic view that the baptism of John was not Christian baptism. Early Reformed writers like Turretin took Calvin's side in the debate, but later writers tend to agree with the Roman Catholic view. Thus, Turretin expresses himself in language that is basically similar to Calvin, though this is only found in a polemic against Roman Catholic views of baptism rather than in a positive exposition of Christian baptism.

> The baptism of Christ ought not to differ from the baptism of believers, because he is the head and believers are the members; and because he ought to sanctify the use and sacrament of our baptism in his own; and because baptism is the symbol of the unity of believers in one mystical body (Eph. 4:5), not only with each other, but also with Christ, the head (1 Cor. 12:13; Gal. 3:27); and because his circumcision was the same as that of the Jewish people.[16]

Wollebius also follows the old Reformed view that the baptism of John and Christ are fundamentally the same, but he says nothing in his discussion of baptism about the baptism of Jesus by John.[17] When we come to later Reformed writers, like Charles[18] and A. A. Hodge,[19] Robert Lewis Dabney,[20] and John Murray,[21] Calvin's view is openly repudiated.[22] A. A. Hodge clearly expounds the differences between John's baptism

---

16. Turretin, *Institutes,* 3:400. The quotation above is from the third in a list of five reasons for regarding the baptism of John as identical with Christian baptism. However, Turretin admits "that some difference should be made between John's baptism and Christ's; but accidental with respect to circumstances and degrees, not substantial and specific with respect to essence; by reason of the mode of exhibition and measure of gifts and not by reason of the thing itself" (3:399).

17. *Beardslee, Reformed Dogmatics,* 129–32.

18. Hodge, *Systematic Theology,* 1:425.

19. Ibid., 603–4.

20. Dabney, *Lectures in Systematic Theology,* 763–64.

21. Murray, *Christian Baptism,* 1–2.

22. William G. T. Shedd is an exception to the rule (*Dogmatic Theology,* 823).

and Christian baptism, affirming that they are essentially diverse, one belonging to the old covenant, the other to the new.[23]

Louis Berkhof summarizes the debate and attempts, it seems, to hold a mediating position:

> Another question that calls for consideration, is that of the relation of the baptism of John to that of Jesus. The Roman Catholic Church in the Canons of Trent curses those who say that the baptism of John equalled that of Jesus in efficacy, and regards it, along with the Old Testament sacraments, as purely typical. It claims that those who were baptized by John did not receive real baptismal grace in this baptism, and were at a later time re-baptized, or, more correctly expressed, baptized for the first time in the Christian manner. The older Lutheran theologians maintained that the two were identical as far as *purpose* and *efficacy* were concerned, while some of the later ones rejected what they considered to be a complete and essential identity of the two. Something similar may be said of Reformed theologians. The older theologians generally identified the two baptisms, while those of a more recent date direct attention to certain differences. John himself would seem to call attention to a point of difference in Matt. 3:11. Some also find a proof for the essential difference of the two in Acts 19:1–6, which, according to them, records a case in which some, who were baptized by John, were re-baptized. But this interpretation is subject to doubt. It would seem to be correct to say that the two are *essentially* identical, though differing in some points. The baptism of John, like the Christian baptism, (a) was instituted by God Himself, Matt. 21:25; John 1:33; (b) was connected with a radical change of life, Luke 1:1–17; John 1:20–30; (c) stood in sacramental relation to the forgiveness of sins, Matt. 3:7, 8; Mark 1:4; Luke 3:3 (comp. Acts 2:28) and (d) employed the same material element, namely, water. At the same time there were several points of difference: (a) the baptism of John still belonged to the old dispensation, and as such pointed forward to Christ; (b) in harmony with the dispensation of the law in general, it stressed the necessity of repentance, though not entirely to the exclusion of faith; (c) it was intended for the Jews only, and therefore represented the Old Testament particularism rather than the New Testament universalism; and (d) since the Holy Spirit had not yet been poured out in pentecostal fulness, it

---

23. Hodge, *Outlines of Theology*, 603–4.

was not yet accompanied with as great a measure of spiritual gifts as the later Christian baptism.[24]

We have, then, a case of a Reformation debate in which something like the older Roman Catholic view is now espoused by most Reformed theologians, while at least a few Roman Catholic theologians now hold to something like Calvin's view of the baptism of Jesus, though of course with nuances that Calvin would not acknowledge.[25] In this essay, I hope to show that both Calvin and his Reformed critics are correct in different ways. On the one hand, I agree with Calvin's view of the baptism of Jesus as essential to our understanding of Christian baptism, especially with my understanding of covenant initiation. On the other hand, however, I also believe that, understanding the baptism of Jesus in the larger context of covenantal history, later Reformed writers are correct in asserting that the baptism of John the Baptizer was indeed fundamentally different from Christian baptism. One key to my view is to distinguish the baptism of Jesus by John the Baptizer from his ordinary practice of a baptism of repentance.

James D. G. Dunn's View

No study of the baptism of Jesus and the work of the Spirit can afford to neglect James D. G. Dunn's classic work on the baptism of the Holy Spirit. Dunn, one of the most respected and prolific New Testament scholars of our day, wrote this book in 1970 and it remains one of the most rewarding studies in print because of its rich exegetical and theological insights.

Dunn's inquiry into the New Testament doctrine of the baptism of the Holy Spirit aims primarily to respond to the Pentecostal doctrine. Through detailed attention to the New Testament teaching about the gift of the Spirit, Dunn shows that the notion of a second blessing is not biblically grounded. But Dunn also attempts to refute traditional "sacramental" understanding of baptism, by demonstrating that water baptism and the gift of the Spirit are not only basically distinct, but "antithetical." On this point, I believe, his work is seriously flawed.

Let me begin by quoting some of the concluding words of his section on the baptism of Jesus by John:

---

24. William G. T. Shedd is an exception to the rule (*Dogmatic Theology*, 823).
25. See McDonnell, *Baptism of Jesus*.

> It is quite evident, therefore, that much theologizing about the relation between baptism and the Spirit has been based on a fundamental mistake. Indeed, the false conclusions drawn from "the baptism of Jesus" have been the chief source of the unscriptural views about Christian baptism which for far too long have discomforted the Church's understanding of the Holy Spirit. It must be stated emphatically, that the baptism of Jesus and the descent of the Spirit are two distinct events—closely related, but distinct. Moreover, the emphasis in any theologizing on these events should fall on the descent of the Spirit: the baptism is only a preliminary to it—a necessary preliminary perhaps, but a preliminary. John's baptism remains in the role and with the significance John himself gave it—essentially preparatory for and antithetical to the imminent Spirit-baptism. It was not water-baptism which initiated into the messianic office, but only the baptism in Spirit.[26]

Here we see, I believe, one aspect[27] of Dunn's theological agenda for his study of baptism and the Holy Spirit. He intends to set the record straight and deliver us from what he sees as a "fundamental mistake" and as "false conclusions" that have led the Church to an unscriptural doctrine of baptism.

Similarly, the introduction to this section of his book[28] also urges us to firmly reject the ancient view that Jesus' baptism is "the prototype of Christian baptism." The following quotation includes the basic structure of Dunn's argument, including the implication that clerics have not been honest with the text.

> We turn now to those who talk of Jesus being given the Spirit in, or even through his baptism, and of this baptism in water-and-Spirit as the prototype of Christian baptism. This interpretation must be firmly rejected. I have deliberately refrained from entitling this chapter "The Baptism of Jesus," for an examination of each of the four Gospels makes it quite plain that Jesus' baptism at the hands of John was not the principal interest. Nor can the concertina be expanded to make "baptism" embrace the whole event. The Fourth Gospel does not even mention the baptism, and the three Synoptics speak of the baptism as a completed act (all aorists) which preceded the main action of the pericope.

---

26. Dunn, *Baptism in the Holy Spirit*, 35.

27. As I said previously, his book is *primarily* aimed at investigating the Pentecostal interpretation of Holy Spirit baptism.

28. Dunn, *Baptism in the Holy Spirit*, 32–37.

> As elsewhere "baptism" means no more than the act or rite of immersion. To entitle this paragraph "The Baptism of Jesus" is therefore a misnomer. It reflects the interest of later ecclesiastics rather than the emphasis of the Evangelists.[29]

Though Dunn no doubt knows as well as anyone else that theology and exegesis cannot be neatly separated, he nevertheless implies that his view is exegetically rather than theologically motivated, in contradistinction to certain "later ecclesiastics." But, of course, Dunn's view is no less obviously theologically motivated. What I intend to demonstrate is that Dunn's exegesis of the relevant passages overemphasizes certain features while neglecting other important aspects, suggesting that it may be Dunn, rather than the clerics he refers to, who has not given due account to the text of Scripture.

Dunn claims that the ancient tradition of the Church was mistaken in believing the gift of the Spirit was an aspect of the baptism of Jesus. According to him, what the Gospels actually present are two distinct events. First, there is the baptism of Jesus by John. When this event is over, another event follows close behind. The heavens are opened, the Spirit descends, and the Father speaks His word of approval. Though Dunn acknowledges that the two events are related,[30] he also refers to them as "antithetical," fundamentally challenging the traditional reading of the text. If he is correct, our understanding of the baptism of Jesus and its meaning for His life and ministry may be very different. More than that, our understanding of the implications of Jesus' baptism for Christian baptism will certainly differ from the view of the ancient Church and that of Calvin referred to above.

Restating the arguments in the quoted paragraph from Dunn, we arrive at the following:

1. Baptism is not the principal interest.
2. Baptism is not broad enough to embrace the whole event.
3. John's Gospel does not even mention the baptism.
4. The synoptic Gospels speak of the baptism as a completed act (aorists).
5. Baptism means no more than the act of immersion.

---

29. Ibid., 32–33.
30. Ibid., 35–36.

Of the five points above, 1 and 2 are more assertions of his point than arguments to support it. Whether or not baptism is of principal interest is just the issue in question; it is the subject of the debate. To say Jesus' baptism cannot be conceived of broadly enough to embrace the whole event is simply an assertion of Dunn's conclusion about the limited meaning of the baptism. Those who disagree with Dunn are quite certain that baptism embraces the whole event without forcing the concertina to be unduly expanded.

The presupposition in point 5 that the mode of baptism must be immersion is debated by Christians of various denominations, but even if one could prove that baptism was not by immersion but by pouring, it would not change the nature of Dunn's argument. His point is that, whatever the mode, the act of baptizing is over and finished. The ceremony itself was a completed event. Therefore, the rending of the heavens, the gift of the Spirit, and the declaration of the Father constitute a separate event.

It seems to me, however, that this proves too much. If baptism is just the "water-rite" and nothing more, what about the words pronounced in Christian baptism when the minister says, "I baptize you in the name of the Father, the Son, and the Holy Spirit"? Certainly the words that accompany the baptism are part of the rite. Prayer before or after the act of baptizing would usually be considered part of the baptismal ceremony as well. When we consider the passages in detail, I think it will become clear that the synoptic Gospels record what Dunn sees as a separate event as, in fact, a necessary response to Jesus' baptism, bringing it to completion.

Dunn's real arguments are expressed in points 3 and 4 above. He devotes only one paragraph to point 3, but almost four pages to the exegesis of the synoptic Gospels, which point 4 summarizes. Concerning the Gospel of John (point 3), Dunn says, "Far from implying that this [the descent of the Spirit] was effected through or by water baptism John focuses attention exclusively on the operation of the Spirit."[31] This conclusion is supported by the fact that the Fourth Gospel does not even mention that John the Baptizer baptized Jesus. Also, two other verses in John that allude to the gift of the Spirit to Jesus make no mention of His being baptized by John (3:34; 6:27). So, for Dunn, the idea that John could see a connection between Christian baptism and the

---

31. Ibid., 33.

baptism of Jesus and nevertheless not even mention Jesus' baptism "is incomprehensible."[32]

This seems to me to be a very partial reading of John's Gospel and one that assumes that John is not self-consciously building on the Synoptics. What if, rather than repeating what has already been said three times, John intends to supplement? Consider the context in which the descent of the Spirit upon Jesus is introduced:

> "I did not recognize Him, but so that He might be manifested to Israel, I came baptizing in water." John testified saying, "I have seen the Spirit descending as a dove out of heaven, and He remained upon Him. I did not recognize Him, but He who sent me to baptize in water said to me, 'He upon whom you see the Spirit descending and remaining upon Him, this is the One who baptizes in the Holy Spirit.' I myself have seen, and have testified that this is the Son of God." (John 1:31–34 NASB)

The conversation about John's baptizing activity begins in verse 19 when men sent from the Pharisees ask John who he is. When they cannot get a satisfactory answer to bring back to their leaders, they become more specific in verse 25, "Why then are you baptizing if you are not the Christ, nor Elijah, nor the Prophet?" (NASB). It was John's baptizing in the Jordan that troubled the Jewish leaders in Jerusalem because so many people were flocking to him. John the Evangelist puts significant emphasis on the ministry of John the Baptizer, though he relates incidents not recorded in the synoptic Gospels. Thus, we should read John as an Evangelist who knows of and presupposes the content of the Synoptics—a perfectly naturally reading, since other apostles are aware of other New Testament epistles, such as Paul who quotes from Luke's Gospel and Peter who alludes to Paul's epistles. There is no reason to suppose that the Evangelist neglects the baptism of Jesus. John is leaving out part of the story that he knows his audience is familiar with and telling another story they may not know.

The proof of this is seen in the fact that John's Gospel not only does not mention the baptism of Jesus by John, but also does not mention the rending of the heavens or the voice of God. Why should the Fourth Gospel leave these profoundly significant details out of the story? Certainly not out of a desire to downplay them. The best answer is that John presupposes the Synoptics and his readers' familiarity with them,

---

32. Ibid., 33.

so that it is not necessary for him to repeat the whole story. What John does instead is tell us what John the Baptizer said the next day, after the baptism was over—his understanding of and reflection upon the baptism of Jesus, something we don't find in the Synoptics.

First, John the Baptizer says that he came baptizing so that the Messiah could be made manifest. In other words, he says in the most unmistakably clear language that his work of water baptism *resulted in* the manifestation of the Messiah. What specifically is he referring to? Some might say John is speaking of the fact that his baptism unto repentance prepared the way for the Messiah. That is no doubt true. But if John had not baptized Jesus in the Jordan with all the accompanying miraculous testimony, how would John's work of baptizing have identified Jesus as Messiah? The climax of John's baptizing work, the end for which it all aimed was achieved when he baptized Jesus and the Spirit of God came down upon Him, publicly identifying Him as the Messiah.

Second, John adds his own testimony to Jesus in the place of the declaration of God the Father. John the Baptizer was sent to baptize in order that the Messiah may be manifest to Israel. The Holy Spirit descended on Jesus, bringing John the Baptizer's work to its climactic fulfillment. In the Fourth Gospel, it is the Baptizer who boldly proclaims that Jesus is the Son of God, repeating God the Father's words, and associating that declaration with his own work of baptizing.

In addition, John's Gospel includes an allusion to Christian baptism which suggests that Old Testament prophecy about the gift of the Spirit is fulfilled in Christian baptism. Only John records the story of Jesus' conversation with Nicodemus in which Jesus says, "Truly, truly, I say to you, unless one is born of water and the Spirit he cannot enter into the kingdom of God" (John 3:5 NASB). Here water baptism and the gift of the Spirit are explicitly brought together in a context in which Jesus clearly says this is something that a teacher of the Old Testament should understand.

Contrary to Dunn, therefore, we have to conclude that John is not reluctant to join water baptism with Spirit baptism, nor does he simply not mention the baptism of Jesus. Rather the Fourth Gospel presupposes the Synoptic accounts and offers an account of John the Baptizer's testimony that emphasizes the significance of the baptism of Jesus, but instead of actually recording the event itself, John documents the Baptizer's reflection on his baptism of Jesus, the coming of the Spirit, and

Introduction 17

the Father's declaration. A careful reading of John's Gospel that assumes John is aware of the Synoptic accounts and in adding to them gives a very different picture than the one suggested by Dunn.

Dunn's discussion of the synoptic Gospels and his development of argument 4 constitutes the bulk of his demonstration that the baptism of Jesus and the coming of the Spirit are two events, not one. He begins with Luke 3:21–22 and says that Jesus' baptism is "passed over in an aorist participle." Dunn explains further:

> The aorist participle, of course, often signifies coincident action, but here the action of βαπτισθέντος obviously precedes in time the action of the *present* participle προσευχομένου. Had Luke wished to link the descent of the Spirit directly with the baptism he would have said βαπτιζομένου. As it is, he evidently intends us to understand that the descent of the Spirit coincided with the praying of Jesus, not with his baptism, which had already been completed. For Luke the Spirit is given in response to prayer, and neither in nor through baptism.[33]

This may sound very solid, but looking back at Luke and re-reading the single sentence in which all of these verbs appear hardly leads one easily to Dunn's conclusion. Here is the whole sentence, verses 21–22, in the literal translation by Young and two recent translations:

> And it came to pass, in all the people being baptised, Jesus also being baptised, and praying, the heaven was opened, and the Holy Spirit came down in a bodily appearance, as if a dove, upon him, and a voice came out of heaven, saying, "Thou art My Son—the Beloved, in thee I did delight." (YLT)

> Now when all the people were baptized, and when Jesus also had been baptized and was praying, the heavens were opened, and the Holy Spirit descended on him in bodily form, like a dove; and a voice came from heaven, "You are my beloved Son; with you I am well pleased." (ESV)

> When all the people were baptized, it came to pass that Jesus also was baptized; and while He prayed, the heaven was opened. And the Holy Spirit descended in bodily form like a dove upon Him,

---

33. Ibid., 33–34. John Nolland agrees with Dunn. "No longer do we have a report of Jesus' baptism. The baptism is stripped of all its details, is subordinated, linked to the baptism of all the people, and set into the past. The report is of what happened while Jesus was praying after his baptism" (*Luke 1—9:20*, 160).

and a voice came from heaven which said, "You are My beloved Son; in You I am well pleased." (NKJV)

Dunn is correct that the baptism of Jesus is presented as past and His praying as present, but that hardly requires us to infer that the event that immediately follows the baptism is not part of a complex of events logically related to the baptism. The three translations above each indicate how closely the various actions are interconnected. When all the people were baptized, Jesus was, too. When Jesus was praying immediately after His baptism, the heavens were opened, the Spirit descended, and the Father declared His love for the Son. Dunn's analysis of the participles is correct, but that should not blind us to the fact that this is all included in a single complex sentence. If Luke shared Dunn's view that there are two very distinct events being presented, perhaps he would have written at least two sentences to describe them.

Jesus own baptism is clearly associated with the baptism of the people, indicating that He is baptized as a representative. It seems, then, that on the one hand we have to say that Jesus' baptism is not altogether different from that of the people. On the other hand, however, we have to immediately add that Luke also points to a fundamental distinction in meaning and purpose. More than anything else, this is made clear by the fact that only Jesus' baptism is linked with a response from God and the pouring out of the Spirit. Though Jesus identifies with the people who are repenting of their sins, His baptism, unlike theirs, results in the gift of the Spirit and a blessing from the Father. The full meaning of that is what I hope to introduce in the next chapters, but for now the point is that the two verses in Luke are a single sentence describing a complex set of actions that are presented as a unified whole.

No doubt the emphasis is on the gift of the Spirit rather than the baptismal rite itself, but that does not imply that the gift of the Spirit is not part of the baptism, broadly conceived. In fact, through the prayer of Jesus, which only Luke records, Luke ties Jesus' baptism to the gift of the Spirit. Jesus' prayer at His baptism has not been concluded when the heavens burst open and the Father and Spirit appear. In that sense, we can almost say that in Luke the baptism of Jesus is still in progress when the heavens are opened and the Spirit descends.

Dunn treats Matthew and Mark together and admits that they associate the baptism and the gift of the Spirit more closely than Luke does.³⁴ He does not treat Matthew at length, but concerning Mark, Dunn makes a number of observations.³⁵

1. The use of εὐθὺς—"immediately" (Mark 1:10)—should not be given much weight since Mark uses it so frequently.
2. The present participle ἀναβαίνων—"coming up"—"does not describe the emergence above the surface of the water that follows the complete immersion; it describes rather the climbing out of the river and on to the bank after the rite has been completed."³⁶
3. Mark emphasizes the "antithesis" between water and Spirit baptism: "I baptized you in water; but He shall baptize you in the Holy Spirit"(Mark 1:8).
4. In Mark, there are three passages in sequence that "are bound together by the theme of the Spirit," from which Dunn infers that the Spirit is the central concern, not baptism.

In response to Dunn's first and second points, it seems to me that though the translation "immediately" might legitimately be watered down to "then" or "so then" in many instances, as Dunn argues, it is much more difficult to escape the implication of immediacy when εὐθὺς is used with a present participle. I believe the New Revised Standard Version translates the verse in line with the nuance of the original: "And just as he was coming up out of the water . . ." (Mark 1:10).

Dunn is correct that the participle does not refer to Jesus' emerging from the water after being immersed but rather to His emerging from the river, but the point to note is that Jesus was not yet out of the water when He saw the heavens opened. Dunn himself recognizes this: "Mark's picture is of the heaven opening and the Spirit descending actually while Jesus was climbing out of the water onto the bank, with his baptism completed."³⁷

Dunn's claim that Mark emphasizes the "antithesis" between water and Spirit baptism is a misreading of the text. What Mark actually emphasizes is significantly different. In the Greek of Mark 1:8, both the pronouns "I" and "he" in John's statement are specifically for emphasis and

---

34. Ibid., 34.
35. Ibid., 34–35.
36. Ibid., 34. Dunn points out here that Matthew says that Jesus left the water. Considering Matthew and Mark together, Mark's meaning is clear beyond dispute.
37. Ibid., 34.

contrast.[38] The antithesis, here, then is not between water and the Spirit, but between John the Baptizer and Jesus. Neither Mark nor his original readers would have understood 1:8 to assert a fundamental contrast between baptism by water and baptism by the Spirit, certainly not an antithesis that would be determinative for a Christian doctrine of water baptism. As for the fourth point—his view that the Spirit is the central concern of the passage—I concur. But that does not really demonstrate that what we have is two different events.

Having presented the relevant material in the synoptic Gospels, Dunn offers a three points to conclude his discussion, the third of which is worth quoting in full.

> Third, in all three Synoptics the eschatological features appear after the baptism. It was what happened *after* the baptism which brought in the new age. The baptism is not part of the eschaton or of its inbreaking. It is still the baptism of John, still the preparatory rite whose fulfilment lies not in itself but awaits the future. That the fulfilment follows the performance of the rite in the case of Jesus is due not to the rite but to the person involved in it....[39]

A detailed consideration of the Synoptics might rather lead to the conclusion that the eschatological features appear *in response to* the baptism. The baptism of Jesus brings in the new age because of what happened when He was baptized, distinguishing His baptism from the baptism of others. While Jesus was praying and before He had even completely stepped out of the water, the heavens are ripped open so that Spirit and Father can complete the baptismal consecration of the Messiah, bringing in the new age. They finish what John the Baptizer had begun. For John the Baptizer was sent to baptize in order that the Messiah would be revealed to Israel (John 1:31). The baptism of Jesus by John the Baptizer is therefore linked with the revelation of the Messiah and the coming of the Spirit (cf. John 1:32).

A verse that Dunn barely discusses is most important for understanding the baptism of Jesus. In Matthew 3:14–15, we have Jesus own testimony about the meaning of His baptism.

> John would have prevented him, saying, "I need to be baptized by you, and do you come to me?" But Jesus answered him, "Let it be

---

38. Guelich, *Mark 1—8:26*, 24.
39. Dunn, *Baptism in the Holy Spirit*, 35.

so now; for it is proper for us in this way to fulfill all righteousness." Then he consented. (Matt 3:14–15 NRSV)

Dunn refers to various aspects of Jesus' baptism and includes the idea of "submission to the will of God" with Matthew 3:15 as his text, but that is all he has to say about this important text. More than the other Synoptics, it is Matthew who show us clearly how the baptism of Jesus is related to the baptism of Jews by John the Baptizer, on the one hand, and to the subsequent coming of the Spirit, on the other, enabling us to arrive at the theology of the whole event.[40]

Note, first, that Matthew's Gospel associates the baptism of Jesus with the baptism of repentant Jews because Jesus specifically seeks out John in order to be baptized. Matthew recorded this after devoting twelve verses to describing what John's baptism was all about. It is clear, then, that in one sense, Jesus came to John like other Jews. Second, at the same time, Matthew brings the baptism of Jesus into sharp contrast with that of the repentant Jews, because he records John's attempt to prevent Jesus from receiving baptism. It was only when Jesus redefined His baptism that John was willing to continue. Third, John's baptism of Jesus is said to be a "fulfillment," a word Matthew uses often. To say that Jesus baptism is a "fulfillment" suggests an Old Testament prophetic or typological background. Fourth, Jesus defines His baptism by John as a "fulfillment of righteousness." Whatever exactly Jesus meant by this—a topic I will discuss later—it sets the baptism of Jesus in an Old Testament framework in which the issue is righteousness rather than repentance. John the Baptizer realized that what he was doing when he baptized Jesus was related to his baptism of the Jews, but also *qualitatively different* from it.

In addition to the details of the Gospel accounts, one must consider the broader New Testament witness concerning baptism. The descent of the Spirit on Jesus is called an anointing (Luke 4:18; Acts 4:27; 10:38). The baptism of the Spirit given to the Church is also called an anointing

---

40. Dunn holds to the primacy of Mark's Gospel and makes much of the so-called "antithesis" he finds in Mark. But suppose we held to the primacy of Matthew's Gospel. This was the view of the ancient Church and it has been argued for effectively by John Wenham. If we consider Matthew's Gospel as the first written record, then Mark and Luke presuppose the perspective already provided by Matthew. I would not want to build too much on this, but it is worth mentioning that on internal grounds alone, the priority of Matthew is no less plausible than the priority of Mark, but the theory of Matthew's priority has in its favor the unanimous testimony of the early Church. See Wenham, *Redating Matthew, Mark and Luke*.

(1 Cor 1:21; 1 John 2:20, 27). The parallel between the gift of the Spirit to Jesus and Jesus' sending of the Spirit to the Church is close enough to say that the Father "baptized" with the Holy Spirit. The close association of the gift of the Spirit with water baptism for the Church suggests similarly that the gift of the Spirit is given to Jesus in association with His water baptism. These parallels will be explored later. For now, it is sufficient to point out that Dunn is artificially putting asunder and calling antithetical what the New Testament clearly joined.

If we combine the testimony of the four Gospel accounts, we see that when Jesus was about thirty years of age, He sought out John the Baptizer to be baptized; that John, however, realized that he was not worthy to baptize Jesus and that Jesus did not need his baptism; that Jesus persuaded John to perform the ceremony on different grounds from others, grounds to be found in Old Testament prophecy or typology; that John did perform the baptism, as Jesus told him to; that when John baptized Jesus, Jesus prayed to His Father; that as Jesus was coming out of the river with John and was still praying to the Heavenly Father, the heavens were ripped open, the Spirit of God descended, and the Father declared His love for His Son.

Jesus' baptism is thus distinguished from the baptism of repentant Jews in two ways: first, by the conversation between John and Jesus before He was baptized; second, by what God did after He was baptized. But it is all a single baptismal scene. We cannot understand the baptism of Jesus without considering the whole. The fact that Jesus' baptism parallels the baptism of Christians in associating baptism by water and the Spirit provides a larger theological context in which the baptism of Jesus must be considered.

CONCLUSION

In this introduction, we have seen that the baptism of Jesus by John the Baptizer, though relatively neglected in recent Reformed theology, was seen by John Calvin as basic to the Christian doctrine of baptism, for Christ received baptism so that "he might consecrate baptism in his own body, that we might have it in common with him." Calvin's view of the baptism of Jesus by John the Baptizer needs revision in the light of the insights culled from recent biblical theology, but his view holds promise in rethinking the doctrine of baptism.

Dunn's attempt to set water baptism and Spirit baptism in antithetical relationship fails to accurately represent the accounts in the Gospels. His minute exegesis is challenging, but in the end he proves his point by exaggerating some details and neglecting others. In particular, he has not given due account to Matthew 3:14–15. He has also not given due consideration to the larger New Testament witness which indicates parallels between the baptism of Jesus and the baptism of Christians. In the chapters that follow, I hope to show that, contrary to Dunn, without the response of the Father and the Spirit to the Son, the baptism of Jesus would not make sense as the fulfillment of all righteousness. Also that Jesus' baptism is indeed the prototype or paradigm of Christian baptism. Indeed, it is the most succinct and concrete picture of new covenant baptism in the Bible.

2

The Messianic Dimension

In this chapter, I argue that Jesus' baptism in the Jordan was the inauguration of His Messianic ministry. In other words, though administered by John the Baptizer as part of his ministry of baptizing Jews unto repentance, Jesus' baptism was unique, fundamentally different in character from that of the Jews. That this was so appears clearly enough from the Gospel accounts themselves, but it becomes even more apparent when we consider the Old Testament background for John's ministry as a baptizer.

Of course, the decisive issue is to discover how Jesus' baptism in water by John is related to the coming of the Spirit and the declaration of the Father. We must, therefore, consider both of these matters in some detail as well. In the end, I believe it will become clear not only that the baptism in water, the coming of the Spirit, and the voice of the Father all belong together as one complex event—Jesus' ordination ceremony—but also that this event is the commencement of a new age, the beginning of the new covenant era, the definitive arrival of the kingdom of God. For in His baptism, Jesus the Messiah is anointed as King and Priest.

MINISTRY OF JOHN THE BAPTIZER

The ministry of John the Baptizer stands out in the Gospel accounts, not only as the introduction to the ministry of Jesus, but also as the link between the old covenant Israel and the new covenant ministry of the Messiah.

The Gospel Accounts

Each of the four Gospels begins the story of Jesus' ministry with the account of John the Baptizer's labor and each quotes Isaiah 40:3, referring to John the Baptizer as the one to prepare the way for Yahweh (Matt 3:3; Mark 1:3; Luke 3:4; John 1:23). Also, each shows that John's ministry found its purpose in introducing Jesus the Messiah to Israel. The three Synoptics record that, later in His ministry, some people thought Jesus might actually be John the Baptizer (Matt 16:14; Mark 8:28; Luke 9:19; cf. Matt 14:2; Luke 9:7–9), which indicates how close John and Jesus were in the minds of the Jews. The Gospel accounts overlap, but however similar they are, each Gospel presents John the Baptizer's ministry in its own distinct way.

Matthew emphasizes that Jesus' ministry is in continuity with the ministry of John the Baptizer by having Jesus declare in 4:17 exactly, word for word, what John had in 3:2: "Repent ye; for the kingdom of heaven is at hand" (μετανοεῖτε· ἤγγικεν γὰρ ἡ βασιλεία τῶν οὐρανῶν).

Matthew also includes a confrontation between John the Baptizer and the Pharisees and Sadducees, in which John the Baptizer calls them a brood of vipers, striking at the heart of their racial pride, "Say not to yourselves, 'We have Abraham as our father'" (Matt 3:9). Matthew obviously intends for us to note the parallel to Jesus' similar confrontations with these groups (Matt 5:20; 9:10–13, 32–34; 12:1–8, 14, 38–40; 15:1–9, 12–14; 16:1–4, 6, 11–12; 19:3; 22:15, 34, 41; 23:2–7, 13–15, 23, 25, 27, 29), since he uses the relatively rare Greek expression γεννήματα ἐχιδνῶν—"brood of vipers"—only three times, once on the lips of John the Baptizer (3:7) and twice in sayings of Jesus (12:34; 23:33), all referring to the Pharisees.[1] There is a further connection in Matthew 12, where Jesus almost copies John's earlier sermon. Just as John the Baptizer called the Pharisees a brood of vipers and warned them that good trees must produce good fruit (Matt 3:7–8, 10), Jesus calls the Pharisees a brood of vipers and warns them that they will be judged by the fruit their trees bear (Matt 12:33–34).[2] The continuity between Jesus and John the Baptizer is thus Matthew's distinct emphasis.

---

1. The word ἔχιδνα is used only five times in the New Testament (Matt 3:7; 12:34; 23:33; Luke 3:7; Acts 28:3). The whole expression "brood of vipers" (γεννήματα ἐχιδνῶν) is used only four times (Matt 3:7; 12:34; 23:33; Luke 3:7). Outside of Matthew, Luke is the only author who uses the word "viper," once in the Gospel and once in Acts (Luke 3:7; Acts 28:3). In the Gospel of Luke, John the Baptizer is denouncing the *crowds* as a "brood of vipers," and neither Mark nor Luke includes this word in Jesus' denunciation of the Pharisees. Thus only Matthew uses this expression to make a direct link between Jesus' and John the Baptizer's similar confrontations with the Pharisees.

2. In Mark and Luke, these connections are not made. Only Matthew puts the same

Among the Synoptics, Mark's account of John's ministry is the briefest. Though he basically follows Matthew, he emphasizes the *difference* between John the Baptizer's baptism and Jesus' baptism in a short sentence that puts the two prophets in sharp contrast. As I pointed out in previously, Mark is not making water and Spirit baptism antithetical, for the contrast is primarily between "I" and "He," rather than between the elements of water and Spirit (Mark 1:8).[3]

It is also noteworthy that whereas Matthew emphasizes the similarity of Jesus and John the Baptizer, Mark reports Jesus' gospel message in words that draw attention to the fact that Jesus fulfilled John's ministry.[4] Thus, for Mark the beginning of Jesus' ministry is set in Galilee, after John is imprisoned, and Jesus' call to repentance begins with the words "The time is fulfilled": "The time is fulfilled, and the kingdom of God is at hand: repent ye, and believe in the gospel" (Mark 1:15).

The kingdom that John the Baptizer had announced is here declared as present in the ministry of Jesus, for "the time is fulfilled." Though all of the Gospel accounts imply this, Mark places this emphatically at the beginning of his Gospel.

As much as we learn of John the Baptizer from the testimony of Matthew and Mark, compared to Luke, the information they provide is minimal. Only Luke gives us the fuller story of John, telling us that he was miraculously born to a family whose father and mother were both from the tribe of Levi (Luke 1:5); that he was named by the angel Gabriel, who also announced from the beginning that he would be the prophet like Elijah (Luke 1:17; cf. Mal 4:5–6); that he was six months older than Jesus (Luke 1:26); that his mother and Jesus' mother were related (Luke 1:36); that John the Baptizer first greeted Jesus when he was still in his mother's womb (Luke 1:41, 44); that his father prophesied at his birth that he would prepare the way of the Lord (Luke 1:76; cf. Isa 40:3); that he lived in the desert until the day he began his official ministry (Luke 1:80)—which implies that his ordination to the priesthood

---

sayings about a brood of vipers and fruit-bearing together on the lips of both Jesus and John the Baptizer, emphasizing the close relationship between them.

3. The use of the personal pronouns ἐγὼ and αὐτὸς ("I" and "he") is clearly emphatic.

4. The fact that John is merely introducing Jesus is a theme in all four Gospels. I am pointing here to distinctive emphases.

was extraordinary and not at the temple as a normal priest[5] —and that concerning John the Baptizer, "the people were in a state of expectation and all were wondering in their hearts about John, as to whether he was the Christ" (Luke 3:15). To this John "answers" the people in words that point to the one who comes after him, who is greater (Luke 3:16). In effect, John says, "No, I am not the Messiah, but He is coming soon." This places the baptism of Jesus in the context of Messianic expectation and strongly implies that it was Messianic anointing (cf. Luke 4:18).[6] As we shall see, this is corroborated by numerous details.

All of this is more than any other Gospel tells us, but Luke has an unusual way of both emphasizing and de-emphasizing the importance of John the Baptizer. On the one hand, Luke gives us the long account of John's birth, teaching us most of what we know about John the Baptizer. On the other hand, when Jesus comes to be baptized, Luke does not even mention that He met, spoke to, or was baptized by John the Baptizer. Though it is clear in the context, it is remarkable that Luke does not explicitly speak of John the Baptizer's involvement. After a proleptic report of John's imprisonment by Herod (Luke 3:19–20),[7] Luke returns to the baptism of Jesus, without mentioning John:

> Now it came to pass, when all the people were baptized, that, Jesus also having been baptized, and praying, the heaven was opened, and the Holy Spirit descended in a bodily form, as a dove, upon him, and a voice came out of heaven, Thou art my beloved Son: in thee I am well pleased. (Luke 3:21–22)

Here in a single sentence that does not mention John the Baptizer, Luke not only gives us the account of Jesus' baptism by John, but also tells us that Jesus was praying when the heavens opened and the Spirit descended as a dove "in bodily form." The emphasis, therefore, is entirely on the Father, Son, and Spirit, with the Jordan river and John the Baptizer not included in the long sentence that records the great event.

---

5. We know from John's Gospel that John the Baptizer was ordained by God (John 1:6).

6. See Strauss, *Davidic Messiah*, 200ff.

7. The exact chronology of the Gospels is extremely difficult, but there is no doubt about the fact that John was imprisoned long after Jesus' baptism. It may have been about a year later. Thus, Luke's presentation is intentionally "theological," bringing the ministry of John to an end as the ministry of Jesus begins.

Taken together, the Synoptic Gospels present John the Baptizer as a prophet from a line of priests, who grew up in the desert and ministered a Jewish cleansing rite out of the bounds of the temple authorities. John the Baptizer practiced a baptism of repentance, leading the Jewish people back to God. He was called to prepare the way of Yahweh, which meant that, like Elijah, his mission was to lead sinful Jews to repent, creating a remnant of true followers within the mostly apostate nation.

The identification of John with Elijah cannot be overemphasized for interpreting his place and ministry. It indicates clearly the dire spiritual state of the people and their need for repentance. But, as Matthew specifically stresses, Jesus' baptism cannot fit that mold, for He was anything but a sinful Jew who needed baptism to be restored to God. This provokes the question, If Jesus' baptism was not a baptism of repentance, what sort of baptism was it? Why did Jesus seek baptism?

Here is a question John the Baptizer himself could not initially answer. When John saw Jesus, he confessed that he should seek baptism from Jesus (Matt 3:14), obviously implying that he knew that Jesus did not need repentance but that he himself did. Jesus did not need John's water baptism, but John needed the baptism of the Spirit. In his confusion, John was attempting to prevent Jesus from being baptized. He must have known Jesus personally and regarded Him as far more righteous than himself. However he came to know it, he knew that he was unworthy to baptize Jesus. Perhaps John also suspected that Jesus was the Messiah. If that is true, it was still only a hope, because it was not until he saw the Spirit descend on Jesus that John was certain that Jesus was the Messiah, as the fourth Gospel, to which we now turn, sets forth clearly:

> On the morrow he seeth Jesus coming unto him, and saith, Behold, the Lamb of God, that taketh away the sin of the world! This is he of whom I said, After me cometh a man who is become before me: for he was before me. And I knew him not; but that he should be made manifest to Israel. For this cause came I baptizing in water. And bare witness, saying, I have beheld the Spirit descending as a dove out of heaven; and it abode upon him. And I knew him not: but he that sent me to baptize in water, he said unto me, Upon whomsoever thou shalt see the Spirit descending, and abiding upon him, the same is he that baptizeth in the Holy Spirit. And I have seen, and have borne witness that this is the Son of God. (John 1:29–34)

The fourth Gospel gives us a fuller picture of John's ministry as the one who fulfilled Isaiah 40:3. John came to baptize, preparing the way of Yahweh by creating a believing remnant to serve Him, ultimately in order that the Messiah could be manifest to Israel. This also explains why Jesus, who needed no repentance, came to John in order to be baptized (Matt 3:13). At the right time, when He was thirty years of age (Luke 3:23), Jesus initiated the fulfillment of God's will so that His Messianic ministry could begin.

In this context, it is important to note the intimate connection between water baptism and the gift of the Spirit. From John's testimony, it is clear that the manifestation to Israel was not primarily through the baptism in water—though John's ministry of water baptism was necessary—but through the descent of the Spirit onto Jesus, which fulfilled and finished the work that had begun in the water. The question then is, How are the two related? To answer this question, we need to first discover the meaning of cleansing rites in the Mosaic Law and see which, if any, is similar to John's baptism.

The Old Testament Background

The baptism of John the Baptizer obviously has its roots in the Old Testament, for when John began baptizing in the Jordan, Jews flocked to him, not to ask what baptism was or what it meant, but to be baptized. They must have thought they understood what John was doing, and they clearly believed they needed his baptism. Something in the culture of the first century Jews informed them of John's rite and it did not come from Greece or Rome. Neither the Essences nor the community at Qumran offer light.[8] The most reasonable place to look for the roots of John's baptism is in the Old Testament.[9] In fact, even the use of the word "baptism"

---

8. Both of these groups are so far out that the Gospels do not even address them. Jesus and the apostles do not treat them as a faithful remnant. On the contrary, they utterly ignore them. It is highly doubtful, therefore, that either of these groups provide background explanation for the ministry of John the Baptizer. As Aiden Kavanagh writes, "It is not a means for making gentiles Jews, as was proselyte baptism, nor is it wholly bounded by the bathing ablutions of the Essene ascetics or Qumran. It is its own distinctive thing, subsequently viewed by New Testament authors as the opening of a new order of things without actually being included in it" (*Shape of Baptism*, 10).

9. In this I disagree with Beasley-Murray, who claims, "The Old Testament Scriptures that John the Baptist appears to have had in mind in his adaptation of the lustrations are connected with the prophetic expectations of divine cleansing, and the refining and

in the New Testament points to an Old Testament background, since one of the Greek words for "baptism"[10] is also used in contexts that point to Mosaic ceremonial washings as "baptisms" (Mark 7:4; Heb 9:10).

What I am referring to are two especially relevant uses of the word βαπτισμός that must be taken into account:

> ...and when they come from the market-place, except they bathe themselves, they eat not; and many other things there are, which they have received to hold, washings (βαπτισμός) of cups, and pots, and brasen vessels. (Mark 7:4)

> ...being only (with meats and drinks and divers washings [βαπτισμός]), carnal ordinances, imposed until a time of reformation. (Heb 9:10)

Mark refers to a Jewish custom that was based upon the teaching of the law of Moses, even if it had been distorted by the Pharisees in Jesus' day. The law of Moses speaks repeatedly of the ceremonial washing of defiled clothing (e.g., Lev 11:25; 14:47; 15:5–8, 10–11, 13) and specifies that household articles of various sorts may be defiled by the dead bodies of "creeping" or "swarming" things (animals like mice and lizards).

> And upon whatsoever any of them, when they are dead, doth fall, it shall be unclean; whether it be any vessel of wood, or raiment, or skin, or sack, whatsoever vessel it be, wherewith any work is done, it must be put into water, and it shall be unclean until the even; then shall it be clean. (Lev 11:32)

---

judging work of the Messiah, rather than with the typology of Sinai and the ritual of the covenant" (Beasley-Murray, *Baptism in the New Testament*, 41). His discussion of the Old Testament antecedents for Christian baptism completely neglects the distinction between lustrations that are self-applied and those applied by others, thereby failing to treat the most relevant of the Old Testament rites, that of initiation to office.

10. The Greek noun βάπτισμα is only used nineteen times in the New Testament (Matt 3:7; 21:25; Mark 1:4; 10:38–39; 11:30; Luke 3:3; 7:29; 12:50; 20:4; Acts 1:22; 10:37; 13:24; 18:25; 19:3–4; Rom 6:4; Eph 4:5; 1 Pet 3:21). A related noun, βαπτισμός, is used only four times (Mark 7:4; Col 2:12; Heb 6:2; 9:10), one time clearly of Christian baptism (Col 2:12) and two times of Jewish washings (Mark 7:4; Heb 9:10); the fourth reference is disputed (Heb 6:2). The Greek verb βαπτίζω is used over seventy-five times in the New Testament (Matt 3:6, 11, 13–14, 16; 28:19; Mark 1:4–5, 8–9; 6:14, 24; 7:4; 10:38–39; 16:16; Luke 3:7, 12, 16, 21; 7:29–30; 11:38; 12:50; John 1:25–26, 28, 31, 33; 3:22–23, 26; 4:1–2; 10:40; Acts 1:5; 2:38, 41; 8:12–13, 16, 36–38; 9:18; 10:47–48; 11:16; 16:15, 33; 18:8; 19:3–5; 22:16; Rom 6:3; 1 Cor 1:13–17; 10:2; 12:13; 15:29; Gal 3:27).

Hebrews 9:10 refers to all the ceremonial washings of the law as "baptisms." This includes the baptism of household articles, the baptism of clothes, and the baptism of people when they become unclean, which would have been a relatively regular occurrence given the many possible sources of uncleanness. A Jew who took the law of Moses seriously would practice baptism for various reasons with relative frequency. If the law were literally practiced, it is hard to imagine an entire week going by without the need for at least one baptism on the part of at least one member of a Jewish family.

Though this shows clearly that old covenant washings were actually referred to as "baptisms," thereby pointing to the law as a possible source for understanding John, it is still not sufficient as background for John's baptism. Why? Because Old Testament Jewish baptisms were virtually all self-administered. Baptizing clothes, oneself, and household utensils did not require the ministry of a priest. It was done by the individual. Though these references to old covenant baptisms indicate a cultural context in which Jewish people were accustomed to the idea of ceremonial washing and frequently practiced it, they do not give us an answer to why Jewish people in Jesus' day would have understood what John was doing and responded in great numbers. There must be something more.

And there is. The law of Moses prescribed two initiatory baptisms that were performed by someone other than the person being baptized.[11] One was the baptism of the priest at his ordination (Lev 8). The second was the baptism of the Levite when set apart for tabernacle service (Num 8:5–15). In the law of Moses, only these two baptisms were rites of initiation performed by another. There is a third washing that is similar to the ordination of the priest—the cleansing of a leper (Lev 14:1–32). Even though the washing aspect of the leper's cleansing is performed by the leper himself (Lev 14:8), his representative bird is baptized and he is baptized by sprinkling with bloody water (Lev 14:6–7). But could these be related to the baptism of John? The answer to that question may be found through a consideration of the meaning of priestly baptism.[12]

---

11. The law also prescribed baptism to cleanse someone who had touched a corpse. This could be performed by any clean person and it included baptizing the tent in which the person died and all the utensils (Num 19:11–22). Obviously, this is not an initiatory rite and in certain circumstances it would be repeated.

12. As I have indicated previously, my entire argument relies heavily on Leithart's thesis in *Priesthood of the Plebs*.

To begin with, let us consider the ordination ceremony. We see from the book of Leviticus that it is a complex rite. In Leviticus 8, the ceremony is divided into seven sections, the heptamerous pattern suggesting that the ordination of the priest is an act of re-creation, one that corresponds to the re-creation theme as it appears in the Exodus narrative as a whole and in particular in the building of the tabernacle.[13] Samuel E. Balentine introduces his comments on the ordination ceremony with the following observations:

> The transfer of authority from God to the priests comprises seven steps, each one propitiously marked by Moses' faithful enactment of what "the Lord has commanded" (vv. 4, 9, 13, 17, 21, 29, 36): assembling the materials and the persons (vv. 1–5); washing the priests and clothing Aaron (vv. 6–9); anointing the sanctuary and Aaron and clothing his sons (vv. 10–13); the presentation of the purification offering (vv. 14–17); the presentation of the burnt offering (vv. 18–21); the presentation of the ordination offering (vv. 22–30); and final instructions concerning the consumption of the offerings and the duration of the ordination ritual (vv. 31–36). The seven-step process that "creates" a consecrated priesthood recalls, enacts, and ritually extends God's seven-day process of creating a world that is blessed with the possibility of being "very good." That possibility, from the priestly perspective, is part of an ongoing process. Its journey toward completion is marked by interlinked intervals of sacred "sevens": seven divine speeches that create the world (Gen. 1:1—2:4a); seven acts of obedience through which Moses completes the sanctuary (Exod. 40:19–32); seven divine speeches setting forth instructions for the holy sacrifices (Leviticus 1–7); and now seven consecrated acts that enable ordinary persons to become priests, holy stewards of sacred hopes and visions (Leviticus 8). Inside this heptadic world of ritual enactment, the ordination of Aaron and his sons is a major move founded on the hope that the world of God's creation can in fact be all that God created it to be.[14]

Priestly baptism, then, is one aspect of a more elaborate ceremony by which Aaron and his sons are ordained into the priesthood. First,

---

13. James Jordan ("The Tabernacle: A New Creation") shows that the narrative of the tabernacle construction in the book of Exodus is replete with allusions to Genesis 1, indicating clearly that the gift of the tabernacle to Israel in the wilderness constituted a "new creation."

14. Balentine, *Leviticus*, 70–71.

they are anointed with water when Moses bathes them, then with oil, and finally with the blood of the ram of ordination (Lev 8:6, 12–13, 23–24). This threefold anointing consecrates them for ministry by washing away uncleanness, empowering them with the Spirit, and removing guilt of sin.

As Peter Leithart argues in detail, in ancient Israel to be a priest means to be an attendant in Yahweh's house, serving both Yahweh Himself and His people.[15] Leithart explains the ordination bath and relates it to the baptism of John the Baptizer:

> Like Christian baptism, the washing at the beginning of the ordination rite was an administered initiation, and in these respects the ordination bath was unique in the Levitical system. While most Old Testament ablutions were self-washings, Moses washed Aaron and his sons (Exod. 29:4; Lev. 8:6; cf. Lev. 14:8; 15:16–18, 27); while most cleansing rites were repeated as often as one became unclean, the ordination washing was once-for-all. Though priests washed their hands and feet before approaching the altar or entering the tent (Exod. 30:20), this self-washing was not a repetition of the ordination bath since it was partial and not administered. Similarly, when the Levites were set apart to help the priests in tabernacle service, Moses sprinkled them with water, then they shaved themselves and washed their clothes before being installed through a sacrificial rite and the laying on of hands (Num. 8:5–15). The ordination bath and the closely related sprinkling of the Levites were the *only administered initiatory water "baptisms" in the Levitical system.* Tracing the form of Johannine and Christian baptism to priestly ordination and Levitical consecration is thus more plausible than the rival explanations. Baptism was described under other typologies, but its form points to a connection with ordination.[16]

Here we need to introduce one more feature of the Mosaic background for John's baptism. Leithart shows that the ceremony for cleansing a leper is parallel to the rite of ordination, meaning that a leper's reinstatement into the covenant community was a sort of priestly ordination because Israel as a whole was a nation of priests (Exod 19:6).

> Proof of the priestly status of lay Israelites is found in the rite for cleansing skin disease (Lev. 14). The overall trajectory of the

---

15. Leithart, *Priesthood*, 48–86.
16. Ibid., 95–96.

rite is the same as that of ordination. Lepers were cut off from the liturgical assembly of Israel, and the rite reintroduced them to tabernacle, just as priests in the ordination rite moved from the outskirts into the house. In several details, the cleansing rite duplicates the rite of filling:

1. Both rites began with washings, Lev. 14:8–9; 8:6.

2. Both followed a 7 + 1 day structure, 14:9–10; 8:33 and 9:1.

3. In both, blood was smeared on the right ear lobe, thumb, and toe, 14:14; 8:23–24.

4. Both High Priest and leper were anointed on the head, 14:8; 8:12.

These parallels suggest that the rites were mutually interpreting. Ordination cleansed Aaron and his sons from defiling affliction, and the cleansing rite inducted the leper into a kind of priestly ministry. Cleansed lepers were not, however, made priests for the first time, for that would have positively encouraged the proliferation of skin disease as a means of ascending Israel's liturgico-social hierarchy. The cleansing rite *restored* lepers to a priestly standing from which their uncleanness separated them. When did leper first receive this priestly standing? A clue to the answer is found in the temporal structure of the cleansing ritual: The main rite took place on the eighth day after the priest pronounced the leper clean (Lev. 14:10), and this recalls the eighth-day rite of circumcision (Gen. 17:12). Cleansing a leper, then, renewed his circumcision, as the priestly ordination was an extension of circumcision to the four corners of the priest's body.[17]

To summarize Leithart's research: (1) the baptism of the priest as part of his ordination service and the baptism of a Levite in preparation for temple service are the only two initiatory baptisms administered by another, and (2) the cleansing of the leper, which includes both self-administered washing and sprinkling by the priest, is parallel to the ordination of the priest, restoring the leper to the priestly community of Israel. Add to this what Balentine points out, that priestly ordination is a new creation ceremony.

This appears to be the old covenant background for the baptism of John the Baptizer. If John's baptism of repentance is more that just cleansing—that is, if it is cleansing as part of an ordination ceremony—

---

17. Ibid., 148–49.

then we can also understand why it is not repeated like most Levitical washings. According to Leithart, John baptized Jews not only to cleanse them of sin, but to define a remnant people by reinstating the baptized ones to their priestly calling under God. The question is, Does the New Testament description of John's baptism fit this picture?

The Old and New Together

To bring together the old covenant background and the witness of the Gospel accounts and to confirm what we have asserted about the Gospel accounts, we must take another look at the enigmatic figure of John the Baptizer. His ministry raises a number of questions:

1. Why do the Gospel accounts draw attention to his clothes and diet?
2. Why is the son of a priest not associating with the temple?
3. Why is he working in the wilderness around the Jordan river?
4. What is the significance of Isaiah 40 for John's ministry?
5. What is the significance of the prophecies in Malachi 3 and 4 for John's ministry?

Matthew and Mark both tell us that John wore a camel's hair garment and a leather belt around his waist, that he ate locusts and wild honey, and that he ministered in the wilderness (Matt 3:4; Mark 1:6). It may seem odd to take note of the Baptizer's sartorial inelegance and his strange appetite for bugs and honey, but the Gospel writers are not recording facts to fascinate the readers. Even in this scant information, there is a clear echo of Elijah, the hairy man with the leather belt who ministered in the wilderness.

We know this understanding is correct because Luke tells us that the angel Gabriel announced to Zacharias that John would be a prophet like Elijah (Luke 1:17), and this is confirmed by Christ Himself later in the Gospels (Matt 11:12–14; 17:10–13; Mark 9:11–13). The Gospel of John offers a much subtler association of the Baptizer with Elijah, mentioning only that he was sent by God (cf. Mal 4:5) and that his work, like Elijah's, was in the wilderness beyond the Jordan.

What kind of ministry did Elijah have? Elijah ministered in a time of apostasy calling a remnant back to God when the nation as a whole had departed. He ministered in the wilderness because that was where Israel had begun, in the wilderness with God. That was her birthplace. The wilderness ministry, then, constituted a call to a new beginning.

It was the same when John the Baptizer, a prophet like Elijah, summoned the Jews of his day to repentance and renewal, gathering a remnant of the faithful to serve God in truth. John's clothing, reminiscent of Elijah, helped to identify him to the Jews and to define his ministry. For a prophet to dress like Elijah and appear in the wilderness was at once a condemnation of the current system and an invitation to a new start.

It seems clear that the Gospels connect John's ministry with Elijah's, but we need to consider what exactly is being established by linking the ministry of these two prophets. At least three interrelated answers come to mind. First, though John himself denies that he is Elijah (John 1:21)—which presumably means that he is not Elijah in the sense the Jews of his day expected—Jesus clearly indicates that he is the one who fulfills the prophecy of Malachi:

> Behold, I will send you Elijah the prophet
> Before the great and dreadful day of Yahweh come.
> And he shall turn
> The heart of the fathers to the children,
> And the heart of the children to their fathers;
> Lest I come and smite the earth with a curse. (Mal 4:5–6)

This is nothing other than special preparation for the last days and the coming of the Messiah. John was sent by God (John 1:6) to prepare the way for Jesus by calling sinners to be reconciled with God and one another.

Second, if John the Baptizer is like Elijah, he is a prophet of exceptional stature. Again this is confirmed by Jesus when He says that John the Baptizer is the greatest prophet of the old covenant era:

> And when the messengers of John were departed, he began to say unto the multitudes concerning John, "What went ye out into the wilderness to behold? a reed shaken with the wind? But what went ye out to see? a man clothed in soft raiment? Behold, they that are gorgeously apparelled, and live delicately, are in king's courts. But what went ye out to see? a prophet? Yea, I say unto you, and much more than a prophet. This is he of whom it is written,

> Behold, I send my messenger before thy face,
> Who shall prepare thy way before thee.
>
> I say unto you, Among them that are born of women there is none greater than John: yet he that is but little in the kingdom of God is greater than he." And all the people when they heard, and the publicans, justified God, being baptized with the baptism of John. But the Pharisees and the lawyers rejected for themselves the counsel of God, being not baptized of him. (Luke 7:24–30)

Of course, this passage also indicates the connection between the prophecies of Malachi 3 and 4. There is one man, like Elijah but even greater, whose ministry will fulfill both.

Third, if the ministry of John the Baptizer is to be like that of Elijah, it is also implied that the time in which John lived is parallel to the days of Elijah, a time of gross national apostasy, especially on the part of the leaders. John's rebuke of Herod for his wicked wife conjures up images of Elijah rebuking Ahab and Jezebel. In both cases, the perversity of the leaders was typical of the spiritual condition of the whole nation.

With this in mind, we are in a better position to reflect on the ministry in the wilderness beyond the Jordan. Here we need first to recall that Joshua led the children of Israel across the Jordan to bring them into the promised land, a miraculous crossing reminiscent of the Red Sea, revealing again God's special presence with His people. This provides the essential historical setting for Elijah's return to the wilderness. In Elijah's day, northern Israel had turned so far from God that Elijah seemed to think there was not even a remnant:

> And he said, I have been very jealous for Yahweh, the God of hosts; for the children of Israel have forsaken thy covenant, thrown down thine altars, and slain thy prophets with the sword: and I, even I only, am left; and they seek my life, to take it away. (1 Kgs 19:10, 14)

This wilderness ministry of Elijah supplies the essential historical setting for understanding John the Baptizer's work. It was John himself who invited the associations with his ministry and Elijah's. For the Jews of his day, John's ministry in the wilderness around the Jordan was intended to evoke a complex set of historical memories that would communicate to them the spiritual status of their generation and the call for a faithful remnant. This means that John's choice of clothes and place for ministry, no doubt directed by God, were prophetic actions, like the odd, attention-getting conduct of prophets like Hosea (1:2), Ezekiel (cf. 4:1ff.), and Jeremiah (cf. 19:1ff.; 28:10). When a prophet entered a conspicuously inadvisable marriage, lay on his side for over a year laying siege to a clay model, or broke a potter's vessel in the presence of the leaders of Jerusalem, he was making a statement by his deeds. Of course, preaching usually accompanied the prophetic act.

A prophet like Elijah, ministering around the Jordan and asking Jews to get into the water of the Jordan for baptism is obviously suggesting that the Israel of the day has departed from God and needs a new start, a new exodus. John the Baptizer is calling out a remnant—a true Israel within the larger apostate Israel—and is searching for the seven thousand who have not yet bowed the knee to Baal. The remnant needs to re-cross the Jordan and once again become the people of God. Something like this should have been in the minds of Jews who reflected on what John the Baptizer was doing.

Of course, it was ambiguous to some degree, at least for those who did not want to accept John's testimony. That is why the Pharisees sent men to John to ask him whether his actions were a claim to be the Messiah or to be Elijah or to be "the prophet" (John 1:19–22). Perhaps the Pharisees reasoned like this: John's clothing and location recall Elijah, but baptizing Jews in the Jordan could have greater meaning. He could be claiming to be the Messiah and using baptism to gather the remnant around himself. Among the common Jews also, there were those who thought that John the Baptizer might be the Messiah (Luke 3:15).

Luke indicates how important the baptism of John the Baptizer was for the Israel of Jesus' day:

> And all the people when they heard, and the publicans, justified God, being baptized with the baptism of John. But the Pharisees and the lawyers rejected for themselves the counsel of God, being not baptized of him. (Luke 7:29–30)

Those who had submitted to the baptism of John "justified God" or "acknowledged God's justice," in contrast to the Pharisees and lawyers who rejected John's baptism and therefore also refused to submit to God's will. John the Baptizer was sent by God on a mission to prepare for the coming of Messiah. All who rejected his baptism were refusing the cleansing rite that was essential for membership in the faithful remnant that would become the people of the Messiah. John's ministry, like Elijah's, was definitive for true membership in the people of God. But John's ministry was also greater than Elijah's because John was not merely calling people back to the covenant, but introducing them to the fulfillment of all the covenant promises in the Messiah: "Repent for the kingdom of God is near." The time had come that all the prophets longed for.

However, Israel was not ready. She had become so defiled by her sin and apostasy that her temple had become a den of thieves rather than a house of prayer for all peoples. Like a leper, she was not qualified to enter the house of God. She needed to leave the spiritual Egypt she had created for herself and go to the wilderness to renew her covenant with God. She needed a cleansing bath and prophet to lead her to cross the Jordan river all over again to make a new start as a renewed priestly people, consecrated to her covenant Lord. In this way, the ministry of John the Baptizer prepared a special people for the coming Messiah. As the prophet who cleansed the believing remnant, he brought to a close the ministry of the old covenant priesthood by reinstating the defiled remnant to its status as the priestly nation.

N. T. Wright summarizes this well:

> [A]nyone collecting people in the Jordan wilderness was symbolically saying: this is the new exodus. Anybody offering water-baptism for the forgiveness of sins was saying: you can have, here and now, what you would normally get through the Temple cult. Anybody inviting those who wished to do so to pass through an initiatory rite of this kind was symbolically saying: here is the true Israel that is to be vindicated by YHWH. By implication, those who did not join in had forfeited the right to be regarded as the covenant people. In these ways, completely credibly within the history of first-century Judaism, what John was doing must be seen, and can only be seen, as a prophetic renewal movement within Judaism—a renewal, however, that aimed not a renewing the existing structures, but at replacing them.[18]

Note, as Wright emphasizes, that John the Baptizer's ministry is not aimed at renewing existing structures but at replacing them. John aims at something new. The people must be anointed with water not only because they have been defiled and need a cleansing bath, but because

---

18. Wright, *Jesus and the Victory of God*, 160.

they are being anointed with reference to the soon-to-come kingdom of God John was announcing. The people of the kingdom are defined as the anointed people. John's preliminary baptism was the promise of the greater baptism to come. "He shall baptize you with the Holy Spirit!"

When the baptism of Jesus is seen in the larger context of what John is doing, we understand well why Jesus was baptized at thirty, since that was the age for a priest to enter the ministry. We also understand why Jesus said that He had to be baptized to fulfill all righteousness, for it is necessary for the Messiah, both as king and as priest, to identify with the people and to be consecrated to service. Finally, it becomes clear why the word from the Father and the gift of the Spirit came at the very moment Jesus had been washed, since the baptism of Jesus in water was part of the larger and more complex process of His priestly ordination. Without the participation of the Father and Spirit, Jesus' baptism by John would have to be subsumed under John's gathering of a remnant people and Jesus would be just another member of the remnant, an idea that John himself found out of place (Matt 3:14). The declaration of the Father and the coming of the Spirit do not erase the old covenant context for Jesus' baptism by John; they place Jesus' baptism in a distinctly higher sphere.

THE FATHER'S WORD AND SPIRIT'S COMING

The baptism of the repentant remnant by John/Elijah was to reinstate Jews into their ministry as a priestly people, so the rite was simply a ceremonial washing, a special covenant renewal rite ordained by God for the situation of the first century Jewish people in preparation for the coming of Messiah. The Messiah's baptism, however, would have to be different. He could not be viewed simply another member of the renewed nation. Beyond identification with the people, His baptism must also publicly designate Him as Messiah. For the Messiah's anointing, the Mosaic law implies the need for the Spirit and the prophetic promise explicitly demands a greater anointing than that of the Aaronic priests, namely, the pouring out of the Spirit. Moreover, the Messiah would have to be ordained as a priest after the order of Melchizedek, the Messianic priesthood that David prophesied in Psalm 110.

Therefore, the rending of the heavens, the voice of the Father, and the descent of the Spirit belong with the baptism by water as essential aspects of the Messianic ordination rite. In this rite, Jesus is publicly declared Messiah and officially empowered for His office, just as Aaron and his sons at their ordination were publicly declared priests and symbolically empowered by the anointing with oil. The fact that the Father speaks and pours out the Spirit on Jesus just as He comes up from the water and in answer to His prayer confirms the connection with Aaronic ordination, for the declaration and the coming of the Spirit fit with the complex nature of the ordination ceremony and correspond to Moses' declaration and instructions and the pouring out of oil on Aaron and his sons. But it goes beyond Aaronic anointing because the Spirit must be given to the Messiah in fulfillment of prophecy (Isa 42:1).

The Father's Messianic Word

The Father's declaration clearly indicates that Jesus' baptism was His Messianic ordination. The heavens opened—or as Mark says, were rent asunder—so that the Father could speak and the Spirit descend. The same Greek expression is used twice in the Septuagint, once when Isaiah prays God would rend the heavens and come down (Isa 64:1 [63:19 LXX]) and, more significantly, when Yahweh appeared to Ezekiel to commission him for ministry. Ezekiel says "the heavens were opened and I saw visions of God" (Ezek 1:1). Just as for Ezekiel, the opening of the heavens brought John the Baptizer and Jesus, and probably others present as well, into the presence of the glory cloud of God. In that way, the Spirit descended from the temple and glory above to anoint Jesus at the open doorway of the heavenly temple, as Aaron was anointed before the doorway of the earthly tabernacle (Lev 8:4) and as the kings of Judah were apparently anointed at the pillar before the temple (cf. 2 Chr 23:8–11, 13).

In contrast to Ezekiel's ordination, however, at Jesus' baptism we are not told of anything further in the way of a vision. Rather the descent of the Spirit as a dove is the only visible sign that is given. The voice of the Father declaring Jesus to be the Messiah is what interprets the coming of the Spirit for us.

Nolland observes that a voice from heaven already implies a commissioning:

> The voice from heaven is a familiar apocalyptic theme in Revelation (4:1; 10:4, 8; 11:12; 14:13 and cf. Isa 6:4, 8; Ezek 1:25, 28; *4 Ezra* 6.13) where it is uniformly involved in giving directives. That is not immediately the case here, though in the larger Lukan structure a directive is obviously implied (cf. Luke 4:18).

Even before attending to the words of the voice it is clear that we are dealing with a divine commissioning of Jesus.[19]

The words that the Father speaks confirm this impression, especially when associated with the pouring out of the Spirit. The gift of the Spirit in the form of a dove will occupy our attention later. For now what is important is to note that the Spirit is given to the Son, after which words are pronounced that indicate the meaning of the gift, or baptism, of the Spirit.

When we consider the words of the Father, it is profoundly significant that He refers to previously written Scriptures, for these words have a broad old covenant context. To put it differently, the exact words of the Father must be understood as an allusion that constitutes the tip of a literary iceberg or a link to a vast network of texts and themes, for the Father's words for this ceremonial occasion must have been carefully chosen with reference to the larger context and the related themes.[20] Though all Scripture is given by inspiration of the Holy Spirit so that every instance of an allusion to previous Scripture is God alluding to His own Word, still there is something special about God the Father quoting Scripture in the ritual commissioning of God the Son as Messiah.

To which verses are allusions being made? Though there is relatively broad agreement, there is some debate about exactly which Scriptures are being referred to.[21] In order to consider this in detail, it will be helpful to begin with a literal translation of the words of the Father in Mark 1:11, divided into three parts as follows:

σὺ εἶ ὁ υἱός μου—You are My Son
ὁ ἀγαπητός— the Beloved
ἐν σοὶ εὐδόκησα— In You I am well pleased

There are at least three possible views on which Scriptures are being alluded to. First, it is possible to see two passages being alluded to (Ps 2:7; Isa 42:1). Second, it is possible to see one passage being alluded to (Isa 42:1). Third, it is possible to see three passages being alluded to (Ps 2:7; Gen 22:2; Isa 42:1). I hope to show that careful attention to the details—

---

19. Nolland, *Luke 1—9:20*, 162.

20. I say more about literary allusion and its importance for the narrative of Jesus' baptism in chapter 3.

21. Nolland, *Luke 1—9:20*, 162–65.

both in the words themselves, as well as the narrative context—points in the direction of the third view.

The first words, "You are My Son," are usually understood as an allusion to Psalm 2:7 and the last words, "In You I am well pleased," as an allusion to Isaiah 42:1 ("Behold, my servant, whom I uphold; my chosen *in whom my soul delighteth*"). The Messianic Servant is described as the one in whom "My soul delights." The wording is only slightly changed in Mark 1:11 to "in You I am well pleased." Thus, most commentators see an allusion here to two passages from the Old Testament.

But the modification from "in whom My soul delights" to "in You I am well pleased" suggests that similar modifications may occur in the other two expressions. Some suggest, then, that "My servant" in Isaiah 42 has been reworded in Mark as "My Son" and "My chosen" in Isaiah 42 has become "the Beloved" in Mark 1. All three sections then, would allude, not to several different passages but to one passage, Isaiah 42:1.

The possibility that "the beloved" is an allusion to Isaiah 42:1 is supported by another verse in Matthew (12:18a), where there is an allusion to the opening words of Isaiah 42:1:

ἰδοὺ ὁ παῖς μου ὃν ᾑρέτισα—Behold My Servant whom I have chosen

ὁ ἀγπητός μου—My beloved

εἰς ὃν εὐδάκησεν ἡ ψυχή μου—In whom My soul is well pleased

Note, by contrast the Septuagint[22] and the original Hebrew of Isaiah 42:1:

Ιακωβ ὁ παῖς μου—Iakob is My servant

ἀντιλήμψομαι αὐτου—I will lay hold of him

Ισραηλ ὁ ἐκλεκτός μου—Israel is My chosen

προσεδέξατο αὐτὸν ἡ ψυχή μου—My soul has accepted him

הֵן עַבְדִּי אֶתְמָךְ־בּוֹ—Behold My Servant, whom I uphold

בְּחִירִי רָצְתָה נַפְשִׁי—My Chosen, in whom My soul delights

Clearly Matthew 12:18a is not following the Septuagint, but neither is it offering a literal rendition of the Hebrew. A. B. Bruce describes it this way:

---

22. The English translation employed here is Moisés Silva's in Pietersma and Wright, *Septuagint*, 856.

> The quotation is a very free reproduction from the Hebrew, with occasional side glances at the Sept. It has been suggested that the evangelist drew neither from the Hebrew nor from the Sept., but from a Chaldee Targum in use in his time (Lutteroth).[23]

Whatever Matthew may be doing, what is important for our study is the fact that he translates the Hebrew for "My chosen" (בְּחִירִי)—which the Septuagint makes "My elect one"—as "My beloved" (ὁ ἀγπητός μου). If this was common or if Matthew is using a translation that was typical among early Christians, then it may be that the words "the beloved" (ὁ ἀγπητός) in Mark 1:11 also allude to Isaiah 42:1. However that may be, in Mark 1:11 in the words "in whom I am well pleased," there is undeniably an allusion to Isaiah 42:1.

What makes the allusion to Isaiah 42:1 so unquestionably clear in Matthew 12:18a is the key expression which introduces the quotation, "Behold My Servant," in connection with "My chosen." There is no other possible passage that it could be referring to.

But that is not the case in Mark 1:11. Here the key opening expression is "Thou art My Son." Again, the opening words point to a specific verse in the Old Testament, even though the Septuagint is not quoted exactly, for there is no other relevant passage in the Old Testament that is as close to the opening words of Mark 1:11 as Psalm 2:7.[24] By contrast, the Septuagint for Isaiah 42:1, as we saw above, says "Jacob is My servant." In the opening expression, "Thou art My Son," a reference to Psalm 2:7 seems nearly certain. There are, then, at least two passages being alluded to in the words of the Father in Mark 1.

Is there a third allusion? It seems quite possible that the words "the Beloved," allude to a distinct passage, though this is disguised in our English translations when we translate it as "Thou art my beloved Son." If we separate the three expressions as I have done in the literal translation above, the second part stands out, "the Beloved." What might the allusion be? In the Septuagint, ἀγπητός (beloved) is relatively rare, appearing only twenty-four times, but it is repeated for emphasis three times in one of

---

23. Bruce, "Matthew," 1:185. I have quoted only the first words of the verse, since it is only this portion that is relevant for the discussion of Mark 1:11, but the rest of the quotation is characterized by peculiarities that suggest that Matthew may be doing his own paraphrastic translation.

24. The exact expression in Mark 1:11 and Luke 3:22, σὺ εἶ ὁ υἱός μου, is found in the Septuagint in Genesis 27:21, 24, but it is highly unlikely that these verses provide relevant background.

the most famous stories of the Old Testament—Abraham's offering of Isaac, his "beloved" son (Gen 22:2, 12, 16). R. T. France points out that the wording in Mark 1:11 is closer to the Septuagint of Genesis 22:2 than to any of the other references.[25]

What further supports the possibility of an allusion to the story of Isaac is the use of the word "baptism" in the Gospels as a reference to the sacrifice of Christ. By recalling the story of Isaac, the beloved son who was sacrificed as a type of the Messiah, an allusion to Genesis 22:2 would suggest that Jesus' baptism with water by John and the gift of the Spirit from the Father were a consecration for a sacrificial self-giving on the cross—the ultimate baptism to which He was called (Mark 10:38-39; Luke 12:50).

If the words "the beloved" are intended to point back to Genesis 22:2, then there are three verses of Scripture (Ps 2:7; Gen 22:2; Isa 42:1)—or rather, three Old Testament contexts (Ps 2:1-12; Gen 22:1-18; Isa 42:1-9)—that resonate in the background. Each allusion recalls an entire narrative context relevant to the meaning of Jesus' baptism as Messiah and must be understood in that context.

Returning, then, to the most obvious of the allusions, Isaiah 42:1, it must be stressed that the full meaning of the allusion can be appreciated only by considering at least the rest of the paragraph beginning from Isaiah 42:1. More probably one should even include the entire context of the Servant Songs in Isaiah 42-53, not to mention the even larger context of Old Testament Messianic prophecy. The immediate paragraph is Isaiah 42:1-7:

> Behold, my servant, whom I uphold;
> my chosen, in whom my soul delighteth:
> I have put my Spirit upon him;
> he will bring forth justice to the Gentiles.
> He will not cry, nor lift up his voice,
> nor cause it to be heard in the street.
> A bruised reed will he not break,
> and a dimly burning wick will he not quench:
> he will bring forth justice in truth.
> He will not fail nor be discouraged,
> till he have set justice in the earth;

---

25. France, *The Gospel of Mark*, 80–82. However, France entirely misses the significance of the dove as an Old Testament sacrificial animal, which supports an allusion to Genesis 22:2 (78–79).

> and the isles shall wait for his law.
> Thus saith Yahweh God,
> he that created the heavens, and stretched them forth;
> he that spread abroad the earth and that which cometh out of it;
> he that giveth breath unto the people upon it,
> and spirit to them that walk therein:
> I, Yahweh, have called thee in righteousness,
> and will hold thy hand, and will keep thee,
> and give thee for a covenant of the people,
> for a light of the Gentiles;
> to open the blind eyes,
> to bring out the prisoners from the dungeon,
> and them that sit in darkness out of the prison-house.
> (Isa 42:1–7)

The paragraph before us contains faint, but nonetheless clear, allusions to the Abrahamic and Davidic covenants as well as to the original promise in the Garden and to prophesies of the Messiah in many other passages. What is most important for our present purpose is to note that the Creator Yahweh declares that His Servant will be endowed with the Spirit and empowered to bring salvation to the nations of the world. In other words, the section of Scripture to which the Father points speaks of the Messiah—the Servant of Yahweh—as being called ("I have called you") and commissioned ("I will appoint you") to do a particular work ("a light to the nations") and of the gift of the Spirit ("I have put My Spirit upon Him") as the special divine provision that enables Him to accomplish His task. The baptism of Jesus by John the Baptist and the connected gift of the Spirit and declaration of the Father, therefore, must be understood as the anointing and ordination of the Messiah for His saving work.

This is further confirmed by the allusion to Psalm 2:7 in the very first words of the Father in Mark 1:11, "You are My Son." Again, though the words quoted are only part of verse 7, we must read the whole Psalm to appreciate the point of the allusion.

> Why are the nations in an uproar
> And the peoples devising a vain thing?
> The kings of the earth take their stand
> And the rulers take counsel together
> Against Yahweh and against His Anointed, saying,
> "Let us tear their fetters apart
> And cast away their cords from us!"

The Messianic Dimension

> He who sits in the heavens laughs,
> Yahweh scoffs at them.
> Then He will speak to them in His anger
> And terrify them in His fury, saying,
> "But as for Me, I have installed My King
> Upon Zion, My holy mountain."
> "I will surely tell of the decree of the LORD:
> He said to Me, 'You are My Son,
> Today I have begotten You.
> Ask of Me, and I will surely give the nations as Your inheritance,
> And the very ends of the earth as Your possession.
> You shall break them with a rod of iron,
> You shall shatter them like earthenware.'"
> Now therefore, O kings, show discernment;
> Take warning, O judges of the earth.
> Worship Yahweh with reverence
> And rejoice with trembling.
> Do homage to the Son, that He not become angry, and you perish in the way,
> For His wrath may soon be kindled.
> How blessed are all who take refuge in Him! (Ps 2:1–12 NASB)

On the surface this is a Psalm about the Messiah, Yahweh's Anointed, and it concerns His installation as King.[26] Jesus' actual enthronement does not occur until His ascension when, as the book of Acts indicates, Jesus took His place on the throne at the right hand of the Father. The quotation of this Psalm at Jesus' baptism indicates that He was ordained and anointed as King and Priest at His baptism in order to be installed at His ascension, rather like David who was anointed by Samuel as king many years before he actually was able to reign on the throne in Zion (1Sam 16:12–13; 2 Sam 5:1–5).

---

26. Mark L. Strauss recognizes the strongly Messianic character of the Father's declaration and emphasizes especially that the Messiah is a Davidic figure, though his exegesis of the details is different from mine (*Davidic Messiah*, 203–7). Contrary to Van Groningen and most modern interpreters, I agree with Hengstenberg that this entire Psalm is straightforward Messianic prophecy. The entire context, therefore, is especially important for understanding the words of the Father (cf. Van Groningen, *Messianic Revelation*, 333ff., and Hengstenberg, *Commentary on the Psalms*, 1:18–39). Hengstenberg writes, "There are the clearest grounds for asserting, that by the King, the Anointed, or Son of God, no other can be understood than the Messias. It is generally admitted, that this exposition was the prevailing one among the older Jews, and that in later times they were led to abandon it only for polemical reasons against the Christians" (*Commentary on the Psalms*, 1:19).

If we assume an allusion to Genesis 22 in the words "the beloved," then we have three allusions to Messianic passages in the Old Testament,[27] two of which speak of Messiah as king with global lordship and one of which specifically speaks of the gift of the Spirit to enable the Messiah to bring the world under His dominion. By including the third typological reference in Genesis 22, the declaration of the Father connects the cross with the crown at Jesus' baptism—most appropriately since Jesus is being baptized for a Messianic work that is fulfilled on the cross. I believe the Spirit's descent supports an allusion to Genesis 22 here and is evidence for including a prophetic view of the cross in the Messianic ordination rite, for the Spirit descends in the form of a dove.

The Spirit's Coming as a Dove

Commentaries often express puzzlement at the picture of the Spirit as a dove, and some seem to despair of a solution. Robert L. Webb, for example, cites numerous studies attempting to explain the Spirit's descent as a dove, but he apparently finds all of them less than persuasive:

> A third mitigating factor is the presence in the theophany narrative of the description "like a dove" (Matt 3:16 = Mark 1:10 = Luke 3:22; cf. John 1:32). Much ink has been spilled discussing the possible origins and significance of this imagery, but none has been entirely satisfactory.[28]

Robert A. Guelich goes so far as to say the following:

> Although the dove has subsequently become a popular symbol for the Holy Spirit, the occurrence of the imagery in 1:10 appears to stand without previous parallel, a fact that should discourage any attempt at finding a symbolic meaning behind this reference. The importance of the event lies in the Spirit's coming.[29]

Disappointingly, even Darrell L. Bock concludes along similar lines:

> These attempts to make a theological symbol out of the dove seem flawed. . . . It seems best to leave the figure of the dove as

---

27. I do not assume that a single passage must allude to only one passage. It may allude to more than one.
28. Webb, "Jesus' Baptism," 276–77.
29. Guelich, *Mark 1–8:26*, 35.

a simple metaphor without theological significance. The Spirit descended on Jesus with the grace of a dove.[30]

This agnostic consensus is strange, for even though the image is unusual, it is not at all as unprecedented as it is assumed to be. When the heavens opened above and the Spirit descended, we are told that He came as a sign to John the Baptist to identify the Messiah. Now, to be a *sign* for John, the Spirit had to descend in some *visible* form. The question is, What form might be fitting?

In the Old Testament, God appears in various forms, but only a few of them would be appropriate for a context in which the Spirit is seen to descend from heaven. Three stand out. First, the Spirit could have descended like a cloud, as God descended on Mount Sinai or the tabernacle. Second, the Spirit could have descended as fire, as He later descended on the apostles in Acts 2. Third, the Spirit could descend like a bird, since He is pictured as a bird in creation and redemption (Gen 1:2; Exod 19:4; Deut 32:11; Ruth 2:12; Pss 17:8; 36:7; 57:1; 61:4; 63:7; 91:4). No doubt there are other possibilities, but these seem the most obvious.

The next question is, Why, out of these possibilities, would God choose to send the Spirit in the form of a dove? Even if descent in the form of a bird seems most appropriate out of the three basic possibilities sketched above, there are other birds. God is compared to an eagle more than once (Exod 19:4; Deut 32:11), why should the Spirit descend as a dove? Contrary to skeptical commentaries, considering the whole range of Old Testament references to doves provides ample indication of why the Spirit would appear in this form at Jesus' baptism.

First, as we have seen, there is clear Old Testament background for the association of the Holy Spirit with a bird. The metaphor appears in the second verse of Scripture at the beginning of the story of creation, making this a foundationally important symbol.

If we ask, what is the most appropriate form for the Spirit to descend upon Jesus? The very first answer that should occur to us is that the Spirit might appear as a bird, as He did at the very beginning: "The Spirit of God was hovering over the surface of the waters" (Gen 1:2b).

---

30. Bock, *Luke 1:1—9:50*, 339. Bock's language utterly baffles me. It is hard to conceive of metaphor being used without theological significance in any work of serious literature. But the Bible in particular is not the kind of book in which metaphor could be used without theological significance, for it teaches us to see the whole world in metaphorical terms and constantly speaks of God through metaphors.

The Hebrew verb rendered "hovering," when used in the piel stem, refers to the fluttering of a bird's wings[31] and is used only three times in the entire Old Testament (Gen 1:2; Deut 32:11; Jer 23:9), two of which are metaphorical depictions of God as a bird. Since this metaphor appears in the creation story and again in the song of Israel's redemption, it should be considered the most important symbolic way of picturing the Spirit of God. Both in the original creation and in redemption, which is re-creation, God the Spirit is the one who hovers over the world, powerfully working the Father's will. The imagery of a bird hovering suggests nurture in Genesis 1:2, and in Deuteronomy 32:11 protection.[32]

Bird imagery, thus, seems to be the basic background for the descent of the Spirit,[33] but this must be connected specifically with Old Testament references to the dove. The first explicit reference to a dove in the Bible confirms the creation/re-creation theme suggested by the word "hover." In the story of the flood, Noah sends out a dove three times to see if the world is ready to be re-inhabited. It is the dove that brings Noah the message that the waters have abated (Gen 8:8–11) and then, by not returning, gives Noah the assurance that the new world is ready for man and animals (Gen 8:12). In the flood narrative, the dove is thus associated with redemption and new creation.

To get a full picture of the Old Testament background, we must briefly consider both the Hebrew word for dove (יוֹנָה) and that for turtle-dove (תּוֹר). All together, they are used forty-seven times in thirty-seven verses.[34] Many of the uses provide scant help at best for understanding the picture of the Spirit as a dove, especially the reference to Ephraim being as silly as a dove (Hos 7:11). Other passages, however, are significant.

---

31. For the piel stem of רחף, Koehler and Baumgartner have "to set quivering, meaning to hover with fluttering wings, characteristic flying behaviour of birds of prey" (Koehler and Baumgartner, *Hebrew and Aramaic Lexicon*, 3:1220).

32. Also, bird imagery is related to the glory cloud, as even a cursory reading of Ezekiel 1:4–28 makes abundantly clear.

33. In Jewish tradition, the Spirit in Genesis 1:2 has occasionally been thought to be a dove, as in the Babylonian Talmud and Simon b. Zoma. Cf. Capes, "Intertexual Echoes," 46. As well, the Spirit in Genesis 1:2 has been related to the Spirit who will be poured out on the Messiah because of the connection with Isaiah 42:1. Cf. Neuser, *Judaism's Story of Creation*, 184.

34. In the order they appear in the Hebrew Bible, these are Genesis 8:8–12; 15:9; Leviticus 1:14; 5:7, 11; 12:6, 8; 14:22, 30; 15:14, 29; Numbers 6:10; 2 Kings 6:25; Isaiah 38:14; 59:11; 60:8; Jeremiah 8:7; 48:28; Ezekiel 7:16; Hosea 7:11; 11:11; Nahum 2:8; Psalms 55:7; 56:1; 68:14; 74:19; Song 1:15; 2:12, 14; 4:1; 5:2, 12; 6:9.

For example, the Song of Solomon repeatedly refers to the beauty of the dove, which perhaps suggests a humble sort of glory (Song 1:15; 2:12, 14; 4:1; 5:2, 12; 6:9).

Less important but perhaps meaningful are references to the dove as moaning, which may imply repentance and certainly evoke the idea of suffering (Isa 38:14; 59:11; Ezek 7:16; Nah 2:7; cf. Hos 11:11). If repentance is a sub-theme in such verses, they naturally imply that the symbolism of a dove connects with the baptism unto repentance by John the Baptist and also indicate that Jesus' baptism with the Spirit-dove is to be connected with the water baptism of John. The implication of suffering is prominent in Psalm 74:19, where the helpless turtledove is a picture of Israel oppressed by enemies.[35] Also, though this cannot be included in the Old Testament background for the image, our Lord Himself adds to the symbolic importance of depicting the Spirit as a dove when He instructs us to be "wise as serpents, harmless as doves" (Matt 10:16).

Understood with the Father's allusion to Isaiah 42:1, the association of the dove with gentleness, beauty, suffering, and perhaps also repentance, calls to mind the gentleness of the Messiah emphasized in Isaiah 42. Because He is endowed with the dovelike Spirit, He carries out His work in a manner that corresponds:

> He will not cry out, nor raise His voice,
> Nor cause His voice to be heard in the street.
> A bruised reed He will not break,
> And smoking flax He will not quench;
> He will bring forth justice for truth. (Isa 42:2–3 NASB)

For the Spirit who enables the Messiah to accomplish this gentle and gracious work to be pictured as a dove seems perfectly appropriate.

Yet there is one more Old Testament association with the dove—the most important for understanding the gift of the Spirit and His coming upon Jesus as a dove. The dove is specifically the sacrificial animal for the poorest of the people of Israel, those who cannot afford to bring a lamb (Lev 1:14; 5:7, 11; 12:6, 8; 14:22, 30; 15:14, 29). Needless to say, the dove is also the *only* one of the sacrificial animals that would have been appropriate in a picture of the Spirit coming down from heaven,[36] but

---

35. For a discussion of Psalm 74:19 that connects the dove to Jesus' death from a different perspective than mine, see Campbell, "Jesus and His Baptism," 207–8.

36. Bulls, goats, and sheep do not descend from heaven well.

the emphasis on the dove as *the poor man's sacrificial animal* is most typologically appropriate, since Joseph and Mary, who could not afford a lamb, brought doves for Mary's purification (Luke 2:22–24) when she presented Jesus for consecration as the firstborn child.

Baptism by the dove-Spirit, thus, is preeminently baptism by a sacrificial animal, suggesting that Jesus was baptized unto a sacrificial death, an interpretation our Lord seems to confirm by referring to His coming death as a baptism (Mark 10:38–39; Luke 12:50).[37] Also, the Spirit descending as a sacrificial animal corresponds well with an allusion to Genesis 22, identifying the Messiah as the beloved one like Isaac who must die, confirming the idea of a prophetic reference to the cross in Jesus' priestly ordination. Finally, as the animal associated with the poor, it is the dovelike Spirit who anoints Jesus specifically to preach the Gospel to the poor (Luke 4:18; cf. Isa 61:1).

The inherent multivalence of metaphor necessarily suggests a complex reading of the coming of the Spirit as a dove, enabling, if not compelling, us to see in this one symbol cosmic, redemptive-historical, covenantal, and sacrificial themes. We can only state each theme briefly. The *cosmic* theme suggested here is the beginning of a new creation in and through the Messiah, a theme that will be further developed when we consider the Adamic dimension of Jesus' baptism. The *redemptive historical* theme is inauguration of the kingdom of God through the Spirit-anointed-and-commissioned Messiah. Jesus' baptism brings in the kingdom in a definitive manner because the King Himself has come and begins to call men unto Himself. The *covenantal* dimension is complex. Anointed with the Spirit, the Messiah Himself is given as a covenant to the peoples (Isa 42:6), fulfilling the Abrahamic and Davidic covenants and, even in His baptism, bringing in the new covenant, since Jesus is the first man to receive the baptism of the Spirit, the definitive new covenant blessing. Finally, the *sacrificial* theme appears in that Jesus is baptized with a sacrificial animal, consecrating Him to His own sacrificial work, the baptism of the cross. It goes without saying that all of these themes are related in Messianic prophecy, and therefore the Spirit as a dove here in Mark 1 suggests this multiple meaning, drawn from a whole catena of Old Testament references.

---

37. On Luke 12:50, see Campbell, "Jesus and His Baptism," 193ff.

BAPTISM AND RESURRECTION

Jesus Himself teaches us that baptism and death are related when He calls His own death a baptism. As we have seen, the descent of the Spirit in the form of a sacrificial animal and the allusion to Genesis 22 confirm this. But there is more. Jesus' baptism also points to His resurrection, though this is somewhat less clear. In the Gospels, God's declaration at Jesus' transfiguration links His baptism with His resurrection. In the Acts and Epistles, the use of Psalm 2:7 and similar expressions brings Jesus' baptism and resurrection together.

Before turning to the relevant passages, a word about the relationship between the Gospels, Acts, and Epistles is in order. If we assume, contrary to most contemporary scholarship, that Matthew wrote his Gospel first not long after Jesus died, then Paul would be presupposing the stories of the Gospels when he wrote his epistles.[38] With regard to Luke, we know for sure that he presupposed at least his own Gospel when he wrote the book of Acts, and I think we may presume he also knew Matthew and Mark, for he says that he has consulted with the accounts of *many* eyewitnesses who wrote before he did (Luke 1:1–4). If I am correct in the above—and for the Luke/Acts relationship, it is certain—we have to assume that allusions to Psalm 2:7 in the Acts and the Epistles echo the account of Jesus' baptism and His transfiguration. The Gospel testimony is already known and part of the literary matrix within which Psalm 2 would be understand.

Transfiguration in the Synoptics

Jesus' transfiguration is recorded in all three synoptic Gospels (Matt 17:1–8; Mark 9:2–8; Luke 9:28–36). There are variations among them, but among the things that do not vary is the fact that all three accounts clearly echo the story of Jesus' baptism and point forward to His resurrection glory. The unmistakable connection between Jesus' baptism and transfiguration suggest that the declaration of the Father in the baptism of Jesus already implies resurrection victory.

Matthew's Gospel in particular emphasizes the connection between baptism and transfiguration. The words of the Father in 3:17 and 17:5 are identical ("This is My Son, the Beloved"), except that 17:5 adds an exhortation: "Listen to Him!"

---

38. Jordan, "Production of the New Testament Canon."

οὗτός ἐστιν ὁ υἱός μου ὁ ἀγαπητός, ἐν ᾧ εὐδόκησα.
(Matt 3:17)

οὗτός ἐστιν ὁ υἱός μου ὁ ἀγαπητός, ἐν ᾧ εὐδόκησα· ἀκούετε αὐτοῦ. (Matt 17:5)

The two events mutually interpret one another. The Jesus who was baptized by John in the Jordan river, humbling Himself to receive a baptism of repentance to identify with the sinful people, is the same Jesus who is transfigured in terrifying glory before the three disciples. Only Peter, James, and John see the transfigured Messiah and hear the voice of God from heaven. Nevertheless, the transfiguration is a special revelation of Jesus' coming victory for the disciples and a foretaste of the resurrection glory to come.

If we missed the hints implicit in the baptismal account, re-reading it in the light shed by the transfiguration illumines the narrative. The sacrificial dove baptized Jesus unto death, but the Father's declaration that the Son is the beloved, echoing Genesis 22:2, already implies the resurrection. Even more, the quotation of Isaiah 42:1 points beyond death to resurrection, since the context in Isaiah goes on to speak of the victory of the Servant in bringing the justice of God's kingdom to the nations of the world.

The transfiguration in Matthew 17:1–8 is coupled with the resurrection story in Matthew 28:1–20 by numerous parallels. John Nolland points out that

> (1) there are a limited number of disciples (17:1; 28:16);
> (2) there is a mountain setting chosen by Jesus (17:1; 28:16);
> (3) the disciples see Jesus (17:2, 8; 28:17);
> (4) Jesus comes to them (17:7; 28:18);[39]
> (5) Jesus is said to command (17:9; 28:20);
> (6) the word "behold" used in both contexts (17:3; 28:20);
> (7) there are significant ties to Daniel; and
> (8) both passages refer to the resurrection (17:9; 28:6).[40]

Though Matthew's account makes these connections quite explicit, they are present in all the synoptic Gospels. Jesus' baptism includes, therefore, not only prophetic implications of the cross, but also of the

---

39. The exact expression καὶ προσῆλθεν ὁ Ἰησοῦς is used in Matthew 17:7 and 28:18 and nowhere else in the New Testament.

40. Nolland, *Gospel of Matthew*, 706.

resurrection and kingdom victory to follow. In the Gospel accounts, the words of Psalm 2:7, "Thou art My Son" link the baptism, transfiguration, and resurrection of Jesus, indicating clearly that Jesus was baptized as the Messiah who would rule God's kingdom.

Resurrection and Psalm 2:7

Acts 13:16–41 is the first recorded sermon of the apostle Paul. Like Stephen's sermon in Acts 7:2–53, it follows the history of Israel, though the emphasis is different. Stephen focuses more on Moses, Paul on David. In particular, Paul, like Peter on the day of Pentecost (Acts 2:25–28), proclaims the resurrection of Christ as the fulfillment of Psalm 16. In addition, Paul adds Psalm 2:7. However, unlike the Gospel allusions to Psalm 2:7, Paul quotes the entire second half of the verse: "Thou art My Son; this day have I begotten thee."

In the context of the sermon in Acts 13, it is relatively clear that in the words "this day have I begotten thee," Paul sees a prophecy of Jesus' resurrection:[41]

> And we bring you good tidings of the promise made unto the fathers, that God hath fulfilled the same unto our children, in that he raised up Jesus; as also it is written in the second psalm, Thou art my Son, this day have I begotten thee. And as concerning that he raised him up from the dead, now no more to return to corruption, he hath spoken on this wise, I will give you the holy and sure blessings of David. Because he saith also in another psalm, Thou wilt not give Thy Holy One to see corruption. (Acts 13:32–35)

The fact that Luke has already quoted Psalm 2:7 twice in his Gospel before this, both times as the words of the Father, indicates the literary link between the stories of Jesus' baptism, the transfiguration, and the resurrection. At the transfiguration, what had been hidden from view during the time of His humiliation among sinful men was gloriously manifest, though only briefly. In His resurrection, the declaration of the Father that Jesus is His Son finds realization. Only when Jesus has been raised from the dead and seated at the right hand of the Father as Lord and Christ (Acts 2:36) is the meaning of the baptismal declaration ful-

---

41. Though commentators differ, Richard Gaffin is correct when he writes, "No convincing argument exists against a specific reference to the resurrection" (*Resurrection and Redemption*, 113).

filled. Significantly, when Jesus is manifest as Son, He baptizes with the Spirit, as John promised before he baptized Jesus.

Remembering that it was Paul's sermon that Luke was quoting in Acts 13:33 provides important background for understanding Paul's language in Romans 1:3–4:

> concerning his Son, who was born of the seed of David according to the flesh, who was declared to be the Son of God with power, according to the Spirit of holiness, by the resurrection from the dead; even Jesus Christ our Lord.

The echo is faint enough that commentators do not usually pick it up, but Paul here alludes to Psalm 2:7 when he says "declared to be the Son of God." As in Acts 13:33, Paul links the Father's declaration with Jesus' resurrection, but in Romans 1:4 Paul includes the Spirit of God, "the Spirit of holiness." In the words "according to the Spirit of holiness," Paul may be saying that the Holy Spirit is responsible for raising Christ from the dead or he may be referring to the gift of the Spirit, which shows that Jesus is now no longer the Son of God in weakness, but in power.[42] In either case, the Spirit of God is connected with the declaration of the Father, perhaps even with the promised gift of the Spirit by John the Baptizer. In this brief summary of Paul's Gospel, the account of Jesus' baptism, well known to Luke's companion, echoes in the background, as does the transfiguration, where Jesus' power and glory were first manifest to three disciples. The baptism promised the resurrection in its allusion to Psalm 2:7 and Isaiah 42:1. The transfiguration was a prophetic revelation of the glory to come. But only in the resurrection does Jesus' claim to be the Messiah have its initial vindication.

Peter refers to the transfiguration of Christ, testifying that he was an eyewitness to Jesus' majesty when he saw His power and coming (2 Pet 1:16–18). The book of Hebrews adds to the complexity of this literary web by associating Psalm 2:7 with Psalm 110. The association in the book of Hebrews is most natural. Jesus was declared or appointed Son of God at His resurrection and seated at the right hand of God as the Messianic Priest after the order of Melchizedek. When Jesus ascended to the right hand of the Father and took the seat of Messianic authority, He was being appointed Son of God in power (Rom 1:4), both Messiah

---

42. For a discussion of the details, see Moo, *Epistle to the Romans*, 44–51. Moo misses the allusion to Jesus' baptism and transfiguration, but he does mention Psalm 2:7 and Acts 13:33.

and Lord (Acts 2:36). But all of this was already in view in His baptism, when the Father declared, "Thou art my Son, the Beloved, in whom I am well pleased."

Resurrection as Redemption

Richard Gaffin refers to the resurrection of Christ as His "redemption," using the word "redemption" in a broader sense as deliverance.[43] Gaffin explains:

> For him [Paul] the accomplishment of redemption is only first definitively realized in the application to Christ himself (by the Father through the Spirit) at the resurrection of the benefits purchased by his own obedience unto death.[44]

Gaffin sees Romans 1:3–4 as the declarative appointment of Jesus as Son of God in power. The judicial declaration that Jesus is the Son constitutes Jesus as Messiah by adopting Him as the second Adam. Acts 13:33 and Hebrews 1:5 and 5:5 are taken to refer to essentially the same act. Gaffin explains that in the resurrection, Jesus was adopted, just as believers in Christ will someday be adopted bodily by the resurrection from the dead (Rom 8:23).

In 1 Timothy 3:16 Paul says that Jesus was "justified in the Spirit." As Gaffin explains, this refers to Christ's resurrection as His vindication. Jesus is justified in the sense that "the eradication of death in his resurrection is nothing less than the removal of the verdict of condemnation and the effective affirmation of his (adamic) righteousness."[45] On the cross, Jesus was condemned. Without a reversal of that condemnation, Jesus would be perpetually under the sentence of death, as if the penalty had not been fully paid. His resurrection publicly proclaims that He has paid the penalty and defeated sin and death. Hence, it is His justification.

On the basis of Romans 6:1–14, Gaffin even speaks of the resurrection in terms of sanctification. Through baptism, believers in Christ have died to sin and been resurrected to new life. As Gaffin says, "Their freedom from the dominion and power of sin resides specifically in their having been raised with Christ. In other words, (definitive) sanctifica-

---

43. Gaffin, *Resurrection and Redemption*, 114.
44. Ibid., 117.
45. Ibid., 122.

tion is defined here expressly in terms of resurrection."[46] If solidarity with Christ in His resurrection is the basis of our definitive sanctification, then in some sense the analogy suggests that Jesus' resurrection was also His sanctification. What can that mean? Gaffin explains that insofar as Jesus was incarnate as a member of the fleshly order of the Adamic world, He lived in the world of sin and "was exposed to its suffering, weakness (II Cor. 13:4), and death."[47] The resurrection brought Christ fully into the new age and delivered Him from the old age. In that sense, it is His sanctification.

Finally, Gaffin says that the resurrection of Christ is also His glorification. He explains:

> Passages like I Corinthians 15:42ff. and II Corinthians 3:17f.; 4:4–6, as well as the genetic association of glory with the Spirit, show that the pneumatic transformation experienced at Christ's resurrection involves the final and definitive investiture of his person with glory.[48]

The resurrection body of Christ is the body of His glorification. He is the first—and to this date the only—man who has entered fully into the new age. We all await the redemption of our bodies. But His resurrection is the guarantee of ours.

What Gaffin's study shows about the resurrection of Christ is profoundly significant for our understanding of soteriology in general. More than that, his perspective sheds light on the story of Jesus' baptism. Following Gaffin's lead, we can see Jesus' baptism as His adoption, justification, sanctification, and glorification. Jesus was adopted in the sense that the Father declared that Jesus was His Son. He was justified in the sense that the Father proclaims His good pleasure in the Son. He was sanctified in the sense that the Spirit was poured out upon Him to set Him aside for the work that God called Him to do, the work of a Melchizedekian priest. Finally, He was glorified in the sense that the heavens were split open and the Spirit descended from the glory cloud upon Him. Applying each of these categories to the transfiguration follows obviously.

---

46. Ibid., 125.
47. Ibid., 126.
48. Ibid.

Thus, baptism ties to the transfiguration and resurrection. At His baptism, Jesus is declared to be Lord and Christ prophetically. At the transfiguration, this is manifested only to three disciples, but they have given us their testimony about the event and so we are witnesses also. Finally, the resurrection of Jesus is the declarative appointment of the Son of Man to the office of Lord and Christ, seating Him at God's right hand. The New Testament puts these three events together as a single complex testimony to one truth: Jesus is God's Messiah, the Savior of Israel and the world.

CONCLUSION

What I have tried to show in this chapter is that Jesus' water baptism by John was only one aspect of a larger and more complex event, one step in the process of His Messianic ordination. Jesus was baptized at thirty because His baptism was ordination to priesthood by John the Baptizer. In the baptism by water—a preliminary washing in the ordination process—Jesus identified with the covenant people in their sinfulness and their need for repentance. The Son's prayer, the Father's answering voice, and the descent of the Spirit from heaven finished the ordination rite. As the heavens were opened and Jesus stood at the door of the heavenly temple, the Father declared Him to be the Servant of Yahweh who would redeem the world, the Anointed One before whom every king must bow, and the Spirit-filled Savior who would bring justice to the farthest islands of the Gentiles. In accordance with the words of ordination, the dovelike Spirit anointed Jesus with gentle, self-sacrificial power to preach good tidings to the poorest of the poor. Thus, Jesus, by a special anointing ceremony with water and the Spirit was declared by the Father to be the Messiah, a King and Priest after the order of Melchizedek and one appointed to offer up Himself, as the Servant of Yahweh, to redeem His people from their sins.

It should be clear now what Jesus meant when He spoke of fulfilling all righteousness. Baptism by John was necessary for the Messiah to identify with the people of Israel and fulfill Scripture prophecy about the Messiah. For the sinful Jews of the day, John's baptism was a washing that restored their status as God's priestly people. In a similar but distinct way, for Jesus, baptism was inauguration into the Messianic priesthood. By being baptized by John and thereby allowing Himself to be marked out as Messiah according to the sign that God had determined, Jesus was fulfilling all righteousness. More than anything else, by being set apart for the cross by which He would die for the sin of the world, Jesus' baptism fulfilled the righteousness of the old covenant prophecies of the coming Messiah, which John the Baptizer seems to have at least partially understood when he announced, "Behold the Lamb of God." The baptism in water and the gift of the Spirit were both part of a single but complex event that fulfilled old covenant Messianic typology and prophecy.

Fulfilling old covenant Messianic prophecy means the inauguration of the new covenant. Israel's Messiah came as the one who was anointed with the Spirit to bring salvation to the world. Through His sacrifice on the cross, resurrection, and gift of the Spirit to the people He would gather from all nations, Messiah brings in a new age. Baptism with the Spirit as Messiah points to the cosmic significance of Jesus, to which we turn in our next chapter.

3

The Adamic Dimension

WHEN THE APOSTLE PAUL declares that Adam was a type of Christ (Rom 5) and refers to Christ as the second man and last Adam (1 Cor 15:45, 47), he introduces us to a typology that must influence the way we read the whole Bible. Reading the Scriptures through the lens that Paul supplies, we will see the Adam/Christ typology as one of the Bible's most important undercurrents. In effect, Paul is teaching us that included in the Old Testament notion of Messiah is the typology of Adam and the hope of a new Adam.[1]

What does this mean for our understanding of Jesus' baptism? It means that if Jesus was baptized as Messiah, He was baptized as the new Adam, the last Adam. But this theme—the relationship between the Messiah and the last Adam—may be missed even though it is a prominent theme in the Old Testament, because until Paul and outside of Paul it is not explicit.[2] However, *it is virtually omnipresent*, underlying or implied by every theme and motif that calls to mind the original creation and the place of Adam as covenant lord under God.

---

1. Gordon Fee describes three approaches to the typology of Adam and Christ: (1) the minimalist approach, that limits the discussion to the three explicit passages which mention the typology (Rom 5:12–21; 1 Cor 15:21–22; 44b–49); (2) the maximalist approach represented by N. T. Wright and James D. G. Dunn; and (3) a middling approach, which is Fee's own position (*Pauline Christology*, 513–14). Fee might call the approach in this chapter super-maximalist. I argue that the Adam-Christ typology is central to the whole matrix of old creation/new creation symbolism and typology. The best introduction to biblical typology is Jordan's *Through New Eyes*.

2. For examples of complete neglect, see Hasel, *Old Testament Theology*; Von Rad, *Old Testament Theology*; and House, *Old Testament Theology*. See also Waltke, *Old Testament Theology*, 296–302. Waltke recognizes the theme of the new Adam, but his view is quite limited, for though he sees Noah and Israel as new Adams that foreshadow Christ, the whole topic is covered very briefly as a secondary theme at best.

In this chapter, I intend to paint a basic picture of the Adam/Messiah typology. Without going into details of argument, this chapter implicitly stands against three views. First, by showing the breadth and depth of the Adam typology, I will be arguing against the general neglect of the theme of the new Adam and attempting to show how vital and fundamental it is to biblical theology. Second, my discussion contrasts sharply to that of James D. G. Dunn, though he is certainly correct when he writes that "Adam plays a larger role in Paul's theology than is usually realized—and even when that role is taken into account it is often misunderstood."[3] Unfortunately, Dunn himself contributes to the confusion. For, though his discussion of Adam and Christ is helpful in many places, in the end Dunn himself misunderstands Paul when he argues that Christ's role as last Adam does not begin until the resurrection.[4] Third, this chapter runs contrary to N. T. Wright's penetrating discussion of Adam and Israel, full of insight as it is. I believe Wright gets the picture backwards when he claims that "the apocalyptic belief that Israel is the last Adam is the correct background against which to understand Paul's Adam-christology."[5] On the contrary, as I think this chapter will show, Paul's understanding of Genesis 1–3, the covenant with Noah (Gen 9:1–17), and the call of Abraham (Gen 12:1–3) is the background for his understanding of Israel's relationship to Adam, which means that the Adam/Messiah typology is prior to and more fundamental than the Adam/Israel typology.[6]

If we begin with Genesis 1–3 and build from there, it becomes clear that we find the new Adam theme implicitly whenever we encounter a new covenant, a new leader of humanity, or the promise of a global savior and a new world. Each of these themes is associated with and presupposed by the others because the original Adam was the head of the first covenant, the guardian and lord of the first world, the father and leader of humanity. For there to be a new world, a new covenant, or a savior means that there will be a new covenant head, a

---

3. Dunn, *Christology in the Making*, 101; cf., for the whole discussion, 98–128.
4. Ibid., 108.
5. Wright, *The Climax of the Covenant*, 39.
6. Wright's exposition of the Messiah as Israel is on target. What I want to add is that ancient Israel saw itself as a new Adam. Wright's narrative seems to begin with Abraham. The biblical narrative line begins with Adam and his story echoes in the background of every other story.

new Adam. The Messiah is the last Adam, the one who undoes what the first Adam did, saving the race that has been plunged into sin and judgment. Even more, He leads a new race of mankind to fulfill the mandate given to the first Adam.

After examining this background briefly, I hope to show that the Gospels themselves intend us to understand that Jesus was baptized to be consecrated as the head of a new humanity. Though this is inescapably involved in being baptized as Messiah, it needs separate emphasis because of its profound significance for our whole theology. The topic is so large that we might even say that it was the ancient Pharisees' misunderstanding of the Messiah as something other than a new Adam that betrayed them into racial narrowness. And we might also say that the neglect of this truth in our day is one aspect of the misunderstanding of the meaning and mission of the Church. For if we see the Church as the new humanity under a new head, we know that she cannot be a mere sect, nor can she retreat from the world and wait for the end.

MESSIAH AS THE NEW ADAM IN PAUL

Paul explicitly identifies Adam and the Messiah in two passages. First, Jesus is called "the last Adam" in 1 Corinthians 15:45, and the larger context views the last Adam as the head of a new humanity and Lord of a new creation. Second, in Romans 5:14 Paul tells us that Adam was a type of Christ. Considering Romans 5:12–21 in the light of other passages in Paul's letters, especially 1 Corinthians 15, suggests that Paul sees the Adam/Christ typology as having fuller implications than just the contrast of the Garden and the Cross. Even in Romans 5, there seems to be a wider application, for in the context in which we are told Adam is a type of Christ, Paul twice speaks of Jesus' righteousness resulting in dominion (5:17, 21). How can we not be reminded of Adam as the king of the original creation who was given priestly duties to guard the Garden (cf. Gen 1:26–28; 2:15–17) and who had prophetic responsibilities to teach Eve? Is there not here an echo of the promise that the Seed would crush the head of the serpent (Gen 3:15)?

Other passages in Paul allude to Adam without mentioning him. One of the most obvious is Colossians 1:15: "who is the image of the invisible God, the firstborn of all creation." Adam was, of course, the literal firstborn man in all history, created by God as His image. The rest of humanity is born as God's image and likeness. In the Bible, however, as many stories in Genesis show, "firstborn" can indicate position or rank rather than literal birth order. This is illustrated in the Psalms also, where David is promised that he will be made "firstborn" of the kings of the earth:

> I also shall make him my firstborn,
> The highest of the kings of the earth. (Ps 89:27)

Here "firstborn" is a position of rank, which the parallel expression in the latter part of the verse expounds as "highest of the kings of the earth." As in Genesis and Psalm 89, Colossians 1 is speaking of the position or rank of Messiah. When he says that Christ is "the image" and "the firstborn," Paul obviously has in mind the original man who was image and firstborn, whose place Jesus inherited and whose task Jesus fulfilled.

Another important passage that alludes to Adam is Philippians 2:5–11. N. T. Wright discusses this at length, showing that Paul is alluding both to the Genesis creation account and to Psalm 8, as well as directly quoting Isaiah 45:23. Furthermore, there is an implied contrast between Adam and Christ in Philippians 2:6. When Paul says that Jesus did not grasp for what was rightfully His, he is alluding to Adam's grasping for what was forbidden.[7] As Wright explains, Paul's view of Messiah as a new Adam is related to his view of Messiah as the one who fulfills God's will for Israel.[8]

Taken altogether, then, it is clear that Christ as the new Adam underlies Paul's view of the Messiah, especially since Romans 5 and 1 Corinthians 15 are pivotal for Paul's understanding of Jesus as Messiah and are definitive of His saving work. Thus, there is no debate about whether or not Paul regarded Jesus as the new Adam. But was Paul's view something new, a revelation given to him that is read back into Scriptures that otherwise would not support it? Is there a larger picture into which Paul's insight may be integrated, making it part of the structure of biblical theology as a whole?

I argue that Paul is not making an isolated statement about Adam and Christ, but rather is pointing to a paradigm that underlies biblical history. From the time of the fall, godly men were waiting and longing for the "new Adam," the leader who would defeat the dragon/serpent and save them (cf. Gen 3:15). Every hero who brought deliverance to

---

7. Ibid., 56–98.
8. Ibid.

the people of God should be seen in the light of that larger framework which inspired Israel's hope, though only the Messiah could truly satisfy the demands of the promise. In the same way that every anointed one in Israel's history pointed forward to the true Anointed One, so also every new Adamic leader pointed forward to the final new Adam who would crush the head of the serpent and save the woman and her seed. If we read the Bible with this basic theme in mind, we will notice it in places we might ordinarily overlook and we will see the promises of Israel's Messiah in connection with the promise of a new creation. In other words, a new Adam implies cosmic salvation.

We will return to the central passages in Paul when we consider the significance of the new Adam typology. For now, I want to emphasize that the typological relationship between Adam and Christ, which underlies the Old Testament doctrine of the Messiah, is made explicit by Paul. If we had reservations about reading the Old Testament or the rest of the New Testament in the light of such a typology, Paul's clear statement that Adam was a type of Christ not only relieves our hesitation, but also *compels us to read the whole Bible and its teaching about Christ with this typology in mind.*

LITERARY ALLUSION, ECHO, INTERTEXTUALITY, AND METALEPSIS

To appreciate the importance of the new Adam theme in the Old Testament, we must first understand the place of literary allusion in the Bible, for the Bible was the earliest work of true literature in world history[9] and its literary conventions are the foundation for all Western literature.[10] To the degree that these conventions express what is natural to man as God's image, they are foundations for any literary enterprise, inescapable

---

9. James Jordan argues that Genesis is based on records that are much earlier than Moses and that the definitive edition of Genesis may have been put together and edited by Joseph. Assuming that the records which stand behind Genesis were literary compositions including short poetic fragments and an exalted style of writing, Genesis as we have it is based on and includes the oldest example of human literature. See James B. Jordan, "Sequence of Events." Sumerian myths are usually thought to be the oldest world literature and they may antedate the final form of Genesis, but they would not be older than the records on which Genesis was based nor do they compare with the literary quality of Genesis.

10. This assumes the accuracy of biblical chronology. See James B. Jordan's *Biblical Chronology* newsletter, online at www.biblicalhorizons.com.

features of human thought and feeling, though expressed differently in various cultures. But in no work of ancient literature outside the Bible and in no work of the ancient world before the Bible was there literary artistry comparable to the artistry that abounds in the Scriptures.[11]

In other words, the Bible is *distinctly literary*. Before we delve into this, it may help to review what literary allusion is. Robert Alter, a Jewish literary scholar, explains it well:

> Nothing confirms the literary character of biblical narrative and biblical poetry more strikingly than their constant, resourceful, and necessary recourse to allusion. Now, it is obvious that, because the members of any culture carry around in their heads bits and pieces of all sorts of texts, allusion also occurs quite abundantly in nonliterary discourse, both written and spoken. A newspaper article, say, about the collapse of an African government may invoke T. S. Eliot's "not with a bang but a whimper," or a phrase from Lincoln's Gettysburg Address, or a line from Hamlet, or a prescription from Robert's Rules of Order. On the whole, such allusions to familiar texts in ordinary speech, journalism, and most expository writing work as rhetorical embellishments; there is rarely a sense that they are dictated by the necessity of the form of expression in which they occur.
>
> The case is quite different with literature. A person inevitably composes a story or poem—and it makes no difference whether the composition is written or oral—out of the awareness of a preexisting body of textual objects, stories or poems, in which the composition at hand will constitute a new member. Thus, every writer not only emulates certain models but is compelled to define a relationship—competitive, admiring, revisionist, elaborative—to at least certain elements of antecedent literary tradition. Allusion, then, is not an embellishment but a fundamental necessity of literary expression: the writer, scarcely able to ignore the texts that have anticipated him and in some sense given him the very idea of writing, appropriates fragments of them, quali-

---

11. There are too many books written on the Bible and its relationship to literature to offer an adequate list of references here. The best place to begin for the interested student is to read ancient literature and compare it with the Bible. As for English literature, the influence of the Bible is well known. In one of the most often quoted studies, Northrop Frye writes, "I soon realized that a student of English literature who does not know the Bible does not understand a good deal of what is going on in what he reads: the most conscientious student will be continually misconstruing the implications, even the meaning" (*Great Code*, x). See also Norton, *Bible as Literature*.

fies or transforms them, uses them to give his own work both a genealogy and a resonant background.[12]

In his books on biblical literature, Alter describes various techniques of allusion and shows how richly and necessarily allusive Old Testament literature is.[13] More recently, scholars like Richard Hays have emphasized the importance of understanding literary allusion in order to rightly interpret the epistles of Paul. Hays, like Alter, is applying techniques of literary analysis that come from outside the disciplines of biblical studies. In particular, Hays builds on the work of semiotic scholars like Julia Kristeva and Roland Barthes, Jewish biblical and literary scholars like Michael Fishbane's *Biblical Interpretation in Ancient Israel*, and, especially, the literary scholar John Hollander's *The Figure of Echo: A Mode of Allusion in Milton and After*.

Hays adds to the complexity of our understanding of how allusion might work in the Bible when he explains the kind of allusion he calls "echo":

> Allusive echo can function as a diachronic trope to which Hollander applies the name of *transumption*, or *metalepsis*. When a literary echo links the text in which it occurs to an earlier text, the figurative effect of the echo can lie in the unstated or suppressed (transumed) points of resonance between the two texts.... Hollander sums up in a compact formula the demand that this sort of effect places upon criticism: "the interpretation of a metalepsis entails the recovery of the transumed material." Allusive echo functions to suggest to the reader that text B should be understood in light of a broad interplay with text A, encompassing aspects of A beyond those explicitly echoed. This sort of metaleptic figuration is the antithesis of the metaphysical conceit, in which the poet's imagination seizes a metaphor and explicitly wrings out of it all manner of unforeseeable significations. Metalepsis, by contrast places the reader within a field of whispered or unstated correspondences.[14]

In the nature of the case, Hays's notion of "echo" is more difficult to apply than the broader and sometimes quite straightforward device

---

12. Alter, *World of Biblical Literature*, 107–8.

13. In addition to the work cited above, Alter has also written *The Art of Biblical Narrative* (1981) and *The Art of Biblical Poetry* (1985).

14. Hays, *Echoes of Scripture*, 20.

of literary allusion.[15] It should be added, though, that although Hays is relying on literary scholars, he clearly distances himself from the philosophical presuppositions of semiotic theorists like Kristeva and Barthes or scholars like Harold Bloom, who use the notion of intertextuality to demonstrate the inescapable fluidity of a text's meaning.[16] What is important to see from Hays is that allusion in the Bible can be extremely subtle and may, in some cases, require the reader to recall not only the passage alluded to, but also a whole network of passages or even a theme of Scripture not explicitly mentioned but presupposed in the passage alluded to.

Steve Moyise suggests the following simple definitions for various kinds of literary reference:

1. Quotation: "generally, a quotation involves a self-conscious break from the author's style to introduce words from another context."

2. Allusion: Allusions, Moyise says, are "usually woven into the text rather than 'quoted,' and often rather less precise in terms of wording."

3. Echo: Echoes are "faint traces of texts that are probably quite unconscious but emerge from minds soaked in the scriptural heritage of Israel."[17]

I have to disagree with Moyise's view that the faint traces of texts that he labels "echo" would probably be unconscious. On the contrary,

---

15. What this means can be illustrated by Hays's view of the echo of Scripture found in 2 Corinthians 3, where Paul compares and contrasts his own ministry with that of Moses. Hays says that Paul "simultaneously posits and undercuts the glory of Moses' ministry." Steve Moyise explains, "According to Hays, this is achieved by Paul's allusive use of Scripture, which 'leaves enough silence for the voice of Scripture to answer back.' Paul does not fill in all the 'intertextual space with explanations' but 'encourages the reader to listen to more of Scripture's message than he himself voices. The word that Scripture speaks where Paul falls silent is a word that still has the power to contend against him'" (Moyise, "Intertextuality," 26). I am not comfortable with this language in that I do not imagine Paul and Scripture contending with one another. But there is no question that Paul's use of Scripture is complex and requires us to consider larger contexts, underlying themes, whispered correspondences, and "intertextual space."

16. Hays, *Conversion of the Imagination*, 172–74.

17. Moyise, "Intertextuality," 18–19. In the original essay, these definitions are part of his discussion of what he calls an "intertextual echo," but the larger discussion is not important for my purposes.

biblical writers like Paul, saturated in the Scriptures, would naturally use the language of previously written Scripture in subtle ways that they would normally be fully conscious of. Of course, there is no theological problem with a Scripture writer saying more than he intended, since the ultimate author of Scripture is the Holy Spirit. It just seems unlikely that a man like Paul would miss very much.

Consider, for example, what Moyise says shortly after providing these definitions:

> It is not difficult to see why studies on the "Old Testament in the New" have often focused on quotations. There is not usually much controversy as to the source text and the author is clearly "intending" the reader to acknowledge the citation by drawing attention to it. However, if a subtext is well known, the slightest of allusions is sometimes sufficient to evoke its presence. A popular game show on television required contestants to guess the title of a piece of a music from its opening bars. Sometimes, the winner managed this from just two notes. Similarly, not many words are necessary to evoke Israel's Passover or Exile.[18]

If the winners of a TV game show—no doubt some of whom are less intellectually and spiritually gifted than the apostle Paul—can recognize a song from hearing only the first two opening bars, then I think we should assume that the authors of Scripture, who are carefully constructing their writings as servants of God filled with the knowledge of Scripture, were almost always conscious of the background music and at least *usually* intended their echoes no less than their quotations. But the crux of the matter is that reference to previously written Scripture is a category much broader than mere quotation. Allusions and echoes play a significant part in the way later Scripture refers to and interacts with earlier Scripture.[19]

18. Ibid., 19.

19. Moyise suggests that in Romans 8:20, Paul's reference to the creation subjected to futility may be an echo of the book of Ecclesiastes. He writes, "Is it then an echo or an unconscious allusion? Sanday and Headlam note that ματαιότης is the constant refrain of Ecclesiastes and therefore Paul's use of the word is 'appropriately used of the *disappointing* character of present existence, which nowhere reaches the perfection of which it is capable.' The implication of this appears to be that while Paul is not consciously alluding to Ecclesiastes, he has nevertheless chosen a word that is thoroughly appropriate, given its particular usage in that book. In terms of a theory of echo, we might say that Ecclesiastes is the 'cave of resonant signification,' to use one of Hollander's terms. The reader is not specifically directed to the book of Ecclesiastes but the haunting prose of

Of course, in all of this, we have not even begun to take account of the Divine Author of Scripture. If we believe that God is triune and that He is a God who communicates because that is His essential nature, then our views of Scripture—including phenomena such as intertextuality—and our hermeneutics in general must be grounded in a view of language and interpretation that includes God as the ever-present Lord of history. The meaning of any particular text may include ramifications that extend far beyond what the original human author intended but not beyond what the Divine Author planned.[20]

In other words, the complexity of meaning in the biblical text is a special case within literature, because *only the Bible is equally the word of God and the word of man*. Behind the surplus of meaning in the God-inspired text is the reality of the triune God Himself. The Son is the exact image of the Father, a perfect and exact reproduction of all that the Father is as the Father. And yet, He is an exact image as Son, not as a clone of the Father or an attempted replacement for the Father. The Spirit, too, is ontologically one with Father and Son because the Three are one God, sharing the same essence and attributes. Nevertheless, the Spirit is perfectly distinct as Spirit. In His person, there is something special that conditions all He is and does. The sameness within difference and difference within sameness that characterizes the persons of

---

that book *accompanies* a reading of Romans 8 as 'shading of voice.' Or, as Hays puts it, it 'places the reader within a field of whispered or unstated correspondences.' At any rate, Barrett says that the reader of Romans 8.20 'recalls at once passages such as Eccles.i.2'" (Moyise, "Intertextuality," 23–24).

This discussion is supposed to illustrate what Moyise means when he says that an echo may be unconscious, but the example itself is doubtful from more than one perspective. If in Romans 8:20 there is an echo of Solomon's theme of "vanity," we need to ask the question: If the echo is obvious enough that many commentators feel obligated to consider it, why should we assume that Paul would have missed it? Unless, of course, there is no echo at all and we are relating themes that are not really connected in the way we may be thinking. In either case, there is no reason to assume that Paul missed what was going on in his own epistle. Indeed the rest of Moyise's discussion makes far better sense on the assumption of a self-conscious allusion to Ecclesiastes, for the profound theological reading he suggests could hardly come from a text by a writer unconscious of not one but multiple echoes and the theology implied by them.

20. Poythress, "Course Materials on Biblical Hermeneutics" offers valuable material. Peter Leithart's recent book, *Deep Exegesis*, explains typological interpretation and extends it to literature outside of the Bible as well, though the interpretation of the Bible is his main concern. The book was published after I had this one almost completed, so I can only mention it here, but it is must reading for anyone considering intertextuality and related topics.

the Trinity is the rich ontological background for God's communication to man and man's communication to God and other men. The interpersonal communion in God is a fellowship of love in which each person wholly gives Himself to the others—a communion of self-giving love that grounds all communication within the triune God.

In the word that the triune God speaks to us, therefore, there must be an infinite surplus of meaning, for it is the Word of the Creator, who inspires the words of the prophets and controls all history, guiding the minds and hearts of every man to the end of the world. More importantly and before all, Scripture is the Word of the Creator who speaks within Himself every word He gives to man, for His word is settled from eternity: "Forever, O Yahweh, Thy word is settled in heaven" (Ps 119:89). All that God speaks to man and through man has been planned before the foundation of the world. In a way, it is first of all the word of God to God because Christ who is the Word and the Spirit who inspires the Word through man knew every word with the Father before the world began (cf. John 1:1; Rev 13:8; etc.).

The importance of these ideas will become especially clear when we look into the narrative of Jesus' baptism, but before that we must consider the Old Testament background for the biblical idea of the Messiah as a new Adam, an area in which remembering the importance of allusion and echo will help us rightly see the vision of the prophets and hear the Scriptures as they did.

OLD TESTAMENT BACKGROUND FOR ADAM/ MESSIAH TYPOLOGY

The Old Testament background for the Adam/Messiah typology is actually quite broad and multifaceted. Paul's teaching in Romans 5 that Adam was the head of the old race and Jesus the head of a new implies a typology that fundamentally structures revelation. Paul's words compel us to consider various themes related to Adam to discover the full picture. As I pointed out earlier, these include topics such as repeated gifts of a new covenant, the theme of the seed, the promise of global salvation and dominion, references to a renewed nation and new creation, and prophecies of the coming of the Spirit. All of these intertwined and overlapping topics, as well as repeated Old Testament narrative structures, taught old covenant saints to wait for a Messiah who would be a new Adam, the head of God's global kingdom. It will suffice for our purpose here to briefly survey a portion of the old covenant background for the Messiah as head of a new humanity.[21]

New Adams

The earliest records of the Old Testament provide the foundations of the Adam/Messiah typology. To begin with, the curse on the serpent includes a promise of a child of Eve who will deliver man and judge the serpent:

> And I will put enmity
> Between thee and the woman,
> And between thy seed and her seed;
> He shall bruise thy head,
> And thou shalt bruise his heel. (Gen 3:15)

This is commonly and correctly seen to be a promise of a Messiah,[22] but it is important to observe that here, in the very first announcement of a future Savior, there is a literary allusion to an earlier Scripture—God's commission to Adam to *guard* the garden (Gen 2:15).

Adam failed to guard the Garden and his wife and thus led the race into sin. The first prophecy of the Messiah alludes to Adam's original responsibility, though not explicitly. Perhaps this fits into the category

---

21. My approach here is only slightly different from that of N. T. Wright in his chapter "Adam, Israel and the Messiah" in *Climax of the Covenant,* 18–40. Wright argues that "the use of 'Adam' themes in the Jewish literature which may without controversy be considered a part of the background to the New Testament—i.e. the Old Testament, the Scrolls, and the Apocrypha and Pseudepigrapha—consistently makes one large and important point: God's purposes for the human race in general have devolved on to, and will be fulfilled in, Israel in particular. Israel is, or will become, God's true humanity. What God intended for Adam will be given to the seed of Abraham. They will inherit the second Eden, the restored primeval glory. If there is a 'last Adam' in the relevant Jewish literature, he is not an individual, whether Messianic or otherwise. He is the whole eschatological people of God. If we take 'Adam' language out of this context we do not merely distort it; we empty it of its basic content" (20–21). He goes on to explain that he believes Paul rejected the contemporary Jewish understanding of Israel as the "last Adam" because he saw that Jesus Christ fulfilled the role of Adam (*Climax of the Covenant,* 26; cf. also 26–40). Where I differ from Wright is in placing the Messiah as last Adam *before* Israel as the new Adam.

22. Here and throughout, I speak anachronistically in the sense that there is nothing in Genesis 3:15 that implies that the seed of the Woman will be *anointed* to fulfill His task. Most early prophecies are not strictly speaking "Messianic" passages, but the theme of the new Adam and Savior introduced in Genesis 3:15 is further developed in the prophecies of the Anointed One. Referring to earlier passages as Messianic, therefore, is legitimate.

Hays calls *echo*. At any rate, it is clear that the Messiah is depicted as one who will succeed where Adam had failed, for Adam, as the guardian of the Garden, was the one who should have crushed the serpent when it first attempted to lead Eve astray. To describe the Messiah as one who will bruise the serpent's head is to say that a new Adam will take over the original Adam's role as protector and, unlike the first Adam, will be faithful in His work.

When Eve named Cain, she seems to have been thinking of the promise of a deliverer, so here, too, there is probably an allusion to the promise (Gen 4:1). Later in Genesis, the allusion to Adam in the story of Noah is unquestionable. In Genesis 9, the original commission given to Adam is repeated almost word for word in God's covenant with Noah (Gen 9:1ff.), signifying that the new covenant head was, in some respects, a new Adam. Noah, of course, has a special place in this regard because all men after the flood are descended from him, just as all men since creation are descended from Adam.[23] The narrative of the flood, with its depiction of de-creation and re-creation and the repetition of the original covenant in the Garden, point unmistakably to a theme of new creation with all that that involves, including a new Adam, even though the exact expression is not used. With Noah, then, we have a new creation, a new covenant, and a new Adam.

Two theological points are worth emphasizing as well. First, when God said to Noah, "Be fruitful and multiply and fill the earth," He indicated that the original creation mandate was still in force. Mankind had sinned against God, but their historical mission as a race did not change. Though Satan had successfully tempted mankind to sin, he could not derail God's plan for man and the world. Second, there is a development in the theme of the Messiah as a new Adam. As we have seen, in repeating the commission to Noah, God was addressing him as a new Adam. Noah took the place of the first man and became the father of a new race, picking up the theme of the original promise: one born of the woman will be a new leader and savior for the race.

As the story continues, however, it turns out that Noah is too much like Adam: his descendants rebel against God at the tower of Babel, bringing another global judgment and calling for another beginning.[24]

---

23. There is a difference, too, of course, since all women are descended from the original Adam, but not all women are descended from Noah.

24. I do not mean to suggest—like those who believe Noah was drunk and invited God's judgment—that he committed a specific sin that made him like Adam. I am refer-

Thus, the theology of the Messiah becomes more complex. We see that even great covenant leaders like Noah are inadequate to fulfill the promise, though they nevertheless resemble the Messiah in that they do offer real salvation and help in history. They provide a partial salvation that preserves God's people and keeps the promise alive until the right time for the Seed of the Woman to appear.

The next new Adam is Abraham, though the allusion to Adam is less explicit than in the story of Noah. We need to proceed by steps. First, two events of cosmic proportion, the flood and Babel, provide the historical and theological background for God's call to Abraham—the failure of Noah and his descendants calls for a new beginning. By itself, this alerts us to an allusion, which functions behind and beneath all, to the story of creation. If we consider carefully God's promise in Genesis 12:1–3 and related texts, it will become evident that the Abrahamic covenant is a renewal and extension of the creation covenant. We must take careful note of the correspondences to rightly understand the covenant with Abraham, for in Abraham's case, though there is allusion to the themes that appeared in the creation covenant, they sometimes find expression in a different vocabulary.

The most significant aspect of the allusion to creation is this: what were commandments in the creation covenant now become promises. For example, Abraham is promised that he will be the father of a great nation (Gen 12:2). This is connected to the theme of multiplication. In the beginning, what was for Adam a command to be fruitful and multiply is for Abraham the promise that he will be fruitful and multiply: "I will multiply you exceedingly" (Gen 17:2; cf., e.g., 17:5). Again, the promise of land converts the original command for Adam to rule the world into a gift of land that symbolizes and leads to Abraham and his seed possessing the world (cf. Rom 4:13). World dominion is also seen in the promise that those who bless Abraham will be blessed and that those who curse him will be cursed (Gen 12:1–3). The gift of the covenant culminates in the promise that all families of the earth will be blessed in him, confirming that Abraham is a sort of new Adam at the head of a new race of men who are spiritually united through him (Gen 12:3; 28:14). Though the promise of a great name may not be grounded in a command given to Adam, it is a promise of glory, reflecting the glory

---

ring rather to the fact that as Adam's seed departed from God, so did Noah's. This begins with the sin of Ham and Canaan and culminates in the rebellion of Babel.

that Adam originally had in the Garden with God. It specifically alludes to the blessing that the builders of Babel tried to steal from heaven by force (cf. Gen 11:4).

Abraham, therefore, is a new Adam, and the emphasis on the "seed" in the Abrahamic covenant is grounded in the promise to Adam and Eve included in the curse on the serpent. Although he is a new Adam, however, Abraham *himself* is not the one who will actually bring the fulfillment. Like Eve, he is a channel; it is through his seed that salvation will come (Gen 22:18). In the context of the Genesis promise, the implications of this are not difficult to discern: if Abraham's seed is going to bring blessing to all humanity, obviously Abraham's seed is the seed of the woman who will overthrow the serpent. So Paul sees a reference to the Messiah in the fact that the word "seed" is singular rather than plural, making it clear that the Messianic promise is even more fundamental than the role of Israel. Of course, there is also the promise that kings will be born from Abraham (Gen 17:6, 16) and its fulfillment is understood from ancient times to be found in the Messiah, King of kings.

No doubt the most prominent new Adam in the Old Testament is the nation of Israel itself. James B. Jordan discusses the new creation at Sinai and both Israel as a nation and Aaron as the "cosmic man" being the new Adams at Sinai.[25] N. T. Wright has written extensively on Israel as the new Adam and on the fact that Jesus as the new Israel is also the new Adam.[26] Since this topic has been treated in detail by others, I pass over it here since it is not important for my purpose to develop the Adam/Messiah theme further. Noah, Abraham, and the nation of Israel function as "Adams" in a special sense, but there are others, too, who may be regarded as "new Adams" in the Old Testament, even if they are not in the position of heading a new humanity. In other words, every leader who serves in a representative capacity, who sins, and through his sin brings a curse on the people he represents exhibits the paradigm.[27]

---

25. Jordan, "Cosmos Constructors" and "The Tabernacle: A New Creation." These two essays go into the subject in considerable detail and depth.

26. See especially, Wright, *Climax of the Covenant*, 18–40.

27. For one example, see Jordan, "King Saul." Compare also what Jordan says here: "Because all men are made in the image of God, all men bear His imprint. Every man is, thus, in one sense a type of every other man. More importantly, church leaders are to be types or models for kingdom citizens (Philippians 1:7; 1 Thessalonians 1:7; 1 Timothy 4:12; Titus 2:7; 1 Peter 5:3). In terms of a typological view of history, the kingdom of men in the Old Covenant was a type of the New Covenant (1 Corinthians 10:6, 11), and the first Adam was a type of the last (Romans 5:14)" (*Through New Eyes*, 50).

While the people of God repeatedly see great leaders who stand out as new Adams (Saul, David, Solomon), they also repeatedly experience the sequence of promise, hope, but actual failure, which works to create an increasing longing for a new head who will be faithful to God and bring a true fulfillment of the promise. What we have seen here in this brief introduction is that the text of the Old Testament from the very beginning already contains a "new Adam theology." This ties into the later promise of "the Messiah," and both of these prophetic themes find their fulfillment in Jesus.[28]

Younger Brother as Heir

Before we can consider the theme of the younger brother as heir, I must briefly introduce the notion of a conventional story. Simply stated, a conventional story is a type of structuring device for a story, a "grid of conventions, upon which and against which the individual work operates."[29] Stories conforming to the same convention are built on basic elements and a predetermined sequence that form their structure.

For example, in the modern world, TV dramas fit into this mold.[30] Though the contents of the story vary from week to week, the basic elements and sequence remain pretty much the same. From seeing the same sort of story over and over, we naturally have certain expectations when we see a new example that fits the convention. To take an old and simple example, before either of them says a word, we know that the cowboy with the white hat is the good guy and the cowboy with the black hat and long dark mustache the bad guy. We know that the bad guy is going to cause an awful problem, but that the good guy will save the damsel in distress and the people who are victims of the bad guy's evil plan. Somehow, every week, it all works out. The Lone Ranger or Roy Rogers or Marshal Matt Dillon defeats the villains and everyone is happy in the end.[31]

---

28. As I pointed out previously, though Waltke rightly sees that both Noah as an individual and Israel as a nation are "new Adams," he apparently does not regard Abraham as a new Adam. Also, he mistakenly refers to Noah as committing a sin "through drinking in a vineyard" (*Old Testament Theology*, 296–98).

29. Alter, *Art of Biblical Narrative*, 47.

30. My explanation here is a paraphrase of Alter's explanation (*Art of Biblical Narrative*, 48).

31. What the reader may suspect is true: I haven't seen much TV in the last forty years or so, but I think the convention is still known.

The Adamic Dimension

In the Bible, the Exodus story provides perhaps the best and clearest example of such a conventional story. The story of the Exodus from Egypt in the book of Exodus is preceded by similar stories in the life of Abraham, Isaac, and Jacob. It is also followed by similar stories in the Old Testament, but especially the story of the exodus from Babylon, explicitly described by the prophets as a new exodus. The basic elements of the biblical exodus convention have been identified by James Jordan as follows:[32]

1. Threat, an aspect of the curse on sin, drives people from an Eden.
2. Attack on Eve by the Serpent.
3. Use of deception to trick the Serpent and guard the Bride.
4. Blessing to the redeemed; curse upon the wicked.
5. Miraculous intervention for deliverance.
6. Humiliation of false gods.
7. Departure with spoils.
8. Installment in the Holy Land.

Careful readers of the Bible notice that these same elements appear in many biblical stories, though with significant variations. That the Exodus motif is a widely recognized narrative structure illustrates the point that the Bible uses this sort of literary device in telling its stories. When we learn to notice narrative structures and relate them to the larger flow of biblical history, we are doing biblical theology based on how narrative communicates theological themes. Thus, narrative structures or literary conventions are an aspect of typology.

The particular conventional story or narrative structure that I am interested in now is the repeated story in the book of Genesis of the younger brother taking the place of the older brother. There are many examples, the first being, of course, Cain who, though he was the firstborn, was exiled because of his sin, with his younger brother Seth becoming heir instead. Abraham's sons are another famous example. Though the situation is rather different, still, it remains true that Ishmael was firstborn, but Isaac was the heir. Isaac's sons also fit

---

32. What I offer here is a simplified version of what appears in Jordan's *Through New Eyes*, 182–87. On the Exodus motif, see also Leithart, *House for My Name*, 71–81.

the paradigm. His older son Esau was firstborn, but he despised his birthright and sold it to his younger brother Jacob, who became the covenant heir. Jacob himself had twelve sons, which makes the paradigm more complex, but again, the firstborn Reuben lost his blessing through sin and a younger brother inherited. In the story of Jacob, the question is, which younger brother inherited? In one sense, the blessing of the firstborn went to Judah, who is identified as the father of the tribe from which the Messiah will be born (cf. Gen 49:10–12). In the more immediate historical context, Joseph became the heir, since his sons were adopted by Jacob and the two grandsons were given an inheritance with the rest of Jacob's sons. This means that, through Manasseh and Ephraim, Joseph received the inheritance of the firstborn, a double portion (Gen 48:22). We should also note that when he blesses Manasseh and Ephraim, Jacob intentionally reverses their birth order (Gen 48:14–19), again making the second first.[33]

In all of these stories, the firstborn is displaced and rejected. Usually he is disqualified because of his sin and a son born later has to take his place. Once more, something like Hays's notion of an echo is relevant. There is no verbally straightforward reference to Adam in any of these stories. But if we are reading them in the light of the story of the fall, we will see the likeness of Adam, the firstborn of humanity, to the firstborn sons. And we will also hear, through the younger son who becomes heir, an echo of the promise that the seed of the woman, not Adam the firstborn but one born later, would save humanity by crushing the head of the serpent.

It is true that there is nothing explicit in these narratives' retelling of the fall and the promise. However, the story of the fall and the promise of a new Adam reverberate in the background. Or, to put it another way, the story of the fall and the promise of a new Adam provide the only framework that makes sense of the repeated stories of firstborn sons being rejected for the second-born son. Without that background, we would have to wonder, Why is the Bible telling us over and over again about firstborn sons being rejected and later sons set up in their place?

---

33. Jordan calls attention to this theme in various writings. "The older son is often a type of Adam, and the younger of the Second Adam. Thus, Seth replaced Cain, Shem replaced Japheth (Genesis 5:32; 9:24; 11:10), Isaac replaced Ishmael, Jacob replaced Esau, Joseph replaced the older brothers, Ephraim replaced Manasseh (Genesis 48:18), Eleazar and Ithamar replaced Nadab and Abihu (Exodus 6:23; 24:1; Leviticus 10:1–6), David replaced his older brothers, and Jesus replaced Adam" (Jordan, *Through New Eyes*, 188).

However, understood in the light of the Bible's web of allusion, we recognize in the repeated stories of the firstborn being set aside a literary convention with profound theological implications, a conventional story pointing forward to the promise of the Messiah as a new Adam.

New Covenants

The Old Testament can be described as the story of a series of covenants, beginning with creation and progressing gradually until the time of Christ.[34] In Genesis, we see that God created the world originally into a covenant relationship with Himself, with Adam as the head of the covenant and the world placed under his authority and rule. Though Adam broke the covenant and his descendants departed so far from God that the judgment of the universal flood fell upon them, the original covenant was not repealed. Rather, God gave a renewed form of the covenant to Noah (Gen 9:1–17). However, the same pattern of sin and judgment followed, as Noah's descendants built the tower of Babel in rebellion against God. Nevertheless, God in His grace again gave a new covenant to another man, Abraham, along with the promise of salvation for mankind.

Essentially the same story of the covenant is repeated, over and over. Thus, Abraham's descendants also departed from God, worshiping idols in Egypt (cf. Josh 24:14). Because they fell into idolatry, God visited Israel with the judgment of slavery in Egypt. Then, in the fullness of time, God redeemed His people from Egypt and gave them a new covenant at Sinai. But no sooner were they constituted a priestly nation, than the children of Israel in the wilderness sinned like Adam, falling away from God's grace through idolatry. The first generation, therefore, died in the wilderness, but by the grace of God, the second generation was faithful. Even this, however, was not long-lasting. As the book of Judges shows, from the third generation onward the people repeatedly fell into idolatry. Eventually, in the days of the priest Eli, the ark of the covenant was taken away and the whole tabernacle system overturned in judgment.

Some years later, God gave a new covenant to the people through David, a new covenant that expanded the promises of the previous covenants and revealed more clearly the Savior who would come. The temple built by Solomon was the climactic moment of the gift of the Davidic

---

34. See Jordan, *Through New Eyes*; Leithart, *House for My Name*; Smith, *Eternal Covenant*; and Smith, *Covenantal Structure of the Bible*.

new covenant. But Solomon himself stumbled and after him the kings of Israel and Judah sinned even more seriously, leading their people into idolatry with them. The era of the kings ended with the judgments of Assyrian and Babylonian captivity.

Then, after seventy years of captivity, God rescued His people again, as He did in the days of Moses, bringing them back to the promised land and granting them a new covenant, a new temple, and a new priesthood. From the time of Ezra to the time of Jesus, the last phase of the old covenant era saw Israel placed in the midst of Gentile world powers to witness to them and bring them to the true God (Dan 2, 7).

Note that each of these new covenants was actually only a renewed form of the covenant with Adam. Though they all depend upon the promise given at the time of the fall, none of the new covenants provided the redemption that man needed nor the seed who would crush the head of the serpent. On the contrary, each new covenant ended with a repetition of the story of the fall and judgment, as if the point of the narrative is that all of his descendents are just like Adam. The fact that a renewal of the covenant was given, however, meant that God was keeping His promise to Adam and Eve and that eventually there would be a wholly new covenant with a successful covenant head. In the story of Jesus, we finally discover something completely new and different—a man who does not sin and fail. He is an altogether new Adam and He brings a wholly new covenant.

The larger biblical story, then, is a succession of stories each of which follows the same story line: God's gracious gift of a covenant, human sin and failure, God's judgment, and the gracious gift of a new covenant. That repeated pattern contains within it the original promise and gives Israel hope that someday the seed of the woman, a new Adam, will come to rescue her from sin and bring in a truly new covenant. The new covenant in Christ is the fulfillment of all the promises in the covenants of the old era. The new Adam, Jesus, brings a new world and becomes the head of a new race in him. This means, of course, a new creation—another theme that implies a new Adam unlike the first.

New Creation

The idea of a new Adam and a new covenant naturally imply the larger context of a new creation. Again, the most obvious example is the new

The Adamic Dimension

world after the Noahic deluge. In that case, the flood is a de-creation, and the post-flood new beginning is a whole new world, with a new covenant and a new Adam, as we have seen. As a theme, however, a new creation is usually implicit, hinted at by sevenfold sequences or by language alluding to the Garden of Eden or the original creation.[35] But there is one very explicit reference to a new creation in the Old Testament in two passages in Isaiah:

> For behold, I create new heavens and a new earth;
> And the former things shall not be remembered, nor come into mind.
> But be ye glad and rejoice forever in that which I create;
> For behold, I create Jerusalem a rejoicing,
> And her people a joy. (Isa 65:17–18; cf. also, e.g., Isa 41:20; 43:7; 45:8; 48:6–7)

> "For just as the new heavens and the new earth
> which I make, shall remain before Me," saith Yahweh,
> "So shall your seed and your name remain." (Isa 66:22)

Here the theme of a new creation expresses the promise of salvation, which includes restoration to the land and the building of a new Jerusalem in the return from exile. But it looks further to something greater as well, for in the Book of Revelation, John picks up Isaiah's language and shows us that a new creation and a new Jerusalem is the direction of world history. Isaiah linked the return to the land with the ultimate picture of salvation promised in the Garden in so far as he saw the new creation defined as a new Jerusalem, a city filled with people. This means that in the new heavens and earth, the original mandate given to Adam and Eve has been fulfilled, men have multiplied and filled the earth, and the Garden of Eden has been transformed into a great city filled with joy.[36]

The theme of salvation as fulfilled in a new creation is obviously grounded in the promise of Genesis 3:15 and calls to mind the first creation, the place of Adam, the fall into sin, and the horrible consequences for mankind. This means, too, that the theme of the Seed of the woman must be understood as implied. In other words, the biblical network of allusion obligates us to read between the lines. In particular, the new

---

35. See the references in note 25.

36. For a fuller development of the interrelated themes here, see Dumbrell, *End of the Beginning*.

Adam resonates in the background of the promise of the new creation because a new creation in which the former will not be remembered necessarily entails a new Adam who crushes the head of the serpent. Otherwise the former creation would not only be remembered; its pattern of fall and judgment would also dominate history and be repeated in perpetuity as it was throughout the old covenant era.

Universal Messiah

It is remarkable that in the days of Jesus and Paul the majority of the Jews, if not all, looked for a Messiah who would be a mere national savior and hero.[37] They missed the abundant references in the Old Testament to the Messiah as one who would save the Gentiles (cf. Deut 32:43; 2 Sam 22:50; Pss 18:49; 117:1–2; Isa 11:10; 42:1, 6; 49:6; 60:3, 5, 11, 16; 61:6; 62:2; 66:12, 19; Jer 16:19; Mal 1:11). Even more, they ignored the climax of the Abrahamic covenant in which God's ultimate purpose was expressed: "And in you all the families of the earth shall be blessed" (Gen 12:3b).

The strategic place of the Abrahamic promise in the narrative of Genesis cannot be overemphasized. The human race rebelled against God at the tower of Babel and sought to establish a totalitarian idolatrous State. Once again, as at the flood, the whole race of mankind was brought under judgment. And once again, one man was brought out of that judgment to provide a new beginning. But, we have to ask, a new beginning for whom? It must be noted that the new beginning was not merely for Abraham and his physical heirs, for the promise to Abraham was not merely that he and his children would be blessed. Rather, they were explicitly chosen to be a channel of blessing to the world. In other words, the seed-promise given to Adam and Eve would be fulfilled through Abraham and his seed, so that the world could be saved. Just as God saved the race through Noah and the ark, so also through the covenant grace given to Abraham, God was creating a new humanity.

This is clearly seen in the text of the covenant itself as it is first given in Genesis 12:1–3. Though it is true that the covenant includes the phrase "those who curse you will be cursed," that is not the end or climax

---

37. See N. T. Wright's extended discussion of the meaning of Messiahship in *Jesus and the Victory of God*, 477–539. Though the larger paragraph is about the nature of Jewish apocalyptic expectation, Wright includes a sentence that indicates the narrowness of their Messianic hope as well: "Their [Jewish] expectations remained national, territorial, and Temple-centered" (513).

of the covenant. As I pointed out above, the final clause promises that all the families of the earth will be blessed in Abraham (Gen 12:3). All the families and nations that have been dispersed by God's judgment at the tower of Babel will once again be united in blessing through Abraham. This is a vision of a new humanity and a new race of men. The seed that brings this to pass is the Messiah, a universal Savior—not a national but a global Lord.

Though the Jews of Jesus' day seem to have largely forgotten, Isaiah and the other prophets looked forward to a fulfillment of the Abrahamic covenant that included the Gentiles.

> Also the foreigners who join themselves to Yahweh,
> To minister unto him, and to love the name of Yahweh,
> To be his servants, every one that keepeth the sabbath from profaning it
> And holdeth fast my covenant;
> Even them I will bring to my holy mountain
> And make them joyful in my house of prayer.
> Their burnt offerings and their sacrifices shall be accepted on mine altar;
> For my house shall be called a house of prayer for all peoples.
> The Lord Yahweh, who gathereth the outcasts of Israel, declareth,
> I will gather yet others to him, besides those already gathered.
> (Isa 56:6–8)

The ends of the earth will be given to the Messiah (Ps 2:8). Through the victory of the cross, the ends of the earth will remember and all the families of the nations will worship the true God because the kingdom is His (Ps 22:27–28). Solomon's prayer for the king looks forward to the Messiah and His universal dominion (Ps 72). Every knee will bow and every tongue will confess His name (Isa 45:22–23; cf. Phil 2:9–11). The fulfillment of the Abrahamic covenant is the vision of the true Israel, a fulfillment that would come only through a universal Messiah, a new Adam to head a new race:

> And there shall come forth a shoot out of the stock of Jesse,
> and a branch out of his roots shall bear fruit.
> And the Spirit of Yahweh shall rest upon him,
> the Spirit of wisdom and understanding,
> the Spirit of counsel and might,
> the Spirit of knowledge and of the fear of Yahweh.

> And his delight shall be in the fear of Yahweh;
> and he shall not judge after the sight of his eyes,
> neither decide after the hearing of his ears;
> but with righteousness shall he judge the poor,
> and decide with equity for the meek of the earth;
> and he shall smite the earth with the rod of his mouth;
> and with the breath of his lips shall he slay the wicked.
> And righteousness shall be the girdle of his waist,
> and faithfulness the girdle of his loins.
> And the wolf shall dwell with the lamb,
> and the leopard shall lie down with the kid;
> and the calf and the young lion and the fatling together;
> and a little child shall lead them.
> And the cow and the bear shall feed;
> their young ones shall lie down together;
> and the lion shall eat straw like the ox.
> And the sucking child shall play on the hole of the asp,
> and the weaned child shall put his hand on the adder's den.
> They shall not hurt nor destroy in all my holy mountain;
> for the earth shall be full of the knowledge of Yahweh,
> as the waters cover the sea. (Isa 11:1–9)

As we have already seen, God the Father quotes from Isaiah 42:1 at Jesus' baptism. Among other things, this quotation is designed to show that the gift of the Spirit means the beginning of a new world:

> Behold, my servant, whom I uphold;
> my chosen, in whom my soul delighteth:
> I have put my Spirit upon him;
> he will bring forth justice to the Gentiles.
> He will not cry, nor lift up his voice,
> nor cause it to be heard in the street.
> A bruised reed will he not break,
> and a dimly burning wick will he not quench:
> he will bring forth justice in truth.
> He will not fail nor be discouraged,
> till he have set justice in the earth;
> and the isles shall wait for his law. (Isa 42:1–4)

Jesus Himself, after returning from the temptation in the wilderness full of the Spirit, visited Nazareth and announced that He had been anointed with the Spirit—an allusion to His baptism—in order to bring in the kingdom by preaching the gospel to the poor (Luke 4:14–21). It was to Isaiah's promise of the Messianic kingdom that He referred, again making the link between His baptism and kingdom ministry explicit:

> The Spirit of the Lord Yahweh is upon me;
> because Yahweh hath anointed me to preach good tidings unto
> the meek;
> he hath sent me to bind up the broken-hearted,
> to proclaim liberty to the captives,
> and the opening of the prison to them that are bound;
> to proclaim the year of Yahweh's favor,
> and the day of vengeance of our God;
> to comfort all that mourn;
> to appoint unto them that mourn in Zion,
> to give unto them a garland for ashes,
> the oil of joy for mourning,
> the garment of praise for the spirit of heaviness;
> that they may be called trees of righteousness,
> the planting of Yahweh, that he may be glorified. (Isa 61:1–3)

In Isaiah, then, the theme of the gift of the Spirit stands out as a new world theme. This means the Father's quotation of Isaiah 42 must also be understood in the light of the larger emphasis on the Spirit and the new world in Isaiah, who is unique among the prophets in presenting this theme. For prophets like Ezekiel and Joel, the gift of the Spirit is poured out on the people (Ezek 36:26–27; 37:14; 39:29; Joel 2:28–29). Only Isaiah presents the Spirit-filled Messiah as the king of a new world and speaks of Messiah being anointed with the Spirit to fulfill His work. By quoting from Isaiah, then, God the Father draws our attention to the Son as the Messianic king over the whole world, a new and final Adam.

Conclusion

Other related themes point to the Edenic promise as well. For example, when Jael crushes the head of the Serpent, General Sisera (Judg 4:17), we find an allusion to the original promise of the seed of the woman and a reminder that it will be fulfilled.[38] We saw that prophecies of a universal king and a global kingdom are aspects of the doctrine of the Messiah that presuppose the coming of a new Adam, and we could add that these themes are related to Isaiah's prophecies of the Servant of the

---

38. Cf. also the cases of Abimelech, Goliath, and Absalom. All of these men were killed by a head wound. There is in their stories a subtle allusion to the promise in Genesis 3:15, since they were all Satanic leaders who fought against God's kingdom.

Lord, which show the Messiah as the true Israel. Messiah as the New Israel is, thus, another picture of the Messiah as the last Adam.

I have not by any means set forth every theme or structure that includes implicit allusion to the promise of Genesis 3:15 or the theme of a new Adam. I am not even sure that I can. What I have done, I hope, is show clearly that, through various literary devices, the Old Testament repeatedly calls to mind the fall of man and the promise that God granted to humanity in Genesis 3:15. The covenant promises given to Abraham, Israel, and David are, in fact, simply expanded and detailed versions of that original promise.

Moreover, we must assume that a godly and intelligent reader of the Scriptures in the days of Moses or David or Daniel would have understood the kind of allusions and narrative structures mentioned above and would, therefore, have looked forward to the Messiah as a new Adam, a new leader of the race who would not fail as all others had. We must make that assumption because it is the prophetic writers of the ancient Scriptures who are making these various sorts of subtle and multifaceted allusions. It is not modern interpreters who have invented these things, but Moses and the prophets, who were quite self-consciously alluding to, interacting with, commenting upon, and expanding themes in earlier Scriptures through literary devices, most of which were common to the ancient world. Since these literary devices were the authors' method for communicating theological truth, taking account of allusions, echoes, and conventional stories leads not only to a richer and fuller reading of Scripture, but also to the most natural reading, because doing so conforms to ancient literary convention. In other words, taking account of these conventions offers the most truly biblical reading of the Bible.

The whole network of prophecies about the Messiah, through allusions as well as explicit promises, shows us clearly that the Messiah of Israel was never a "nationalist" figure. Contrary to the Pharisees and their pride, the Old Testament vision of the Messiah is the expectation of a new Adam, a final Adam who would crush the serpent and deliver man from bondage. The Messiah of Israel is the seed of the woman who brings about the fulfillment of the Abrahamic promise—He is the Savior of the world. For Jesus to be baptized and consecrated as Messiah, therefore, has a broader meaning than is commonly realized, for to be Messiah is to be a new Adam, the head of a wholly new race of men, men who are like the Messiah—led by the Spirit of God, rather than the flesh of the old Adam (cf. 1 Cor 15:35–49).

MESSIAH AS NEW ADAM IN GOSPELS

The Synoptic Gospels all present Jesus as a new Adam, though in various ways. The most obvious is that they all show Him facing the tempter immediately after He is ordained as Messiah. Just as the first Adam was tempted after he was blessed by God and given his commission to labor for the kingdom, Jesus, the last Adam, was immediately led to the wilderness after He was blessed with the quintessential gift of the new covenant and ordained by the Father for service. The connection between blessing and temptation is a narrative structure that should be obvious to anyone who remembers the story of Adam and notes how often leaders in the Bible face a temptation that will decide whether their own stories will be a tragedy or a comedy.[39]

Of the Synoptics, the Gospel of Luke makes this point with special emphasis by structuring the story to draw attention to Jesus as the last Adam. Unlike Matthew, who places the genealogy of Jesus at the beginning of his narrative, Luke inserts the genealogy of Jesus *after* the account of His baptism, a seemingly odd place for a list of Jesus' ancestors. But Luke does something else that Matthew does not do, he lists the ancestors of Jesus all the way back to Adam, who is designated, "the son of God."

So, after the story of Jesus' baptism where Jesus is identified by the Father as "My Son," we have a genealogy that takes us all the way back to the first man created who is also "the son of God." This clearly links Jesus and Adam. Then, after this theologically pregnant list of Jesus' ancestors that ends with Adam, "the son of God," we read that Jesus was led into the wilderness to be tempted by the devil. Luke invites us to compare Jesus and Adam, the Garden and the wilderness, and the two temptations and their results. Once we recognize the implications of the structure of the narrative, there can be no question about the fact that Luke sees Jesus the Messiah as Jesus the last Adam, the Son of God who has come to crush the head of the serpent.

Moreover, from the beginning of the Gospel of Luke, there are hints of the new Adam theme in the background. When Luke tells us the story

---

39. See Leithart, *Deep Comedy*.

of Mary, he presents her not only as the mother of the man who will bring the fulfillment of the Abrahamic promise but also as the mother of the seed who will destroy the serpent. The hope is expressed, not by a quotation of the words of Scripture, but rather by the emphasis on the mother. Mary is the woman who brings salvation to the world through her son. This ties into and brings fulfillment of the theme that began with Eve herself: "*your* seed shall...."

Careful readers of the Bible from Genesis to Luke will understand the importance of the theme of the mother who miraculously gives birth to a savior. The stories of Samson and Samuel both stand out, but they are not alone in bearing witness to the promise that the seed of *the woman* will save the world from Satan. When we read Luke—and Matthew also, of course, though Luke is more detailed—telling us the story of a woman who will miraculously bring forth a son who will bring salvation to His people and the fulfillment of the promises of God, we should hear the echo of the ancient promise of Genesis 3:15. Mary herself understood the blessing granted her and rejoiced that she was most blessed among women because she would be the mother of the promised one, the last Adam.

The three Synoptic Gospels, all recording Jesus' temptation as immediately subsequent to His baptism, show us Jesus as a new Adam, the one who finally and decisively crushes the head of the serpent at the cross, finishing the work He began in the wilderness. Baptism leads to temptation because, once officially installed in His office as a new Adam, Jesus had to confront Satan. In fact, because in His baptism He was anointed as the Seed of the Woman, meeting Satan in the wilderness had to be the *first item* on His agenda. A literal translation of Mark gives us, "Immediately the Spirit cast Him out into the wilderness." Though Matthew and Luke tell us that Jesus was "led" by the Spirit (Matt 4:1; Luke 4:1), Mark uses the word that typically describes demons being cast out. The Spirit forced Jesus into the wilderness to fight the devil. Whichever word is used, the emphasis on the relationship between the wilderness temptation and the baptism of Jesus is consistent in all the Synoptics and testifies to the fact that Jesus was baptized with the Spirit as the new Adam.

With this in mind, it is not surprising to see the new Adam theme in other parts of the Gospel story, especially at the end of the Savior's life. At the cross, Jesus faces another struggle with Satan in which there are clear allusions to Adam. The very mention of Satan entering Judas and initiating the final struggle recalls Satan approaching Adam and Eve in the Garden to tempt them (Luke 22:3; John 13:2, 27). Add to this Jesus' struggle against temptation in a Garden (John 18:1; Luke 22:39–46), the repeated exhortations to the disciples to pray so that they will not enter temptation, the threefold temptation to come down from the cross, corresponding to the threefold temptation by the devil (Luke 23:35–39), and the reference to paradise (Luke 23:43). The allusion to Adam and the first creation is apparent.

The Gospel of John does not give us the narrative of baptism leading to wilderness temptation, but John has his own way of alluding to Adam. The very first words of his Gospel point back to Genesis 1:1 and in the first section of his Gospel he has an eight-day sequence that suggests a new creation.[40] However, it is at the end of his Gospel where the most interesting picture of the new Adam appears.

> The marriage imagery in the Gospel is an implicit Adam typology, with the Lord awakening in the garden tomb as a new Adam. His wounded side (J[ohn] 19:34) having been healed, Jesus beholds Mary Magdalene, who has become the new Eve. However, the time of Mary's joy must await the day when she will be presented to the Son of Man by Father God (R[ev] 21:2).[41]

We have only scratched the surface here, but the point should be clear that Jesus' ministry is understood in all four Gospels to be the ministry of the new Adam. The official beginning of that ministry at Jesus' baptism constitutes the moment when He is commissioned to undo what the first Adam did and begin to build the kingdom that Adam was disqualified from building.

SIGNIFICANCE OF MESSIAH AS NEW ADAM

The significance of the fact that Jesus is the new Adam is broad and deep, but since it was Paul who makes the theme explicit, it is usually a subject of Pauline study and is not related to the baptism of Jesus. In the two central passages we introduced above—Romans 5:12–21 and 1 Corinthians 15:20–58—Paul brings this theme into relation with the whole sweep of

---

40. For a detailed discussion, see Jordan, "Seven-Fold Covenant Model."
41. Gage, "St. John's Vision," 97.

human history and with the fundamental notion of "mankind." Some of the implications Paul suggests are (1) a dichotomy of the old man in Adam and the new man in Christ; (2) the last Adam as the man of the Spirit; (3) the new Adam as the head of a new humanity; and (4) a new race that fulfills the creation mandate. What is important to note is that each of these Pauline themes is related to the baptism of Jesus and Christian baptism.

In Adam vs. In Christ

Though Paul never speaks of Jesus' baptism, it remains nevertheless true that it is primarily through the apostle Paul that we learn the *significance* of Jesus' baptism as the new Adam, because it is Paul who addresses the theme of the Adam/Christ typology directly. But when Paul introduces the Adam/Christ typology in Romans 5, he is not merely saying Adam is a type of Christ. Rather, Paul sets up the dichotomy of the old man in Adam and the new man in Christ.

There are two opposing humanities in view. Man in Adam is man in rebellion against God; the seed follows the head.[42] Adam is a type only in the sense that he is the head of a race. Jesus is the head of a morally different humanity, but not due to any obedience of their own. Christ is the obedient one who justifies the new race in Him. Grace overcomes sin and death, so that the new humanity in Christ is a people who are justified in Christ and therefore also through Him *reign in life* (5:17; cf. also 5:21). Just as dominion is essential to the covenant in Adam, so it is also in Christ.

The antithesis between these two groups must be absolute in principle (though not in everyday life). Even more, antithesis characterizes the whole course of history and continues in eternity. Though only hinted at by the reference to "reign" in Romans 5—echoing the dominion mandate of Genesis 1:26–28—the victorious rule of Christ comes to the fore in 1 Corinthians, where the conflict of two humanities is explicit since Paul tells us that Jesus will reign till all enemies are brought into subjection (1 Cor 15:25). In the end, Jesus must be victorious, and the old humanity, characterized by the flesh, disobedience, and sin, must die forever. Until the end of history, when Jesus returns, there is spiritual warfare.

---

42. Adam is considered in Romans 5 as a covenant head, not as an individual man. The distinction is important because the historical Adam believed the promise of God, which means, interestingly, that he is now included among those who are "in Christ."

Of course, it is primarily between the two humanities, but because of the remainder of indwelling sin, warfare occurs even among members of the new humanity. So, for example, Paul's epistles are his spiritual battles with sin and error in the churches. They are not primarily directed to the old humanity in Adam—though certainly the churches' obedience to God's word would result in victory against Satan and his seed.

It is important in this connection to remember that the new humanity is a race of men baptized by the same Spirit who came as a dove on Jesus. The weapons of their warfare are Spiritual (Eph 6:10–17; 2 Cor 10:4), not fleshly, because they are the new Holy-Spirit-defined race of mankind. Jesus in the Spirit fights His enemies through the body that is His Church.

There is another dimension of this to consider: the theme of obedience as it relates to the Gospel accounts. Though the obedience of Christ emphasized by Paul is seen throughout Jesus' life and most especially in His death on the cross—Paul's "one act of righteousness" (Rom 5:18)—it had a special beginning at Jesus' baptism and the temptation that immediately followed. For only when He was baptized did Jesus enter the special calling for which He was born and only when He had confronted the devil and won a decisive victory was His obedience truly manifest. Jesus' baptism therefore is the initial step in the path of *specifically* Messianic obedience, the obedience of the last Adam which would bring righteousness and life to a new humanity. Insofar as Jesus' baptism was a baptism unto the death of the cross, the dove-Spirit designating Him as the sacrifice like Isaac, we may say that it was the gift of the Spirit at His baptism that enabled Him to offer Himself up in life and death (cf. Heb 9:14).

What this means for those in Christ is that they are called by the gift of the Spirit to the same sacrificial life of obedience, for they have been baptized by the same dovelike Spirit that baptized Jesus. When the body of Christ walks in the way of Christ, the Spirit of Christ defeats Jesus' enemies and brings in the kingdom.

New Adam and the Spirit

Though we have already alluded to this topic, the gift of the Spirit to the new race of mankind in Christ is fundamental and definitive. The old man, Adam, was the man of flesh but the last Adam is the man of the Spirit. Paul expounds this theme in 1 Corinthians in terms directly related to the subject of Jesus' baptism:

> So also is the resurrection of the dead. It is sown in corruption; it is raised in incorruption: it is sown in dishonor; it is raised in glory: it is sown in weakness; it is raised in power: it is sown a natural body; it is raised a Spiritual body. If there is a natural body, there is also a Spiritual body. So also it is written, The first man Adam became a living soul. The last Adam became a life-giving Spirit. Howbeit that is not first which is Spiritual, but that which is natural; then that which is Spiritual. The first man is of the earth, earthy: the second man is of heaven. As is the earthy, such are they also that are earthy: and as is the heavenly, such are they also that are heavenly. And as we have borne the image of the earthy, we shall also bear the image of the heavenly. (1 Cor 15:42–49)

The word "Spiritual" in the expression "Spiritual body" refers to the Holy Spirit. Paul tells us that the new creation is distinctly and emphatically characterized by the presence and activity of the Holy Spirit, as opposed to the old creation natural body, the body of flesh (1 Cor 15:39, 50). We must be careful to note that when Paul speaks here of flesh and dust, he is not suggesting they are inherently evil. God created Adam good. Rather than suggesting the flesh is evil, Paul speaks eschatologically, implying that the first creation was never meant to be the final stage for man, that God had intended something more than what was given to Adam in the Garden. The gift of the Spirit of God to indwell a new humanity was part of the original plan. The sin of Adam did not alter God's purpose to bring mankind into the higher life of the new creation.[43]

By contrasting the natural body—man as created rather than man as fallen—to the Spiritual body, Paul implies that the new creation is implicit in the first creation. This means that even had there been no fall, there would have been a second Adam. In other words, since the

---

43. See Vos, *Pauline Eschatology*, 166–70. Gaffin explains the two covenantal ages in 1 Corinthians 15 in the language of Paul: "'psychical' and 'spiritual' now describe two comprehensive states of affairs, two orders of existence contrasted temporally. The one follows upon the other and together they encompass the whole of history. Verse 46 is a compressed overview of history. As the era of the first Adam, the psychical order is the preeschatological aeon, the incomplete, transitory, and provisional world-age. As the era of the last Adam, the pneumatic order is the eschatological aeon, the complete, definitive, and final world-age" (*Resurrection and Redemption*, 78–85).

The Adamic Dimension

incarnation of God and the union of God with man was already the aim of creation, the notion of a second and last Adam is implicit in the first creation. The whole typological matrix related to Adam—creation, Garden, covenant, marriage, and so forth—from the beginning already points to the future incarnation of God, before the fall, before Israel. Paul's argument in 1 Corinthians 15:42–49 requires us to see the typology of first and last Adam as fundamental to the symbolism of the original creation and therefore implicit throughout the Scriptures, confirming our reading of various Old Testament themes as pointing to the Messiah as a new Adam.

The question of when Jesus takes on His role as last Adam is also answered implicitly in these verses of 1 Corinthians. In Paul's description of the new creation, the man from heaven—who is the second man and the last Adam—is the man of the Spirit, the man who is indwelt by the Spirit fully. Though from His birth Jesus was filled with the Spirit, something more is bestowed in His baptism. Jesus' baptism was not, as some have suggested, a mere outward sign for John or others to know that He was filled with the Spirit.[44] On the contrary, the Spirit came upon Him in a new way, filling Him and qualifying Him in His humanity to be Messiah, for until His baptism, though Jesus was no doubt always about His Father's business, He had not entered His Messianic office. It was only when Jesus turned thirty and was ready to begin His work as a priest after the order of Melchizedek that the Old Testament prophecies about the Spirit being poured out on the Messiah find their fulfillment in His baptism (e.g., Isa 11:1–2; 42:1). That baptism was what initially characterized Him as the Spiritual man who was also able to bestow the gift of the Spirit. Thus, though the full realization of the new humanity was not initiated until Jesus' resurrection and ascension, we must also say that the baptism of Jesus was the beginning of the kingdom of God and the birth of the new race of Spirit-filled mankind.

To say that the new Spiritual humanity begins with Jesus' baptism is not to speak of an absolute beginning. Or, to put it in other words, there are multiple points that we can call "the beginning." In one sense, the beginning of the new creation and the new human race was at Jesus' birth, for the incarnation of God Himself began a whole new era in history. From the moment of Jesus' conception in Mary's womb, the history

---

44. This is something of an overstatement of Ryle's view but is not entirely inaccurate. Cf. Ryle, *John*, 1:65.

of God and man changed—the second Person of the eternal Trinity was inseparably united with mankind. At His birth, then, Jesus was already Savior, though obviously, the incarnation alone was not enough.

Because Jesus is a true man, He had to grow to maturity and be ordained and empowered for the work that God had called Him to perform. The baptism of Jesus as His priestly ordination to ministry was the beginning of the new creation and the new humanity in the sense that then, for the first time in history, the Spirit of God had been bestowed on a man without measure. From the time the Spirit was poured out on Him, Jesus began His Messianic work and the kingdom of God came into the world.

But, of course, without the cross, His baptism would not have been effective, and without the resurrection, the cross would have been of no benefit. So we must also say that the new world actually began after Jesus' resurrection, when He ascended into heaven and sat at the right hand of the Father, because the kingdom cannot really begin until the King Himself is enthroned and the Spirit is bestowed on His people. Then we know that all authority in heaven and on earth is in His hands.

However, in the New Testament vision of the kingdom of God, even after Jesus' ascension and the gift of the Spirit, the kingdom has not quite arrived, for the New Testament authors all anxiously look forward to and await His vindication as a kingdom-defining event. As long as the temple was standing in Jerusalem, Jesus was not definitively manifest as Messiah, for the Jewish system that rejected and crucified Him appeared to be functioning with God's approval. There is here a repetition of ancient Jewish history, a fulfillment of prophetic typology. Just as in the days of Jeremiah, it took the actual destruction of Jerusalem and the temple to convince many of the Jews that Jeremiah was a true prophet, so also it took the destruction of Jerusalem in AD 70 as Jesus predicted to demonstrate God's wrath against Israel for putting Jesus to death, authenticating Jesus as a prophet and therefore also as Messiah and Son of God.

What this means is that a whole seventy-year period constitutes the coming of the new age in various stages, each of which is essential to the kingdom. But some of these stages have been neglected. Though the incarnation, death, resurrection, and ascension of Jesus are recognized as kingdom-defining events, the destruction of Jerusalem in AD 70 is not properly understood by many, and Jesus' baptism by the Spirit is not often seen in connection with the teaching of Paul that the new humanity is the new race of man characterized by the Spirit. It is true, of course, that Paul is thinking of the resurrected Christ, but just as Jesus offered Himself through the Spirit that was given at His baptism, He was resurrected in the Spirit because He was the Spiritual man. Death could not hold Him because of the life of the Spirit poured out on Him.

To understand this from another perspective, remember Jesus' words to Martha: "I am the resurrection and the life: he that believeth on me, though he die, yet shall he live; and whosoever liveth and believeth on me shall never die. Believest thou this?" (John 11:25–26). Note that Jesus did not say that someday He would *become* the resurrection and the life. As the Spirit-anointed Messiah, He was already the resurrection and the life. That is the reason that He had to resurrect. The Spiritual Man could not be defeated by death because He is life. He is the life-giving Spirit. The age in which we live now is the age of the Spirit because Jesus the last Adam now pours out His Spirit on His people, the new humanity in Him. His baptism in the Spirit was a decisive moment in the coming of the new age of the Spirit in which His people would be baptized by that same Spirit and eventually share in the resurrection life with Spirit-bodies like Christ's.

New Adam, New Humanity

In Romans 5, Paul writes of those in Christ and those in Adam as parallel groups, two races of man:

> So then as through one trespass the judgment came unto all men to condemnation; even so through one act of righteousness the free gift came unto all men to justification of life. For as through the one man's disobedience the many were made sinners, even so through the obedience of the one shall the many be made righteous. (Rom 5:18–19)

Of the new race in Christ, Paul says that where sin abounded, grace much more abounded (Rom 5:20). In Ephesians 2, Paul speaks of reconciled Jews and Gentiles as one new man, a body of believers indwelt by the Spirit of God, constituting a new humanity (2:15). And in 2 Corinthians, Paul speaks of those in Christ as new creatures, a new creation (5:17). There are many other relevant passages, but the idea is familiar enough to proceed into less familiar territory.

The language of a last Adam, a new creation, a new humanity, and a new Jerusalem all combines to give us a picture of a whole new world in Christ. But what does it actually mean? With regard to the idea of a new humanity, for example, we can ask some very concrete questions. What specifically is new about the new humanity, since they are born of the old humanity and look the same? Is the new humanity fewer in number and less in cultural achievement than the old humanity—the culturally retarded remnant of a small, historically insignificant sect? If it is obvious that we must consider the topic of the new Adam in the light of the old Adam, is it not equally obvious that we must consider the new humanity and its task in relation to the old humanity and its task?

New creation passages in the Bible always present the new as something more glorious than the old. The new Jerusalem in the book of Revelation is the clearest example of this. No city on earth has ever been or could ever be so glorious. But the new is not presented as a miraculous replacement for the old, as if the old is simply trashed and the new put in its place. On the contrary, the symbolism of the new Jerusalem connects the new to the old and shows that the new is the *fulfillment* of the old, a fulfillment that transcends our imagination.

In the same way, the theme of a new humanity is ultimately fulfilled in the future resurrection, when God's people will be glorified like Christ. But the new humanity does not *begin* with the resurrection, for death is the *last* enemy that Jesus defeats (1 Cor 15:26). Within history, the new humanity, Christ's body and Church, is built through the work of the Spirit. To see this, we have to consider expressions like last Adam, new creation, and new Jerusalem, in the light of God's promise to save the world.

> For God so loved the world, that he gave his only begotten Son, that whosoever believeth on him should not perish, but have eternal life. For God sent no the Son into the world to judge the world; but that the world should be saved through him. (John 3:16–17)

Benjamin B. Warfield argued long ago that these verses imply the victory of the Gospel in history because these verses make real sense only if the *world*—the vast majority of humanity—is converted.[45] God

---

45. See Benjamin B. Warfield's famous sermon on John 3:16, "God's Immeasurable Love."

loved the world He created, especially His image, mankind. And He sent His Son into the world to save it, not to judge and destroy it. If that is what Jesus came for, it will be accomplished. The question is, How?

The answer is that the one who was baptized by the Spirit is the risen and enthroned Lord who baptizes His people with the Spirit. The eschatological gift of the Spirit of God that the prophets of the old covenant longed for has finally come. Pentecost was the overcoming of Babel, the beginning of a unified race of mankind that speaks a new language, a race of men that will grow and increase until it fills the world, replacing the old humanity and fulfilling the original mandate to be fruitful and multiply. The new race is Jesus' body, consisting of a vast multitude of people filled with the Spirit He poured out upon them, and it is through His body and His Spirit that the resurrected and enthroned Messiah works. It is to that body that He gave the command, "Disciple the nations" (Matt 28:19a), and the promise that He will enable His Church to fulfill His will, "Lo, I am with you always, even to the end of the world" (Matt 28:20b).

Last Adam and the Creation Mandate

The new Adam/new humanity theme in the Bible already answers the question about the last Adam's relationship to the original commission given to mankind in the Garden, but it is worth reflecting specifically on the topic of the Creation Mandate. God called Adam—and through him all mankind—to a specific task. Adam was to rule the world under God and for God. This included working to bring out the potential of the world, finishing the task that God began during the creation week.

In the beginning, the world was dark, without order, and empty (Gen 1:2). God created plants and animals, but only in small numbers. He created only two humans. He gave Adam the task of increasing and ordering, essentially continuing the work God had begun. In other words, mankind was commissioned to nurture the perfect but immature creation into a mature condition. If Adam had not sinned, the old humanity in him would have transformed the world from its original good but immature condition into a condition of glory and beauty.

Again, the picture of the new Jerusalem in the book of Revelation supplies the best illustration. In the New Jerusalem, all the glory and beauty of Eden is amplified and expanded. The jewels that were hidden in Eden's ground have been polished and made into the foundations for the heavenly city. The gold has been mined and made into streets. A river still flows from the center, but it now supplies many trees of life, and the one man and one woman of the Garden have become a multitude that no one can number. What we look forward to as the eternal city is the fulfillment of the Garden.

So who builds the city—and when and how? Does the heavenly city simply appear at the end of a world history that is similar to the story of the old Adam—a succession of one dismal event after another? What is the new Adam doing in heaven now? How does Jesus' earthly body, the Church, relate to the original mandate given to Adam? We know that the original mandate was repeated to Noah (Gen 9:1–7), but does that mean it applies to Christians now? Or has it been done away?

A full answer to these questions would require a book, but what we have seen about Jesus as the new Adam suggests the outline of a biblical answer. The first Adam was given a commission that he and his seed failed to keep. By contrast, the last Adam kept the commandments of God and perfectly fulfilled the work He was given. Furthermore, He is not dead and gone. He rose again from the dead and ascended on high to sit at the right hand of God the Father. From His position at God's right hand, His first official work was to baptize the Church with the same Spirit that baptized Him and enabled Him to fulfill His task.

What, then, should we expect? If the sin and failure of the first Adam dooms those in him, how does the righteousness and victory of the last Adam influence those in Him? Doesn't Paul give us the answer when he says, "where sin abounded, grace did much more abound" (Rom 5:20)? The last Adam has a seed, which is also called His body, through which He works in the world. He is not idly passing by the centuries, waiting for a chance to return. Through His Holy Spirit and in His Church, He is working to bring about the fulfillment of the Great Commission that He gave to the Church. Also, He is working to defeat all His enemies so that, through His body, the Creation Mandate originally given to Adam can be fulfilled.

The Great Commission itself implies this when it says that the disciples are to teach the nations to put into practice "all things whatsoever I have commanded you" (Matt 28:20). Though some, perhaps a very large percentage of modern evangelicals, understand this to be the commandments of the "New Testament" or just the "teaching of Jesus," a proper reading of Jesus' teaching and the rest of the New Testament will not sustain such an interpretation. Jesus' commands include all His teaching from Genesis to Revelation. In fact, if we keep in mind that it is the Second Person of the Trinity that reveals God, we will understand that the command in the Garden is specifically a command of Jesus to the first Adam—one of Jesus' commands that must be obeyed. If the disciples baptize the nations and teach them to submit to Jesus, surely the Christianized world will obey the original command and, through the work of the Spirit who baptized them, bring about the total and final victory of the last Adam.

Unless Jesus' body, the Church, the seed of the last Adam, shares in and brings to historical realization the victory of Christ, the whole typology of Adam and his seed loses its meaning. We would have to say, where sin abounded, grace was frail, lacking the Spiritual strength to overcome. In such a view, the first Adam and his sin dominates not only the history of the world until Christ but also until the end, crippling even the baptized body of the last Adam. The first Adam ruined the world with his sin and those born from him could not escape the power of their birth. But what about the second birth? Is the second birth by the Spirit less powerful and influential than the first birth from Adam? How could that be?

The biblical picture of Christ as the last Adam cannot possibly be a picture of an ineffectual, enfeebled leader whose impact on His seed is minimal compared to that of the first Adam. But that is precisely what many Christians today believe. The common notion, though perhaps not thought through carefully, is that the seed of the last Adam cannot possibly fulfill the commission given to the first Adam and his seed. What is unwittingly included in that idea is the belief that the work of the last Adam on the cross, in His resurrection, and through the baptism of the Spirit from Pentecost onward is ineffectual. The last Adam is found to be less important for the history of the human race than the first. This popular view is exactly the opposite of the biblical picture.

In the Bible, Jesus is the victor over Satan, beginning with His defeat of the devil when He was tempted in the wilderness, continuing throughout His ministry, and climaxing in the cross, resurrection, and ascension. However, Jesus' victory over sin and Satan did not end when He sat at the right hand of God. On the contrary, as the last Adam, He is the father of a seed, a race of men, who have been born of the Spirit of God, which He poured out on Pentecost. And the race of men that He leads will follow their head and, like Him, be successful where the seed of the first Adam failed.

CONCLUSION

We have seen here that the typology of Adam and the Messiah, explicitly identified by the apostle Paul, underlies the whole narrative of the Old Testament and is presupposed in the Gospels. When Jesus was baptized by the Spirit, the quintessential gift of the new covenant, the kingdom of God began in a decisive manner. He was the first man to be filled with the Spirit and the only man to be filled without measure. Since the gift of the Spirit includes all that it means to be in the new covenant, the gift of the Spirit to Jesus at His baptism was a guarantee of the future blessings of the covenant, including His throne and crown. It was necessary, therefore, for Jesus to meet and defeat Satan immediately—which He did.

As the last Adam, Jesus is head of a race of men and they will follow Him because they have also been given the Spirit. The seed of the last Adam have been born of the Holy Spirit, have been baptized by the Holy Spirit, and are indwelt by the Holy Spirit. In various ways, the New Testament tells us that the Church of Jesus Christ is the new race of Spirit-men. Though it is true that the full meaning of the gift of the Spirit waits for the resurrection, just as it also did for Jesus, to be filled with the Spirit here and now in history means that the Church is endowed with the power to accomplish all God has called her to do. Furthermore, Christ is with His Church to enable her to disciple the nations of the world and lead His Church to keep His commandments, increasing His Spirit-led dominion of grace and love until every enemy is defeated.

Understood in the light of the fact that Jesus is the last Adam, the baptism of Jesus is one of the most important events in the history of the world, an event of cosmic significance because in it the history of the whole creation turned from the old covenant to the new—not entirely, but initially and definitively. It took the cross, resurrection, ascension, enthronement, Pentecost, and the judgment of the old covenant temple to complete the transition. But now that the transition is complete, the seed of the last Adam must multiply and increase and have dominion over all creation by the power of the Spirit so that where sin abounded, grace may indeed super-abound.

Many raise the question, What in fact was the nature of this baptism with which the Lord was baptized? What did it amount to, the baptism of our Lord and Savior Jesus Christ, who for the sake of the salvation of all, became human? As such he was to show himself to be the beginning of a certain paradoxical life on account of which he is called Adam, since for Adam's sake and for the rest of those who have arisen from Adam he becomes the beginning of everlasting life, in the same way that Adam was the original of this temporary and moral life.[46]

---

46. Theodore of Mopsuestia, quoted in Simonetti, ed., *Matthew 1–13*, 51.

4

The Trinitarian Dimension

THE STORY OF JESUS' baptism is relevant to the doctrine of the Trinity in two important respects. First, the narrative of Jesus' baptism, recorded in all three Synoptic Gospels and referred to in the Gospel of John, is the only narrative passage in Scripture in which all three persons of the Trinity clearly appear. It offers, therefore, a definitive refutation of one of the two basic ancient Trinitarian heresies, Sabellianism, also called modalism. Second, the narrative of Jesus' baptism offers abundant material for considering how the Trinitarian persons relate to one another.

In order to give adequate consideration to both of these aspects of the story, there are four themes we must consider: (1) the two ancient Trinitarian heresies, with special emphasis on modalism; (2) the motive of Trinitarian heresies, ancient and modern; (3) the distinction between the economic and the ontological Trinity; and (4) the relatively neglected Trinitarian truths that can be gleaned from the narrative of Jesus' baptism.

HERESIES ANCIENT AND MODERN

The two most influential Trinitarian heresies are Arianism and Sabellianism, also called modalism. The history of the early Church's struggle with these heresies is complex, and defining the exact forms these heresies assumed in various times and places is a subject of some controversy. For this essay, a simple outline of each is sufficient for purposes of definition. Sabellianism, clearly refuted by the story of Jesus' baptism, will occupy more of our attention.

Arianism

Arianism must be discussed because it is closely associated, both theologically and historically, with Sabellianism and constitutes one of the most influential and long-lasting heresies that have plagued the Church. Even today, major groups claiming to be Christian hold to a doctrine of Christ that falls within the broad category of Arianism. However, for consideration of the narrative of Christ's baptism, Arianism is a secondary concern. The relevant Scriptures reveal the three persons of the Trinity interacting with one another but do not specifically emphasize the divine nature of the Son and the Spirit. Indeed, from the perspective of Arianism, the fact that God is invisible implies that Son and Spirit cannot be the true God since they may both be visibly manifested, as they were at Jesus' baptism.[1]

A careful historical definition of the Arian heresy is not necessary here. The historical development of the fourth century Trinitarian controversies is extremely complicated and recent scholars have considerably revised the traditional view of what happened, making the term "Arianism" itself suspect. However, I continue to use the term simply because it is traditional, widely known, and for my purposes adequate to express the theological view I address. So, in this book, Arianism is defined as any post-Nicene doctrine of the Son that denies He is eternal and ontologically equal to the Father.[2]

In the modern world, this label would apply to groups like the Jehovah's Witnesses who believe that Christ was a created being, as well as to the many individual teachers and churches that deny Jesus' true divinity. The famous poet John Milton also should be understood as Arian, since he believed that the Son and Spirit were created before the rest of the world and were called "God" only because of their official status, like judges in the Old Testament.[3] Socinianism and forms of modern liberalism that deny of the deity of Christ also fall into the broad category

---

1. Barnes, "Visible Christ," 329–55. I continue to use the common designation "Arianism" though Barnes prefers not to for reasons of historical accuracy.

2. Of course, the problem began before Nicea, but until the First Council of Nicea in 325, the view now commonly called Arian was not clearly defined as heretical. According to Lewis Ayres (*Nicea and Its Legacy*), it was not until the 360s that the Nicene Creed came to be widely viewed as a definition of orthodoxy, resulting in the more refined statement of the second Ecumenical Council, the Nicene-Constantinopolitan Creed of 381.

3. For an excellent discussion of Milton's view, see Rumrich, "Milton's Arianism."

of Arianism.[4] In our day, numerous heretical teachers, both within and without traditional churches, deny the deity of Christ.[5]

It is interesting to note that Cornelius Plantinga, Jr., identifies Arianism as tritheism, because even though Arianism does teach that only the Father is the true God, it also usually teaches that the Son and the Spirit are also to be worshiped as God.[6] This would be "tritheist" in the sense that there are three beings to whom worship is to be offered, though they are not regarded as ontologically equal. We may also note that, though ancient Arianism may be described as tritheistic in the sense that Plantinga uses the term, the Arian intention was to preserve the doctrine of God's oneness.

Ancient Modalism

Sabellianism can be defined briefly and in broad terms as the denial of a true personal distinction between Father, Son, and Spirit. It is important for our discussion because modalism, both as a trend within orthodox theology as well as a heretical idea, is quite prevalent in the West, and the narrative of Christ's baptism provides clear biblical refutation of this heresy.

Ancient modalism came in various forms, but the essence of the position is the denial that God is three distinct persons. In its most primitive form, it seems more like confusion about how to think about God than a sophisticated and settled heresy. As confusion and unclear expression of biblical teaching, it seems to have been relatively widespread in the early Church for the simple reason that Christians believed that God was one, passionately rejecting all polytheism, and that Christ

---

4. I am basically following Herman Bavinck's use of the word (*God and Creation*, 290–96), though unlike Bavinck I apply it only to post-Nicene theology.

5. One of the most well-researched and in depth anti-Trinitarian books in recent times is Navas, *Divine Truth or Human Tradition?* Navas skillfully quotes Christian theologians—often without due concern for context—to set their statements against one another, arguing that the doctrine of the Trinity cannot be essential to salvation. If Christian theologians cannot even agree on what the doctrine is, how can it be essential to salvation? The answer is that the Nicene Creed gives us general guidelines for defining truth and heresy. Disagreements among theologians do not undermine the basic truth, which is essential for salvation. However, being able to accurately state or explain the doctrine is not essential for salvation. There is an immeasurable gap between the person who is just confused and the person who is knowingly rejecting biblical truth.

6. Smith, *Paradox and Truth*, 31–32.

was the one true God.[7] If someone suggested that the Father is also God and another person, distinct from the Son, it seemed—at least to some naive Christians with a modalist bent—as if one were asserting a kind of polytheism, believing in two Gods.

Modalism first came to sophisticated and unquestionably heretical expression in the writings of Sabellius, who came to Rome in the early third century while Zephyrinus was pope (199–217). He remained in Rome and apparently taught there until he was declared a heretic by Pope Calistus (217–222).

Sabellius regarded God as a monad, an absolutely unified being. But he also believed that God expressed Himself in three modes of operation. So, "the Father was, as it were, the form or essence, and the Son and the Spirit His modes of self-expression." He also stated his views in a way that seems to imply that God developed. "Thus, the one Godhead regarded as creator and law-giver was Father; for redemption it was projected like a ray of the sun, and was then withdrawn; then, thirdly, the same Godhead operated as Spirit to inspire and bestow grace."

We are not sure, however, of his position, since most of what we know of it comes from a much later time when his theology and that of Marcellus of Ancyra "were hopelessly confused."[8] What we are sure of is that a tendency toward modalism was not uncommon among less educated Christians, for it seemed to preserve the oneness of God and the deity of Christ.

The Modalist Tendency

Robert Letham, following Colin Gunton, identifies modalism as the tendency of Western theology from the time of Augustine.[9] What Letham and Gunton refer to is not a heretical doctrine, but an imbalance in the way orthodox doctrine is stated, leading to a practical deficiency in the life of the Church. This interpretation of the history of Trinitarian theology is not undisputed and may be unfair, at least to theologians like Augustine and Aquinas whose views may be much more complex than the usual summaries reveal, but when we look at the history of the West as a whole, there does seem to be an emphasis on God's oneness in the

---

7. Kelly, *Early Christian Doctrines*, 119–23.

8. All quotations and most of the material for the summary come from Kelly, 119–23.

9. E.g., Letham, *Holy Trinity*, 184–85, 198–200, 408.

practical life of the Church that is not unrelated to the way the doctrine of the Trinity has been explained.

Letham finds Augustine's analogies for the Trinity faulty—at least in the influence they have had[10]—in so far as they seem to favor the unity of God over His triunity, the one essence of God over the three persons. He goes on to describe how Aquinas gives priority to the oneness of God in his theology.[11] Though Letham is aware of scholars like Brian Davies who claim that, for Aquinas, "the heart of Christian teaching is in the doctrine of the Trinity,"[12] and acknowledges that "Aquinas's whole theology is an outworking of his Trinitarianism,"[13] he nevertheless concludes that "Aquinas's full-scale use of the Augustinian model does entail a strong bias in a modalist direction."[14]

Aquinas—who is understood to have set a pattern for the West that is followed down to our day—began his theology proper with a discussion of God's being and attributes, treating God's triune nature last. Though it may not be fair to Aquinas, this has been interpreted to mean that in his theology the Trinity becomes secondary to monotheism. Add to this Aquinas's emphasis on God's simplicity and his doctrine of relations, and the effect of the whole is said to be that the one God is prominent, while the three persons are pushed into the background.[15]

However fair this may or may not be to Aquinas, Reformed theologian Charles Hodge fits the criticized paradigm. His discussion of the Trinity does not appear until he has completed a 250-page exposition of God's existence and attributes. Louis Berkhof and J. I. Packer are also included on Letham's list of theologians who give inadequate attention

---

10. Ibid., 198–200.

11. Ibid., 228–37.

12. Ibid., 228.

13. Ibid., 236–37.

14. Ibid., 236. Letham's view is complex. In the context of the statement quoted above, Letham is disagreeing with John Frame and Cornelius Plantinga who both regard Aquinas as being close to modalism. Letham defends Aquinas to a degree and says that "Aquinas is as concerned with the errors of Sabellius as he is with those of Arius, and he insists that the persons of the Trinity are distinct in a real sense" (Letham, *Holy Trinity*, 235). In his conclusion, however, he agrees that Aquinas leans in the modalist direction.

15. Part of the problem is that Aquinas, like Augustine, wrote so much that unless one specializes in him, it is difficult to do justice to his thought. His commentaries, for example, contain much about the Trinity that points in the direction of a richer view of the persons. See, for example, Gilles Emory, *Trinitarian Theology*, 19, 185–92.

The Trinitarian Dimension

to the Trinity.[16] More importantly, Letham believes that at the popular level the tendency toward modalism prevails.[17]

> Today most Western Christians are practical modalists. The usual way of referring to God is "God" or, particularly at the popular level, "the Lord." ... This practical modalism goes in tandem with a general lack of understanding of the historic doctrine of the Trinity.[18]

Nor is Letham merely commenting on a lack of understanding in the pew. An anecdote he cites betrays remarkable ignorance of the theology of the Trinity on the part of a Christian minister, David Prior, a well-known evangelical Anglican who described the Trinity by an illustration that clearly reduces to modalism.[19]

One is reminded of similar statements by other theologians, especially the often quoted words of Karl Rahner:

> Thus the treatise on the Trinity occupies a rather isolated position in the total dogmatic system. To put it crassly, and not without exaggeration, when the treatise is concluded, its subject is never brought up again. Its function in the whole dogmatic construction is not clearly perceived. It is as though this mystery has been revealed for its own sake, and that even after it has been made known to us, it remains, as a reality, locked up within itself. We make statements about it, but as a reality it has nothing to do with us at all.[20]

If the knowledge of God is the supreme knowledge to which man can attain and if true knowledge of God necessarily means knowledge of

---

16. Letham, *Holy Trinity*, 408.

17. Although it does not serve as evidence for a theological point, still we might ask ourselves how it came about that the oldest church in the United States, the First Parish Church of Plymouth, Massachusetts, as well as Boston's oldest Anglican church, the King's Chapel, are now both Unitarian.

18. Ibid., 5–6.

19. Ibid., 409: "Prior recounted how he was preparing a sermon for Trinity Sunday on the Trinity, searching for some intelligible comparison to help his congregation. He found it on television watching cricket, the Second Test Match between England and Pakistan at Lord's. Ian Salisbury, the English leg spinner, bowled successively a leg break, a googly, and a top spinner. There, said Prior, was a perfect analogy—one person expressing himself in three different ways!" There is not much need to worry about Prior's error, however, as this heresy will fly only in England.

20. Rahner, *The Trinity*, 14.

the triune God, then, assuming Rahner's criticism has *some* validity, the dogmatic systems of our day fail to adequately introduce the Christian view of life and the world, for, however unintentionally, they nevertheless systematically downplay the truth of the Trinity. The question of the Trinity and its place and exposition in dogmatics is not merely an academic question, since the theologians' teaching will be reflected in the life of the Church. The Trinity is the most fundamental truth of the Christian religion, the truth that determines and guides every other truth.[21] If it is true that the Western Church has a weakness here, it is a serious issue.

The accusation that there is a modalist tendency in the West is denied by scholars who specialize in historical theology and who see the great contributions of Augustine and Aquinas and study their works in context.[22] In their expositions of the doctrine of the Trinity and their theology of God, there may indeed be nothing that can properly be described as a modalist inclination. In their expositions of the doctrine of the Trinity and their theology of God, there may indeed be nothing that can properly be described as a tendency toward modalism, but Letham believes that they have been read by their followers in such a way that there results a practical tendency toward modalism.[23]

Whatever may be said about formal theological expositions of the doctrine of the Trinity, there is at least one area in which the Western Church exhibits what has to be called a modalist tendency—the doctrine of God's attributes. In what way? The attributes are understood as

---

21. I have written an introduction to the Christian worldview that outlines how the doctrine of the Trinity informs the whole of Christian theology in my short book, *Trinity and Reality*.

22. On Augustine, for example, Michel René Barnes writes, "In conclusion, I have argued that contemporary systematic appropriations of Augustine are based upon methods and accounts that are preselected for mirroring a widely held hermeneutic or ideology of systematic theology. These methods and accounts typically include an unconscious dependence on de Regnon, a tendency towards a logic of ideas, including a lust (operative even when unfulfilled) for encyclopedic comprehensiveness at the conceptual level coupled with a reductive use of primary sources, a retreat from the polemical genre, with an emphasis on the philosophical content of doctrine. The popular judgment that Augustine's Trinitarian theology sacrificed the oeconomia is presently too burdened by the unreflective use of such hermeneutical presuppositions to be regarded as established or even likely" ("Augustine in Contemporary Trinitarian Theology," 250).

23. Letham, *Holy Trinity*, 198–200.

qualifying the essence of God, without distinction among the persons. What this would seem to mean is that God's love, goodness, faithfulness, and holiness, for example, are not expressed in or by the three persons in distinction or in their relationships with one another, but only by God as God. By identifying the attributes with the essence, theologians teach us to think *not* of the Son or the Father being good to one another, but of God in His single divine nature as being good. Augustine writes:

> Likewise the Father is great, the Son is great, the Holy Spirit too is great; yet there are not three great ones but one great one. It is not, after all, about the Father alone, that scripture says *You alone are the great God* (Ps 86:10), as they perversely consider, but about Father, Son and Holy Spirit. Again, the Father is good, the Son is good, the Holy Spirit too is good; yet there are not three good ones, but one good one, of whom it is said *No one is good but the one God* (Mk 10:18; Lk 18:19)....
>
> So whatever God is called with reference to self is both said three times over about each of the persons, Father, Son and Holy Spirit, and at the same time is said in the singular and not the plural about the trinity. As it is not one thing for God to be and another for him to be great, but being is for Him the same thing as being great, for that reason we do not say three greatnesses any more than we say three beings, but one being and one greatness.[24]

What Augustine writes here provokes certain questions. For example, when we think of the goodness of God in eternity apart from creation, the question that inescapably arises is "Good to whom?" since goodness is a term of relation. Before the foundation of the world, when Father, Son, and Spirit were eternally rejoicing in one another, attributes such as goodness, faithfulness, and love had no possible expression except in their mutual relations. Furthermore, we should expect those qualities to be expressed by each person in a manner appropriate to His relation to the others. Without denying Augustine's teaching that for God to be is to be good, we also have to add that, in their personal relationships with one another, the Father's goodness to the Son is distinct, as is the Son's to the Father and theirs to the Spirit.

If attributes are to be regarded as qualities of the divine essence and not related to the persons, the tendency is for the persons to become abstract, without individual qualities that enhance our appreciation of

---

24. Augustine, *The Trinity*, 195–96.

their interrelationships. The fullness of the Son's personhood can be understood only in relation to the Father and the Spirit, but there must be more involved than the bare fact of generation. Certainly in the Bible, the picture of the Father's relationship to the Son is richer and fuller, as we will see when we consider the accounts of Jesus' baptism.[25]

Recent Theology and Modalism

Some of the leading theologians of the twentieth century exhibit a tendency toward modalism that certainly cannot be blamed on Augustine. Since the Enlightenment, the Bible has been demoted, even among theologians, and its teaching viewed through the skeptical lens of an epistemology that denies the possibility of miracles, especially the miracle of a divinely inspired book. This is true even of those, like Karl Barth, who claim to base their whole theology on the Word of God alone and refuse natural revelation.

In the nineteenth century, the rationalism of the Enlightenment found its theological expression in the work of Friedrich Daniel Ernst Schleiermacher (1768–1834). Schleiermacher's doctrine of God was more the articulation of a philosophical viewpoint than the interpretation of Scripture, but that viewpoint was complex and there is some disagreement among scholars about exactly what he taught. For example, Schleiermacher argued that since anti-Trinitarians could be as pious as Trinitarians, the doctrine of the Trinity "is neither a requirement for nor an expression of Christian faith."[26] Taking this as a starting point, we might say that since Schleiermacher did believe in God in some sense, he should not even be called a modalist, but rather a radical monotheist, believing in a monad something like Allah.

In fairness, however, we have to add that he seems also to claim that, though Jesus is only a man and not an eternal divine person, in

---

25. In the quotation above, when Augustine says, "So whatever God is called with reference to self is both said three times over about each of the persons, Father, Son and Holy Spirit, and at the same time is said in the singular and not the plural about the trinity," I think he might be saying what I am saying in different words. The expression "both said three times over about each of the persons . . . and at the same time is said in the singular and not the plural about the trinity" suggests the possibility of a "both three and also one" perspective on each of the attributes. But that is not the way he is usually read because he does repeat "not three, but one," which ends with the emphasis on the one. At least the "not three but one" seems to carry the traces of a modalist flavor.

26. Powell, *Trinity in German Thought*, 91.

some sense God was in Christ. And the Holy Spirit is God in the Church. So he seems to have an ambiguous kind of Trinitarian interest. However one may label his approach, it remains the case that since God is not three divine persons in one eternal essence, the closest Schleiermacher can come to Trinitarianism would be modalism. Powell summarizes the problems:

> God was in Jesus Christ. The same divine activity that determined the person of Jesus Christ (since the "innermost impulse" of Christ was his "absolute and continuous willing of the Kingdom of God") is present in the church as its corporate spirit. On this basis, Schleiermacher proposed to construct an adequate doctrine of the Trinity. However, Schleiermacher had hitherto demonstrated only that the divine essence had united with human nature twice, in the man Jesus Christ and in the church as a whole. Although stating that the divine essence could be conceived only as creative activity, he had also made statements to the effect that the essence of God in itself is unknowable and that our knowledge of God extends only to what God is in relation to humanity. The problem is that such statements open the possibility of an epistemological gap between God's being in itself and God's being for us, a gap that undermines the importance of revelation. Further, these statements raise the specter of modalism, the view that the Trinitarian persons are mere names for the one divine being. Modalism threatens to render the Trinitarian persons and their revelation unimportant because the divine being remains hidden behind them unchanged while they appear successively in history. To compound this problem, Scheiermacher made no secret of his admiration for Sabellius' view of the Trinity, a view customarily associated with modalism. Schleiermacher's many critics have not been slow to charge him with adopting a modalistic view of the Trinity.[27]

Though Powell goes on to argue that Schleiermacher attempted to establish a sort of Trinitarianism through his doctrine that God is love, Schleiermacher does not, in my opinion, get us beyond Sabellianism, at best. As Powell explains it, Schleiermacher had to demonstrate that the union of God with man in Christ is somehow essential to the divine nature. Love is what makes the link essential for Schleiermacher, but what

---

27. Ibid., 99.

does this view accomplish? In Powell's words, "As a result, God becomes a Trinity in the course of history."[28]

Schleiermacher stands as the supreme example of liberal rationalist theology. Biblical revelation as understood by orthodox Christianity throughout the centuries was rejected in favor of an epistemology that accepted the Enlightenment critique of Christian truth. For such a view, nothing can be more offensive than the idea of an infallible word from God to which man's mind and heart must submit. But, we have to ask, without that Word, who would have come up with the idea of a God who is one in essence and threefold in person?

After Schleiermacher, no single theologian is more important for modern Trinitarian theology than Karl Barth, famous for his rejection of Schleiermacher's liberalism and credited with bringing the doctrine of the Trinity back to the center of Christian theology. His *Church Dogmatics* placed the doctrine of the Trinity at the head of his doctrine of God in the prolegomena of dogmatics, unlike the typical Western approach followed even by the most orthodox theologians. In so doing, Barth made it clear that there is no Christian doctrine of God apart from the Trinity. We cannot set forth the doctrine of God and then add that He is also triune. The fact of His triunity is essential to who He is in every respect. Barth also claimed to base his doctrine of God on Scripture, not natural revelation or mere reason or experience. In these respects, Barth may be said to have rejected—or at least tried to overcome—the Enlightenment view of God.

But Barth's orthodoxy was "new" and not a return to the unerring Scriptures which guided the Reformation and the Church Fathers. Moreover, his doctrine of the Trinity included elements that seem to betray him into modalism, despite his frequent repudiations of it. I am not speaking now of Barth's rejection of the term "person," though that too is problematic, however orthodox his own term is. I am speaking of Barth's dogmatic and repeated affirmation that God is only one subject. This affirmation provokes Jürgen Moltmann's critique of Barth, who says that Barth's speaking of three modes in God who is one subject suggests Sabellianism.[29] Catherine LaCugna spells out this criticism clearly:

---

28. Ibid., 100.
29. Moltmann, *Trinity and Kingdom*, 143.

> Barth suggested that "person" be replaced by "modes of being" (*Seinsweisen*). This is a literal translation of what the early church called *tropoi hyparxeos* and also brought out the dimension of hypostasis as the "one who exists." The irony is that while Barth opposed much of the ethos of the Enlightenment because it seemed to him to make God subject to the creature, Barth clearly operated within the presuppositions of critical philosophy since he regarded God as one personal subject who exists in three modes of revelation, as Father, Son, and Spirit. In fact, he referred to the persons of the Trinity in terms of the formal structure of revelation. God is Revealer, Revelation, and Revealedness; God reveals, God reveals *Godself*, God reveals *through* Godself. Barth equated the divine essence revealed in these three modes of being with God's sovereignty or Lordship.
>
> The result is a form of modalism; whether this modalism is Sabellian could be debated. In any case, Barth's view is a hybrid of the Latin theology of the Trinity in which the one divine substance exists in three persons, and the idea of God as Absolute Subject who exists under the aspects of self differentiation and self-recollection.... For Barth, the essence of God is uni-personal. The God who "distributes" the divine essence in three modes of being is the Sovereign Subject.[30]

William J. Hill also regards Barth's view as leaning toward modalism, though he does not express it so strongly as LeCugna:

> If we ask, "Three what?" we find only the tradition-honored reply of "three *persons*." But Barth aligns himself with Augustine who takes "persons" as a mere convention of speech; to take it literally is to run the risk of tritheism. Barth shares Calvin's polemic against the term.... Melanchthon's preference for it appears to Barth as having "a somewhat suspicious ring." The reason lies in the connotation the word acquires from Schleiermacher's time onward. Schleiermacher himself had used the concept in a way that advanced a form of Neo-Sabellianism. There, Trinity meant only three phenomenal forms behind which stood the one divine reality. "Personality" especially, as a nineteenth-century term, added to this ancient and medieval use of "person" the notion of self-consciousness. This precipitated two opposite courses of thought: (i) to eliminate the term entirely from speech about God on the grounds that as Absolute Spirit he transcended all limitation implicit in consciousness (Fichte and Strauss), or (ii) to continue to use the term but as divested of the new mean-

---

30. LaCugna, *God for Us*, 252.

ing it had acquired. In the ancient Church, somewhat the same problem had been resolved by transforming the Greek πρόσωπον into ὑπόστσις Barth seeks to surmount the dilemma—of tritheism on the one hand when the connotation of self-consciousness is retained, and of mystification and meaninglessness on the other when it is denied—by substituting the phrase "*Seinsweisen*" (modes of being). This is not only "a literal translation of τρόπος ὑπάρξεως already in use in the early Church debates," but also registers the sense of ὑπόστσις insofar as it means "*subsistentia* (not *substantia*), i.e., mode of existence of one who exists."[31]

Letham defends Barth at some length from the charge of modalism, but he still concludes that Barth's Trinitarianism is defective: "Although he avoids modalism, Barth cannot be entirely exonerated from the charge of unipersonality."[32] Hill concludes that Barth's theology is not overtly modalist, but the tendency to modalism is apparent in that Barth denies self-consciousness to Father, Son, and Spirit: "Granting that self-consciousness is a prerequisite for subjectivity, Barth cannot allow that Father, Son, and Spirit are three subjectivities because of the way he locates consciousness on the side of essence and nature."[33]

The crux of all of this is that the most important liberal theologian of the nineteenth century, Schleiermacher, and the most important Trinitarian theologian of the twentieth century, Karl Barth, as well as some of his most influential followers, including Karl Rahner and Robert Jenson, are understood to exhibit a modalist tendency.[34] The modern tendency stems from a different motive from what may have been a historical tendency to overemphasize the oneness of God. But in either case, there is a defect in Western Trinitarian understanding that will be reflected in conservative churches that perpetuate the traditional bias and in "liberal" churches that have been influenced by the Enlightenment epistemology.[35]

---

31. Hill, *Three-Personed God*, 116–17.

32. Letham, *Holy Trinity*, 278. Cf. his discussion of Barth and modalism (275–90).

33. Hill, *Three-Personed God*, 119.

34. Actually, Letham's charge is more severe. He writes of Rahner, "The result is close to pantheism—and Gordon Kaufmann, Robert Jenson, Jürgen Moltmann, various feminists such as Catherine LaCugna and Elizabeth Johnson, and others travel to varying extents along the route charted by Rahner" (*Holy Trinity*, 297).

35. Perhaps we can sum up the differences by analogy to wine. Schleiermacher and liberalism offer us rank modalist and/or Unitarian vinegar. The flavor of the Barth's wine, and that of those influenced by him, is thoroughly characterized by a modalist

The narrative of the baptism of Jesus suggests numerous lines of thought that fundamentally contradict ancient modalism and offer correction to what may have been a vague modalist bias in Western Trinitarianism and to the recent tendency to modalism.

THE MOTIVE OF TRINITARIAN HERESIES

The truth of the Trinity is central to every aspect of the Christian faith, because the doctrine of God touches every other doctrine in some form or other. This makes the narrative of the baptism of Christ especially important, for in it, Father, Son, and Spirit all appear distinct from one another while also relating to one another. However, the testimony of the baptismal narrative is complex. It has been appealed to both by defenders of orthodoxy and by heretics. Heretics such as Paul of Samosata regarded the baptism of Jesus as the time when the logos began to take up residence in Jesus, so that he became the Christ.[36] This sort of heresy is reflected in modern liberal views of Jesus as a mere man who, because of his superior righteousness, was beloved of God.

From ancient times, the orthodox doctrine has been under attack from two heresies usually described as opposite errors, as Michel René Barnes shows when he explains that the Cappadocians "treat Arius only in terms of the need to avoid the opposite errors of Sabellianism and Arianism. . . . This kind of rhetorical or formal pairing off of Arius and Sabellius as two opposite heresies to be avoided appears consistently in pro-Nicene literature from one end of the Empire to the other: Phoebadeus uses it in France, in 358, and the Cappadocians use it twenty (and more) years later."[37] Thus, the two basic errors are thought to pull in

---

imbalance, the tannins and acid overpowering, the aroma smacking of sulfur, and the finish distinctly flat. Augustine and Aquinas, however, present us with a strong bodied complex flavor, a rich bouquet, and long-lasting finish. It is only slightly tainted by occasional hints of the acids and odors of modalism.

36. Pelikan, *Emergence of the Catholic Tradition*, 176. Interestingly, adoptionism or dynamic monarchianism, as this heresy is called, is related to both of the main Trinitarian heresies. On the one hand, adoptionism, as it was called by Harnack, claims that Jesus was a man who so perfectly did God's will that he was adopted into the Godhead. In this sense, it is similar to Arianism, which also taught that Christ was a mere creature, though Arianism had a more exalted view of Christ. On the other hand, as a form of monarchianism—views that stress the monarchy of the Father—it is closely related to modalism, which is also called modal monarchianism.

37. Barnes, "The Fourth Century as Trinitarian Canon," 57.

contrary directions: the Arians, on the one side, emphasized the distinction between and the relationships among the three persons at the expense of God's oneness, and the Sabellians, on the opposite side, denied the distinction of the three persons in their misguided zeal to protect God's oneness.

But in the end, Arianism and Sabellianism both find their motive in the attempt to forge a rationally comprehensible knowledge of God as one, while also confessing some sort of multiplicity. Multiplicity must be acknowledged because the Bible clearly identifies Father, Son, and Spirit as God. But how can this multiplicity be related to God's unity?

In their demand that the doctrine of God fit with human understanding, both Arians and Sabellians reduced multiplicity to unity. Though opposite in some ways, these heresies stem from the same motive and can be regarded as different versions of the same fundamental error. They both conclude that unity overwhelms multiplicity, that God's oneness is more ultimate than His threeness. In these views, the biblical depiction of God as Father, Son, and Spirit must somehow be fit into a form of ultimate unity. Arianism takes one approach, that of ontologically demoting the Son and the Spirit to lesser deities and finding unity in the Father. Sabellianism takes another approach, that of making the Father, Son, and the Spirit to be mere names or roles, three masks worn by the one god, depending on where he is going and what he intends to do.

Thus, though it is legitimate to view Arianism and Sabellianism as heresies pulling in opposite directions, at a deeper level it is more accurate to describe both of these divergent errors as born from a common seed—the demand that the Bible's teaching about God conform to the mind of man. A doctrine of God that is fundamentally inscrutable transgresses the standards of human reason and requires men to relinquish their autonomy in favor of submission to God's revelation. Whichever direction they took, heretics may be rightly described as those who could not tolerate the incomprehensibility of the Trinity. Thus, for example, Thomas G. Weinandy notes that Athanasius regarded the Arians as rationalistic deniers of the mystery of God:

> To the mind of Athanasius it was the Arians who dissolved the Christian mystery in the acid of rationalism. What Nicea had done and what Athanasius strove passionately to do was to articulate faithfully and accurately what the Christian mystery of God as

the Father and Son is. While it is possible to know unmistakably and to express distinctly what the mystery is, it is impossible to fully comprehend that mystery. For Athanasius, God in himself is ineffable and thus the begetting of the Son from the Father is ineffable. The Arians, confronted by the perplexity of God being the Father of the Son, came to disbelieve. However, "it is better to be silent in perplexity and believe, than to disbelieve on account of the perplexity." In the midst of such perplexity one's sure recourse is to ponder, in faith, the truths of Scripture, for it "is able to afford one some relief."[38]

The silence that Athanasius preferred was not a sacrifice of human intellect, but a denial of autonomy. The Church Fathers recognized that the Bible as a whole and its teaching about God in particular requires of us that we use our minds and bodies in the service of the transcendent God, who is far beyond our ability to comprehend. Serving Him is the way to true understanding but not to comprehensive knowledge—something forever beyond the grasp of a creature.

Why should that seem strange? If the world is planned and created by a God of infinite intelligence, how could it be otherwise? If the God of the Bible is the sovereign Lord of the world who created all things according to His eternal plan, then every fact in the world, every event in the history of the universe, has its true meaning in Him and His perfect will. This means that not only is God Himself a mystery, but the whole creation also is a mystery. We know and understand the creation or God Himself only in so far as He chooses to make truth manifest to us.

The good news to which the baptism of Jesus bears witness is that the triune God is a God who delights to reveal Himself. Father, Son, and Spirit are eternally open to one another in their mutual indwelling love. They hold no secrets from one another. Thus, when they created man in their image, they created man to know the eternal God. God intended from the beginning to reveal Himself in, to, and through man, His image, because it is His nature to be self-revealing and because He delights in man, His own image.

But there are boundaries. Even apart from sin, mankind could not ascend to the highest peaks of the knowledge of God. There will always be—and there must always be—mystery for man, unfathomable depths of God and His ways, simply because God is infinite. That does not imply

---

38. Weinandy, *Athanasius*, 78.

that what we know is not true. It only means there are limits, which faith acknowledges and accepts. Pride, however, revolts. And intellectual pride is the essence not only of ancient denial of the Trinity, but of modern denial as well.

> The most successful aspect of the defense of reason in seventeenth-century England is that philosophers made a strong case for the sovereignty of reason over against other criteria of truth, such as Scripture, tradition, and inspiration. This demonstration did not involve showing that reason is the sole and exclusive criterion of truth, or still less that it has some magical yardstick to test the adequacy of all beliefs. All that it established is that we have a right to ask the reasons for the truth of Scripture, tradition, or inspiration. There is no prejudgment whether these reasons are good or bad, what they would be, or where they would come from. But the mere fact that one can demand them put reason above other criteria of intellectual authority. However much authority one cared to give to Scripture, tradition, or inspiration, they could not clam to be the sovereign or ultimate standards of truth, simply because it was possible to assess their authority according to reason. This was a point made time and again by Hooker, the Great Tew circle, the Cambridge Platonists, and the latitudinarians.
>
> It is in just this regard that the postmodern age remains the heir of the seventeenth century. However much it cares to question the claims of reason, there can be little doubt that we still accept reason alone as our final standard of truth in deciding intellectual questions. No one today in tune with the *Zeitgeist* would demand that we accept without question the authority of inspiration, tradition or the Bible.[39]

This view of reason also implies that no one in tune with the *Zeitgeist* of our day can confess the Trinity, because it is entirely a doctrine of special

---

39. Beiser, *The Sovereignty of Reason*, 323. The reference here to Richard Hooker is contestable. Hooker seems to have regarded reason and tradition as secondary sources of authority, under the ultimate authority of Scripture. Nigel Atkinson, for example, writes, "As is so often maintained the Anglican 'genius' that underpins the *via media* is to appeal to Scripture, Tradition and Reason, and one often receives the impression that these three sources of authority are of equal weight and power. Certainly the conclusions that some Reports arrive at seem to suggest that Reason and Tradition have as much significance as Scripture but it would be a gross misreading of Hooker to think that it was Hooker who claimed that Scripture, Tradition and Reason were of equal authority. I shall argue that Hooker's position is almost identical to the one hammered out by the magisterial Reformers in general, and Luther and Calvin in particular" ("Richard Hooker," 61).

revelation, not subject to man's reason as a final standard of truth. From the modern and postmodern perspective as defined above, the baptism of Jesus, also, cannot be taken seriously. In terms of the presuppositions of the Enlightenment, John the Baptizer and Jesus could not have been more than two famous men who met at the Jordan river. The story must have been something like the following. John put some water on Jesus. A dove hovered over Jesus, but there was nothing miraculous about it. Certainly it was a little strange, but, after all, birds will be birds, and they must be allowed to do odd things. The voice from heaven may have been some sort of rumble in the clouds. Perhaps the weather was bad and it was thunder. Whatever the case, there is nothing here demanding a miracle. The Gospel records are merely superstitious interpretation of natural events. For the rationalist, it is imperative to interpret the story in wholly natural terms, eliminating everything that requires us to believe in miracles or a sovereign, Trinitarian God.

The Trinity is the most irritating of all the doctrines that provoke man's pride because it most emphatically requires us to confess that we cannot begin to comprehend either God or His world apart from His self-revelation. Trinitarianism demands that we admit our utter dependence on Him and subject our minds, hearts, and lives to Him. It is, therefore, a fundamental test of faith. However, I hasten to add, not everyone who is befuddled about the Trinity is being rebellious. It is a difficult doctrine and confusion about the Trinity may result from many and diverse influences.

Heresies, on the other hand, are different from confusion. They emerge not from honest intellectual struggle with revelation, nor from difficulties inherent in the subject, nor even from the intellectual tides of the times, but from a stubborn unwillingness to bow the knee to God, from a refusal to think as He commands. Ancients, moderns, or postmoderns, sinful men resist the biblical command to submit their minds to Scripture's authority. The question concerns the ultimate standard for judging truth, and the Christian view stands fundamentally opposed to all non-Christian views in its most basic confession: Christians believe in the triune God. That is where we begin. We begin there because we have seen the face of God in Jesus and we know Him to be Savior and Lord. The testimony of Scripture is the testimony of the Holy Spirit to Jesus our Lord and we accept that testimony in humble faith because we trust Him.[40]

40. For the importance and legitimacy of paradox in the Christian worldview, see

To appreciate the Trinitarian dimension of the baptism of Jesus, we must first give attention to the distinction between the ontological and economic perspectives on the Trinity, for how we interpret this distinction will be fundamental to our understanding of Jesus' baptism.

ECONOMIC AND ONTOLOGICAL TRINITY

The distinction between the economic and ontological Trinity has been important in Trinitarian theology, though there is great debate about the subject and the distinction can be pressed in different directions. Briefly stated, the economic Trinity is God as He is manifest in the economy of salvation, and the ontological or immanent Trinity is God as He exists in Himself from eternity. Again, the economic Trinity is God as He has revealed Himself to us through His acts in history; the ontological Trinity is God as He is in Himself. Defined this way, the distinction between the economic and ontological Trinity does not sound controversial. As is usual in theological discussion, differences arise when one begins to consider the details. In this case, disagreement is the result of attempting to fill out the implications of the distinction, especially with regard to the relationship between the ontological and economic.

Hypothetically, it would at least be possible (1) to deny the distinction;[41] (2) to regard the ontological as decisive for the economic; (3) to regard the economic as decisive for the ontological;[42] (4) to regard the two as identical, but distinct; or (5) to regard the ontological Trinity as the unknowable God and the economic Trinity as the knowable God. There are views that more or less correspond to these simply stated options, but it is not my purpose here to analyze each view in depth. For our purposes, we need to consider only four theologians.

First, the most well-known articulation of the relationship between the two perspectives was by Karl Rahner, famous for his formula, "The economic Trinity *is* the immanent Trinity and the immanent Trinity *is*

Anderson, *Paradox in Christian Theology*. Dale Tuggy ("Trinity") identifies Anderson as the most sophisticated theologian of what he calls the "positive mysterian theory" of the Trinity.

41. "There is neither an economic nor an immanent Trinity; there is only the *oikonomia* that is the concrete realization of the mystery of *theologia* in time, space, history and personality" (LaCugna, *God for Us*, 223).

42. For a consideration of something like both (2) and (3) in the context of discussing Rahner, see Hart, *Beauty of the Infinite*, 156–75.

the economic Trinity."⁴³ There is some debate about exactly what Rahner means by this and whether or not the formula is really helpful.⁴⁴ There can be no doubt that Rahner has been influential. On the best interpretation, what he is saying simply expresses what theologians have commonly believed, that God as He reveals Himself in the economy of salvation is wholly consistent with God as He has existed in eternity. We know the eternal God as He is in Himself through the revelation He gives us in creation and redemption. Understood in this fashion, Rahner's principle is absolutely vital for Christian theology.⁴⁵ If God as He reveals Himself in creation and redemption were not the same as He is in Himself, then we simply would not know God. He would remain hidden and unknown because what seems to be "revelation" would not be consistent with His true nature.

The second theologian to consider is Robert Reymond, who is important because he illustrates a typical kind of mistaken zeal for the Bible. Reymond's objections to reading ontological conclusions from economic revelation are based upon a superficial reading of Scripture—a reading that appears pious, but in fact undermines biblical theology. Reymond denies the doctrine of the procession of the Holy Spirit in the ontological Trinity on the grounds that the major Scripture quoted to support it (John 15:26) refers only to God's economic actions, not directly to His eternal being. Robert Letham comments on the error:

> Robert L. Reymond thinks that referring this [John 15:26] to immanent realities in God is to go beyond the bounds of Scripture. But de Margerie rightly calls this restriction to the temporal mission "a simplistic exegesis that lacks a theological background." It effectively undermines the reality and truthfulness of God's revelation by positing that what God does economically does not necessarily reveal who he is.⁴⁶

---

43. I italicize the "is" as Rahner has done, *The Trinity*, 23.

44. For brief interaction with Rahner's view and bibliographic information, see O'Carroll, *Trinitas*, 94–96. Also, I have a short essay on Rahner here: http://www.berith.org/pdf/against-karl-rahner-s-rule.pdf.

45. Obviously, the belief that God's self-revelation and eternal existence are consistent is not at all new. What made Rahner's statement of the principle seem to be revolutionary was the strong language of identity. Herman Bavinck expressed the traditional view in a succinct statement: "The 'ontological' Trinity is mirrored in the 'economic' Trinity" (Bavinck, *God and Creation*, 318).

46. Letham, *Holy Trinity*, 203.

Reymond, in his attempt to be faithful to the Bible, actually leads us away from a biblical understanding of God, for the Bible often tells us that God's works reveal who He is (e.g., Ps 19:1; Rom 1:18ff.). The Bible also teaches that God is immutable. So when we see Father, Son, and Spirit relating to one another in a particular way in the economy of salvation, we must do a deeper reading of such passages on the assumption that we are seeing how the Trinitarian persons typically relate to one another apart from and before creation. In other words, since the creation of the world and the salvation of man cannot introduce change into the relationships of the three eternal persons, a biblically faithful theology demands that the economic Trinity reveal the ontological Trinity. Contrary to Reymond, we must understand the Father sending the Spirit as a special gift of blessing and love for His people as a revelation of the way Father, Son, and Spirit relate in eternity. If it were not, then the Father's sending of the Spirit would constitute a new way for the persons to relate, a change in God.

To reiterate, then, if God's actions in history did *not* show us who He is in eternity, we would be cut off from the knowledge of God. What we think we know of Him, based as it is on His words and actions in the economy, might be entirely false. Not only would such a view subvert Christian worship, since we could not be sure whom we were approaching, let alone how to approach Him; it would also fundamentally overturn the doctrine of salvation, since we rely on the faithfulness of God's self-revelation as the ground of our eternal hope. Therefore, the principle that God's works in history reveal His eternal nature is not only valid, it is essential for theological knowledge.[47]

The third theologian is Vern Poythress, who offers a summary statement that puts the the question of the economy and ontology in proper perspective:

> Since God is our standard and his word is our standard, there is nothing more ultimate than this revelation of himself. We believe that God is true. He truly reveals himself, not a substitute. We believe it because God says so. Hence we believe that God is in conformity with what he reveals. The Trinity in economic operations reveals the ontological Trinity. Hence, I have not tried to

---

47. Letham points out that modalism presupposes a divide in the revelation of God and His eternal existence. "With modalism, God's revelation in human history as the Father, the Son, and the Holy Spirit does not reveal who he is eternally, and so we have no true knowledge of God" (*Holy Trinity*, 108).

separate in any strict or exhaustive way between functional (economic) and ontological statements. Such separation on the part of a creature would itself be a repudiation of creaturehood. The analogies we explore deal with God in both respects, ontological and economical.[48]

Let me emphasize that Poythress is not saying that the distinction is illegitimate. He is just saying it would be the height of arrogance for us to pretend we can define everything in our own neat categories. We have to approach the subject with the humility of faith. When we do, we will find that the distinction is meaningful and profound, even though we cannot exhaustively spell out distinctions. However, there are basic areas in which the distinction can be clearly stated, which illustrate its importance and necessity.

This brings us to the final theologian, Michael O'Carroll, who states what is perhaps the most important and basic truth in the distinction when he explains that in the ontological Trinity "liberty and necessity are the same thing," whereas in the economy of salvation "God exercises his liberty absolutely, with no necessity arising from his nature."[49] This demonstrates clearly that the distinction between the ontological and economic Trinity is fundamental to our doctrine of God.[50]

Consider: to say that liberty and necessity are the same thing in the ontological Trinity is to say, for example, that the Father generates the Son both because it is essential to who He is to do so *and also* because He freely wills it. The Father could not be the Father without the Son. Thus, generation is necessary. But the Father and Son relationship is not mechanical or impersonal. The Son cannot be generated apart from the Father's personal involvement. Therefore, the Father must freely will to generate the Son. Or, to say it in other words, the Son must be generated in the freedom of love because God is love and He could not generate any other way.

To say that in the economy of salvation "God exercises his liberty absolutely" is to say that God saves sinners simply because He wills to save. There is no necessity in God's nature that makes either creation or the salvation of rebellious man essential. Neither creation nor redemp-

---

48. Poythress, "Reforming Ontology," 196–97.

49. O'Carroll, *Trinitas*, 95.

50. This is also the reason that it is profoundly misleading, at best, to describe the ontological and economic as identical, as in Rahner's rule.

tion can be necessary, for such a necessity would imply that God is dependent on the creation for the realization of His own nature, which would be a denial of God's transcendence. However, this does not mean creation and redemption are arbitrary. Rather, in creating and redeeming, God is freely expressing toward the creation the kind of love that Father, Son, and Spirit share from eternity. Thus, while there is no necessity in God requiring Him to create or redeem, there is an explanation of creation and redemption grounded in His nature.

What does this discussion mean for our view of the baptism of Jesus? It means that, although we are seeing Jesus consecrated as Messiah and anointed with the Spirit to be able to serve God in that capacity, it is not possible for this communion between the Father, the Son, and the Spirit to be limited to God and the man Jesus—though even if it were, the story of Jesus' baptism would still be meaningful for our understanding of the Trinity since it would show how God acts.

Still, why would Jesus' baptism reveal the Trinity? The baptism of Jesus reveals Trinitarian communion because the man Jesus is not a human person; He is the incarnation of the eternal Son—a divine person with two natures. It was the ancient Nestorian error to regard Jesus as two persons, one human and the other divine, and the Church rejected any such understanding as heretical.[51] Chalcedon's formula is clear: two natures, one person.[52]

---

51. According to John Young, Nestorius himself may not have been guilty of Nestorianism. Cf. Young, *By Foot to China*, 45–69.

52. Symbol of Chalcedon (451): "We, then, following the holy Fathers, all with one consent, teach men to confess one and the same Son, our Lord Jesus Christ, the same perfect in Godhead and also perfect in manhood; truly God and truly man, of a reasonable [rational] soul and body; consubstantial [coessential] with the Father according to the Godhead, and consubstantial with us according to the Manhood; in all things like unto us, without sin; begotten before all ages of the Father according to the Godhead, and in these latter days, for us and for our salvation, born of the Virgin Mary, the Mother of God, according to the Manhood; one and the same Christ, Son, Lord, Only-begotten, to be acknowledged in two natures; *inconfusedly, unchangeably, indivisibly, inseparably;* the distinction of natures being by no means taken away by the union, but rather the property of each nature being preserved, and concurring in one Person and one Subsistence, not parted or divided into two persons, but one and the same Son, and only begotten, God the Word, the Lord Jesus Christ, as the prophets from the beginning [have declared] concerning him, and the Lord Jesus Christ himself has taught us, and the Creed of the holy Fathers has handed down to us" (Schaff, ed., *Creeds of Christendom*, 2:62–63, emphasis in original).

The divine person incarnate in Jesus is the same divine person who had lived and still lives with and in the Father and the Spirit in an unbroken fellowship of infinite love. The interaction we see in the Gospels must reflect the eternal relationships among Father, Son, and Spirit because God does not change. Thus the incarnation did not alter either the nature of the Father or the Son or their interpersonal relationship, though it did add a new dimension to that relationship, because the Son since the incarnation became both God and man. We conclude, therefore, that how the Father, Son, and Spirit relate to one another in Jesus' baptism reveals the ontological Trinity and the relationships among the eternal persons.

TRINITARIAN FELLOWSHIP

There are at least five aspects of the Trinitarian fellowship that are revealed implicitly and explicitly in the narrative of Jesus' baptism. Each of the relationships manifest at the baptism of Jesus is an expression of the eternal interaction between the Trinitarian persons, though insofar as they are expressed in visual and auditory forms that reveal God to man, it is more accurate to describe what we see as something analogous to the intratrinitarian fellowship. In the narrative of the baptism of Jesus, we confront the mystery of the Christian God. It is, therefore, vital that we submit our minds to His self-revelation, eschewing the rationalistic spirit of the Enlightenment in all its forms. At the same time, in doing theology we endeavor to express ourselves consistently and coherently, without pretending to be able to unravel the essential paradox the Scriptures present.[53]

Personal Fellowship

In speaking of the fellowship of Father, Son, and Spirit as "personal," I mean that the fellowship evident in the story of Jesus' baptism could occur only among persons—"persons," that is, understood as self-conscious subjects. This is directly contrary to the sort of Trinitarian theology represented by Barth and his followers, who prefer to avoid the term

---

53. Dale Tuggy ("Unfinished Business," 165–83) defines three basic problems for Trinitarian theology: "inconsistency, unintelligibility, and poor fit with the Bible." Turing the problems into a program, I believe the order for Trinitarian study has to be *first* following the Bible, then pursuing consistency and "intelligibility." However, since God is incomprehensible, we cannot escape paradox, nor should we attempt to.

"person" because they consider the word misleading and who deny that there is more than one "subject" in God.

However, the notion of person that has been challenged by Barth and others is distinctly modern. It includes not merely the idea of self-consciousness, but also autonomy and radical freedom.

> From Schleiermacher onwards, at any rate, considerations of the Trinity assume a rationalistic rather than an intellectualist character; the spirit at work is critical and views its subject not as mystery but as problem. When the problem proves to be one that does not yield to rational analysis, the tendency is to reason it away. The crisis came when philosophers of consciousness and the development of psychology as an empirical science gave to the term "person" a meaning that vitiated its traditional use in the trinitarian formula. If person means a center of consciousness, radicated in an autonomous exercise of freedom, then it makes little sense to speak of three Persons of the one Godhead—especially since person, so conceived is frequently understood as self-creating (thus Spinoza, and later Fichte, contend that God's eternity precludes any conception of him as personal), and as finite by definition because of the limitations imposed by other persons.[54]

It should be evident that Christians are not under any particular constraint to subject theological reasoning to the dictates of philosophers of consciousness or modern psychologists. In the main, the practitioners of these disciplines take for granted an evolutionary view of man and the world and assume from the start that the God of the Bible does not exist, that biblical revelation has no part to play in the understanding of man's mind or nature. They also assume that man is "normal" and that direct appeal can be made to his self-consciousness. All of this fundamentally contradicts the biblical worldview. To derive our view of personhood from these sources and apply it to the Christian God would be wrong in every respect. That does not mean, however, that we should give up the term "person" altogether. Rather, Christians should reclaim it and, as much as possible, define it in terms of the Bible.

---

54. Hill, *Three-Personed God*, 254. Hill goes on to outline other aspects of the modern notion of person, including changes in the idea of "nature" and how it is to be related to "person" and relationality. In the modern way of thinking both nature and relationality are understood as essentially temporal and therefore not applicable outside of history.

From a biblical perspective, we must begin with the following two assumptions. First, human beings are persons. Second, man is created in the image of God. Whatever it means, therefore, for a man to be a person must reflect something about the kind of God who created man in His image. To say that the Father, Son, and Spirit are persons is to say that they are the transcendent original from which we were derived. Personhood in God the Creator and man His image must be analogous.

We can say more. For there are certain obvious implications from the Father's words in the Gospel texts: "You are My Son, the Beloved. In You I am well pleased."[55] From these words, the following four inferences seem undeniably clear. First, it is beyond question that the Father is conscious of Himself in distinction from the Son—otherwise He could not meaningfully say "You" or "I." Second, the Father knows Himself as experiencing a definable subjective state—He expresses His own attitude toward the Son. Third, the Father is conscious of the Son as an *other* with whom He has a relationship—He says, "My Son" and describes the relationship as one of love. Fourth, by calling Jesus "My Son," the Father shows that He is conscious of His relationship with the Son as the original from which human father and son relationships derive.

Similar inferences may be drawn from other aspects of the narrative. For example, Luke uniquely draws attention to the fact that the Father's declaration came when Jesus was praying (Luke 3:21), as He was coming up out of the Jordan river (cf. Matt 3:16; Mark 1:10). For Jesus to be praying to the Father implies that He understood Himself and the Father as distinct subjects, since the Father is someone other than Himself who can be addressed in prayer. In the Bible, prayer normally presupposes a relationship of favor and love in which interpersonal verbal communication is possible.

In the same way, the Gospels depict the Spirit and His relationships as personal. Mark tells us that the Spirit who came upon Jesus subsequently "drove" Him into the wilderness to be tempted by the devil (Mark 1:12). Matthew and Luke use the word "led" but in all three Gospels, the Spirit is portrayed as distinct from Jesus and as influencing Jesus, causing Him to go to the wilderness. Though appearance in the form of a dove may seem to be less personal than the verbal interaction

---

55. The words of the Father in Luke 3:22 are identical with Mark 1:11. Matthew 3:17 varies slightly, "This is My Son, the Beloved, in whom I am well pleased." The variation in the expression does not affect the points I make above.

between Father and Son, yet the fact that the Spirit leads Jesus into the wilderness clearly testifies to His deity, since the Son of God cannot be led by anything less than God, and to His personhood, since Jesus would not be led around by an impersonal "force." Or, to put it more accurately, in the biblical worldview, where all creation reveals the one true God in His personal glory, nothing is or can be "impersonal."

This very short narrative reveals much. The Son addresses the Father in prayer and the Father addresses the Son as "Son." The Spirit proceeds from the Father and comes to the Son. The Spirit leads the Son. The Father loves the Son and expresses that love. Though this does not give us a philosophical definition of personhood, all of these forms of interaction describe relations that show what it means to be "persons." Verbal communication, love, and leading describe ways in which human persons interact. Since we are created in God's image and therefore may reason from our own experience to the knowledge of God, when we see God acting in ways that we recognize as personal in our own experience, we naturally apply the word "person" to the Three who love and speak with one another. In fact, it would be very difficult to find a word more appropriate than "person" to describe the Three who reveal themselves in the story of the baptism of Jesus as self-conscious, distinct, and relating in love.

This contradicts all ancient and modern forms of modalism, for in the baptism narrative all three persons of the Trinity appear together at the same time and they are interacting with one another. If Father, Son, and Spirit were merely three names for the one God, the Father could not love the Son, talk to the Son, or give the Spirit to Him. Nor could the Spirit assume temporarily the form of a dove and come down upon the Son. The Son, incarnate as man, stands on the earth, while the Father speaks from heaven and the Spirit descends. In the story itself, the three are as distinct as any three could possibly be, and if we did not have other passages in the Bible that taught us that God is absolutely one, we might easily view these passages from the perspective of tritheism.

Which provokes the question, How does a modalist view these passages? The answer of Oneness Pentecostals—self-conscious, modern-day modalists—is that Jesus in His humanity prayed to the one God, which is Jesus in His divinity. This sounds odd enough, but it gets worse. Jesus' divinity in the voice of the Father talks to Jesus in His humanity and then Jesus as God reveals Himself again in the form of a dove. We are

The Trinitarian Dimension

told that because God is omnipresent, the three different manifestations are not a problem and that, because Jesus is God and man, what we have is interaction between the two natures of Christ.[56]

Even leaving aside its blatant absurdity, this explanation does not account for a number of essential details. How can Jesus' divine nature love His human nature? What would that mean? How can "love" be ascribed to a nature? Natures, not being persons, cannot share a relationship of love. However, if Jesus were two persons, there could be love between them, but that would be outright Nestorianism. Oneness Pentecostals do not seem to understand that Jesus was a divine *person* with a human *nature*. The love expressed between Father and Son cannot be explained away by reference to Jesus having two natures.

Of course, to explain prayer in this passage as Jesus' human nature praying to His divine nature is just as odd as imagining the two natures loving one another. Just as natures do not love, neither do they pray. Persons pray. Again, it seems that something like Nestorianism is being inadvertently presupposed and Jesus is actually being regarded as two persons, rather than one person with two natures. But whatever exactly the Oneness Pentecostals are thinking, they do not have an alternative explanation of the passage that makes exegetical or theological sense.

The historical orthodox understanding is that when the Father declares His love for the Son, He is not speaking of loving a human nature, but the eternal person of the Son whom He has always loved. What the Bible is depicting is interpersonal fellowship of the highest and most intimate sort. The baptism of Jesus reveals the God of the Bible as a God of overflowing love, the infinitely abundant fountain of all goodness and beauty.

Modalism, by teaching that God is only one person, actually undermines the whole idea of a personal God. Its unipersonal god would be like the Muslim Allah. What kind of god would that be? In eternity, the unipersonal god is alone, with none to relate to. Love could not be essential to that god's nature, for in eternity there is none with whom to share love. Revelation would be utterly foreign to its nature, for there would be no other to whom revelation might be made. Having a relationship with another would be something new to this god beginning with the

---

56. This is the explanation given by David K. Bernard in chapter 8 of his book, *The Oneness of God*.

creation—which would mean that creation fundamentally changes the nature of the god.

However a modalist may attempt to answer these problems, it is clear that a god who is only one "person" lacks fundamental prerequisites of personhood and can at best be a sub-personal thing. Modalism, therefore, does not merely deny the richness and beauty of the divine life pictured in story of Jesus' baptism; it reduces the biblical God to an impersonal oneness, an entity who could not have a motive to create and would not know what to do with the world if it could somehow create.

Verbal Fellowship

The story of creation in the book of Genesis makes clear the importance of language in the Christian worldview, for God creates with words.[57] He commands and the world comes into existence. But creation by command may seem odd to us. Certainly we can imagine many ways that God might have created. For example, He could have simply willed the whole world to come into existence in an instant, with no process involved whatsoever. That would have been perhaps the most "efficient" way of creating the world. And we can imagine other possibilities almost without number. So, why did He create by words?

When the Bible tells us that God created the world by speaking, we confront a profoundly significant truth. The Gospel of John adds special emphasis to this when it names Jesus as "Word," tells us that the Word was in the beginning, that the Word is God, and that the Word is Creator. Everything that exists is verbally defined, as it were, by the creative word that brought it into being. The inescapable implication is that the whole creation has meaning that can be expressed in language, though not exhaustively by us.

In the context of this verbal creation, the gift of language to mankind must be seen as definitive for human nature. For in the creation narrative, there is nothing about Adam being taught to speak or learning language subsequent to his being brought into being. Adam is not first a man in God's image and then later endowed with the ability to speak, though, again, we could imagine a story proceeding like that. The fact that the story reports that God created Adam from the beginning with language means that speaking is an aspect of our basic nature, an area of

---

57. For a full discussion of God and language, see Vern Poythress, *In the Beginning Was the Word*.

life in which we reflect the Creator and Lord who spoke the world into existence.

Creation by the Word also means that not only does God's image, Adam, speak from the moment he is made, but the rest of the creation also speaks: "The heavens declare the glory of God" (Ps 19:1). Since Adam was created on the sixth day, the revelation of God in the creation was waiting for him to be fashioned, but it was not silent until then. From the moment they began to exist, the heavens declared the glory of the Father to the Son, of the Son to the Father, and of the Spirit to the Father and the Son. The Father declared everything good that was spoken into existence by the Word through the breath of the Spirit, and the creation responded in praise to its Maker.

With all of this as background—and keeping in mind that the interpersonal relationships between Father, Son, and Spirit do not change—consider again the narrative of Jesus' baptism, for it shows us who God has been, is, and always will be. When the Son spoke to the Father in prayer and the Father declared His love to the Son in response, we have a picture of the fellowship of Father, Son, and Spirit, the rich inner life of God. Of course, God, being a spirit, does not "speak" exactly as we do. He has no vocal cords, tongue, teeth, lungs, or other "equipment" necessary for what we call "speech." And the communication among the persons of the Trinity is not the communication of one person to another "external" to Him. The three fully indwell one another and know one another from the inside, so that we must confess, as Cornelius Van Til points out, that God has both a threefold self-consciousness and also a single self-consciousness.[58]

The interpersonal communication of Father, Son, and Spirit, therefore, confronts us with the mystery of One and Three in a distinct form. On the one hand, the Scripture reveals the Three as interacting verbally. On the other hand, the Scripture also reveals that they indwell one another so perfectly and wholly that the Three *are* the One God. Therefore, there is no "space" between them. The Father has no "inner" life of His own, not open to the Son, just as the Son and the Spirit have no private thoughts or feelings hidden from one another or from the Father.

---

58. In the original context, Van Til's emphasis is somewhat different and the sentence is in the opposite order: "God is a one-conscious being, and yet he is also a tri-conscious being" (*Introduction to Systematic Theology,* 220). I discuss Van Til's view of God's consciousness in more detail in the appendix.

The oneness of the persons is so complete that it would seem to preclude even the possibility of something analogous to communication. Certainly we cannot imagine any *need* for "communication" as we would think of it, especially verbal communication or its analogue. Before the Father could say something, the Son would already know what the Father wants to say and why. But even before this, since God has all knowledge of all things and nothing can be added to His knowledge, the Father and the Son already know all there is to know about all things, a situation in which communication seems to be totally unimaginable. For creatures, communication involves give and take and always results in some sort of change, however infinitesimal or temporary. In an omniscient God for whom the three persons are wholly one, what could possibly be analogous to human communication?

Perhaps we could say that the communication recorded in the Gospels does not reveal God's Trinitarian life but rather God relating to the human nature of Jesus. Would that offer a way out of the dilemma? Not at all. First, even in the incarnation, Jesus is still a divine person. When the Father, directly addressing the Son, says, "You are My beloved Son," it would be absurd to attempt to reduce this to "you have a human nature that I love." Second, if the Father, Son, and Spirit do not have something analogous to communication in their eternal relationships, God could not be a God who would communicate with man, and man, God's image, would not have been created as a communicator. Third, given that God's names reveal His character, a God who does not communicate would not be called by the name, "Word," for that name applies to Him from the beginning before the creation (John 1:1). Fourth, a God in whom there is nothing analogous to communication would not create the world by means of communication. This list could be extended, but the point is clear: from the beginning of Scripture, God is everywhere presented as a God who communicates. The narrative of Jesus' baptism is wholly consistent with the rest of the Bible's revelation of God.

Where does that leave us? Part of the answer is in the ontology of God. The most sublime divine analogue to human communication consists in the eternal generation of the Son and spiration of the Spirit. The Father communicates Himself in generating the Son, and Father and Son together spirate the Spirit in an act of communicating love to one another. The ontology of God is an ontology of communication, but it is not communication of information. It is the communication of self-giving love. In the outworking of God's plan of salvation in the world, we see that the Father gives the Son to the world in His perfect love and grace. The Son gives Himself and His Spirit to the Church. And the Spirit gives the Church to the Son and through the Son to the Father. God's communication to us is the communication of His very person because in God the persons of the Trinity communicate their whole persons to one another.

However, this part of the answer does not solve the dilemma. We still cannot comprehend the meaning that Jesus is the Word in eternity and we cannot even begin to fathom the ontology of eternal generation and spiration, even though we can see in them an analogue to communication. The sum of the matter is that we must confess that we cannot comprehend the mystery of God. We cannot now nor will we ever be able to grasp the God who is so truly three that there can be something like verbal conversation among the persons, each of whom is conscious of Himself and the others as a subject, and at the same time so perfectly one that the three share a single consciousness and constitute one absolute Being. We can only confess the biblically revealed truth of the Trinity and enjoy what it shows us about our God. In respect to communication, the story of Jesus' baptism reveals a rich inner life of movement, sharing, and verbal communication. We are taught to know the persons as giving to one another, enjoying one another, and resting in one another's love.

Loving Fellowship

As we have just seen, communication implies love. What that means in the context of the baptismal narrative may be seen in the following four perspectives on Trinitarian love revealed in the story. First, Jesus submits to baptism to fulfill all righteousness, identifying with sinners and accepting His role as the suffering Messiah and Savior. Second, the Father declares His love for the Son. Third, He gives the Holy Spirit, the gift of love. Fourth, the Spirit comes to anoint the Son with power to accomplish the Father's will. Considering the Trinitarian fellowship of love in the baptism of Jesus is especially important because of what is implied about the attributes of God and the manner in which the attributes of God find distinct expression in the three persons.

As I have pointed out, Jesus was self-consciously submitting to the Father's will for His life and identifying with sinful man. The baptism is the first step on the road to the cross as the dove-Spirit manifests. Though the word "love" does not appear in this passage, Jesus' submission to the Father is a submission of love, as the Gospel of John emphasizes:

> If you love Me, you will keep My commandments.
> (John 14:15 NASB)

> If you keep My commandments, you will abide in My love; just as I have kept My Father's commandments and abide in His love.
> (John 15:10 NASB)

Of course, the connection between obedience and love is something that pervades the Scriptures. But in John's Gospel, we see the basis for that theme in the Trinitarian love of God. Our love for Jesus is the motive for our obedience, because we are created in the image of the triune God, in whom the Son's love for the Father is the motive for His obedience. Of course, the Father accepts and reciprocates that love. When, therefore, we read of Jesus' submission to a baptism that identified Him with sinners, it is the expression of the obedient love of the eternal Son for the Father.

The Father's love for the Son is declared in straightforward terms: "Thou art my beloved Son, in thee I am well pleased" (Mark 1:11). The Father's love and good pleasure in the Son is mentioned more often in the New Testament than we might notice (Matt 3:17; 12:18; 17:5; Mark 1:11; Luke 3:22; John 8:29; Col 1:19; 2 Pet 1:17). In this declaration of love and good pleasure, the Father's joy in the Son virtually overflows into a song of delight. We are reminded of similar words of love the Father declares for His daughter, Zion:

> Yahweh thy God is in the midst of thee,
> a mighty one who will save;
> he will rejoice over thee with joy;
> he will rest in his love;
> he will joy over thee with singing. (Zeph 3:17)

The gift of the Spirit as a gift of love may be less obvious, but this is an area in which God's work in the economy of our salvation reveals truth about the life of the Trinity. To understand the gift of the Spirit to Jesus, we have to consider the parallel example, the gift of the Spirit to us. Paul tells us that when the Father bestows the gift of the Spirit to His people, He is pouring out His love upon us: "And hope putteth not to shame; because the love of God hath been shed abroad in our hearts through the Holy Spirit which was given unto us" (Rom 5:5).

God pours out His love in our hearts by giving His Spirit to us. The gift of the Spirit, in other words, is the gift of love, and He works in our hearts to provide the assurance of God's infinite love for us. For He is the supreme gift the Father bestows, the guarantee that God will finish the work that He has begun in us, the one who opens our hearts to know the love of God and keep us abiding in the one who is love (Luke 11:13; John 3:34; 2 Cor 5:5; Eph 1:17; 3:16–19; 2 Tim 1:7; 1 John 3:24).

What the baptismal narrative draws attention to, then, is that Jesus received baptism at the hands of John in loving submission to the Father's will and that the Father declared His love for Jesus and anointed Jesus with the Spirit of love in order to give Jesus assurance of His great love just before Jesus entered His special time of trial in the wilderness.[59] The declaration was the embrace of a Father sending His Son to war. The gift of the Spirit was the loving provision of all the strength He would need for the battle.

David Bentley Hart sees this declaration by the Father, together with the gift of the Spirit, as an important verse in developing his aesthetic of Christian truth through the knowledge of the beauty of the Infinite.

> When Scripture says God is love, after all, this is certainly not some vague sentiment concerning the presence of God in our emotions, but describes the life of God, the dynamism of his substance, the distance and the dance: the unity of coinherence, but also the interval of appraisal, address, recognition, and pleasure. And if the descent of the dove at Christ's baptism reveals that every act of God, as Basil says, "is inaugurated by the Father, ef-

---

59. For Jonathan Edwards, the fact that the Spirit appeared as a dove is also evidence of God's love. "This is confirmed by the symbol of the Holy Ghost, viz., a dove, which is the emblem of love or a lover, and is so used in Scripture, and especially often so in Solomon's Song, (1:15) 'Behold thou art fair; my love, behold thou art fair; thou hast dove's eyes.' i.e. 'Eyes of love,' and again 4:1, the same words; and 5:12, 'His eyes are as the eyes of doves,' and 5:2, 'My love, my dove,' and 2:14 and 6:9; and this I believe to be the reason that the dove alone of all birds (except the sparrow in the single case of the leprosy) was appointed to be offered in sacrifice because of its innocence and because it is the emblem of love, love being the most acceptable sacrifice to God. It was under this similitude that the Holy Ghost descended from the Father on Christ at His baptism, signifying the infinite love of the Father to the Son, Who is the true David, or beloved, as we said before. The same was signified by what was exhibited to the eye in the appearance there was of the Holy Ghost descending from the Father to the Son in the shape of a dove, as was signified by what was exhibited to the eye [*sic*: ear] in the voice there was at the same time, viz., 'This is my well beloved Son in whom I am well pleased'" (Edwards, *Unpublished Essay on the Trinity*, 103).

fected by the Son, and perfected by the Holy Spirit" (*De Spiritu Sancto* 16.38), it reveals also that God's love is always entirely sufficient in itself: as the third, who receives and returns the love of the Father and the Son, and so witnesses, enjoys, and perfects it, the Spirit is also the one in whom that love most manifestly opens out as sheer delight, generosity, and desire for the other.[60]

But there is something more we must not miss here, something usually overlooked in discussions of God's attributes. In the baptismal narrative, each person of the Trinity expresses His love in a distinct manner. Thus, we are faced again with the paradox of the one and the many, this time in the doctrine of the attributes of God. Of course, the paradox cannot be limited to the attribute of love, though that is what stands out in the baptism of Jesus. But the idea of distinct manifestations of love or any other attribute by Father, Son, and Spirit introduces difficulties in the doctrine of God, beginning with our understanding of a particular attribute, simplicity. For the attribute of simplicity is usually understood to imply that attributes cannot in any sense be described as related to the persons. This requires some explanation.

God is one being and His being is simple, that is, not composed. Therefore each of the attributes of God must be seen as coterminous with His being and with each other. They cannot be thought of as "parts" of God. If each attribute is coterminous with the being of God, they cannot be distinct with the persons, since the three persons share the whole being of God equally and without difference. This basic logic seems solid. It finds expression in the Athanasian Creed:

> But the Godhead of the Father, of the Son, and of the Holy Ghost, is all one: the Glory equal, the Majesty coeternal. Such as the Father is: such is the Son: and such is the Holy Ghost. . . . The Father eternal: the Son eternal: and the Holy Ghost eternal. And yet they are not three eternals: but one eternal. (lines 6–7, 10–11)
>
> So, likewise, the Father is Almighty: the Son Almighty: and the Holy Ghost Almighty. And yet they are not three Almighties but one Almighty. (lines 13–14)[61]

---

60. Hart, *Beauty of the Infinite*, 175.
61. Schaff, *Creeds of Christendom*, 2:66–67.

Charles Hodge shows how the doctrine of God's attributes is related to the problem of the one and the many as it is expressed in the extremes of realism and nominalism, pointing out that Reformed theologians tend to go in the nominalist direction because of their understanding of God's unity and simplicity:

> In attempting to explain the relation in which the attributes of God stand to his essence and to each other, there are two extremes to be avoided. First, we must not represent God as a composite being, composed of different elements; and, secondly, we must not confound the attributes, making them all mean the same thing, which is equivalent to denying them all together. The Realists of the Middle Ages tended to the former of these extremes, and the Nominalists to the other. Realists held that general terms express not merely thoughts, or abstract conceptions in our minds, but real or substantive, objective existence. And hence they were disposed to represent the divine attributes as differing from each other *realiter*, as one *res* or thing differs from another. The Nominalists, on the other hand, said general terms are mere words answering to abstractions formed by the mind. And consequently when we speak of different attributes in God, we only use different words for one and the same thing. . . . The Lutheran and Reformed theologians tended much more to the latter of these extremes than to the former. They generally taught, in the first place, that the unity and simplicity of the divine essence precludes not only all physical composition of constituent elements, or of matter and form, or of subject and accidents; but also all metaphysical distinction as of act and power, essence and existence, nature and personality; and even of logical difference, as genus and specific difference.[62]

Even Cornelius Van Til—in spite of famously emphasizing the equal ultimacy of the one and the many in God and speaking of the persons of the Trinity as subjects who self-consciously relate to one another—does not apply his understanding of the one and the many to the doctrine of God's attributes by distinguishing the love of Father, Son and Spirit. Rather, Van Til agrees with Hodge that attributes pertain to the essence only and are shared equally by the persons, as the following quotations from Hodge and Van Til show:

---

62. Interestingly, it was almost certainly Charles Hodge who was the origin of Cornelius Van Til's unusual language about the Trinity. For a discussion of Van Til's use of Hodge, see my *Paradox and Truth*, 52–54.

The Councils held that the Father, Son, and Spirit are the same in substance, and equal in power and glory. Whatever divine perfection, whether eternity, immutability, infinity, omnipotence, or holiness, justice, goodness, or truth, can be predicated of the one, can in the same sense and measure be predicated of the others. These attributes belonging to the divine essence, and that essence being common to the three persons, the attributes or perfections are in like manner common to each. It is not the Father as such, nor the Son as such, who is self-existent, infinite, and eternal, but the Godhead, or divine essence, which subsists in the three persons.[63]

We come to a discussion of the attributes of God. The problem that faces us at the outset is that of the relation of the virtues or attributes of God to his Being. In dealing with distinctions in the Godhead, we must needs be careful not to do despite to the simplicity of his Being. We cannot divide up the Godhead. But if this is true, must we then conclude that the distinctions we make are made by merely us, and have only subjective value?

There is only one possible answer to this difficulty. Each attribute of God is coterminous with God. God is light, God is love, God is righteousness, God is holiness. Yet God himself has in his revelation instructed us to make distinctions with respect to his Being. These distinctions help us to understand something of the wealth and the richness of his Being.[64]

The problem here is the same that we encounter when we think of God's personhood or His self-consciousness. On the one hand, it is clear in the Bible that God is three persons who relate to one another. If each one is an "I" to Himself, then each is self-conscious, and for the three to relate as persons also requires that each is conscious of the others. If we are going to do justice to the biblical data, we must say that God is three self-conscious subjects. On the other hand, God Himself in the oneness of His being must be absolutely one. He is not a composite. Also, He is not and cannot be impersonal in any aspect of His existence. There is no non-personal substratum of being underlying the persons, nor is there any scintilla of the impersonal in God's essence. In that sense, He must be "one person," as Hodge and Van Til maintain. However, we hasten to add that the meaning of the word "person" is ambiguous here. God is not one person in the same sense that He is three persons, or we would have

---

63. Hodge, *Systematic Theology*, 1:348
64. Van Til, *Introduction to Systematic Theology*, 178.

a quadrinity. Something of the same thing must be said of God's consciousness. God is not conscious of Himself as one person in the same way that the Father is conscious of Himself as the Father of the Son, who loved the Son from before the foundation of the world.[65]

How shall we think of these things? Two aspects of Trinitarian theology offer some aid. First, the biblical doctrine of perichoresis may help us here. The three persons who perfectly indwell one another are so utterly and absolutely one that they may be described as a single person with a single self-consciousness, without in any sense taking away from the reality of their threeness. By their mutual indwelling, they are a single essence which is the one God. Second, we must also remember that the Father begat the Son, and the Father and the Son breathed out the Spirit. The personhood of the three is grounded in the Father. However, even though "begotten" and "spirated," the Son and Spirit, with the Father, *are* the one essence.

In the interest of supposedly following the Bible, some evangelicals, as we saw with Reymond, have denied the doctrine of the generation of the Son and the spiration of the Spirit, because these doctrines seem to them to be based upon inferences from biblical teaching rather than direct statements, in addition to being extremely abstruse notions. However good this may sound at first, it results in a truncated doctrine of the Trinity. We are left with three unrelated persons who are called God. Once we have denied the ontological relationships implied in the names of Son and Spirit—namely generation and spiration—the three Trinitarian persons seem to be separated from one another by undefinable distance, since Father, Son, and Spirit no longer have relationships defined by their names. The three are merely side by side. A jejune reading of the Bible undermines the inherent richness of the biblical doctrine of God and leaves us with three unrelated individuals—the seed of tritheism.

Perichoresis has also been sometimes denied for similar reasons with similar results. When Father, Son, and Spirit are not thought to indwell one another, they seem to be three persons somehow having the same essence, but standing, as it were, beside one another. The same problem of relating the Three appears again. Clearly denial of generation and spiration or of perichoresis tends to undermine basic aspects of the

---

65. Again, see Appendix 1 for a fuller discussion of self-consciousness and consciousness, based largely on William G. T. Shedd's treatment of the topic.

doctrine the Trinity and would push a person either in the direction of tritheism—if the three who stand beside one another were emphasized—or in the direction of modalism—if the single essence were to receive main emphasis. The doctrines of perichoresis and of the eternal generation of the Son and spiration of the Spirit reveal God's nature in a manner that manifests something of the equal ultimacy of the one and the many.

Keeping in mind the dangers of overemphasizing either unity or diversity, there is clearly a need to develop the side of God's threeness in connection with the doctrine of God's attributes. The traditional Christian theological emphasis in the doctrine of God's attributes falls entirely on the side of God's oneness. Of course, we must not deny that God is indeed one in power and glory. But our confession cannot end there. In order for us to say, "God is love," we must also confess that He is three persons who love one another, for unless the love of God is defined in terms of the interpersonal relationships among the Father, Son, and Spirit, God has no "other" to love. This is usually taken for granted in discussions of God's love, but the broader implications for our understanding of God's attributes are ignored.

Let's return to the narrative of Jesus' baptism and consider its implications for understanding God's attributes. Though the story itself is only a few verses long, its concrete depiction of the relationships among the Trinitarian persons suggest distinctions in the way they "hold" various attributes. All three love, but they love according to their personal relation to the others. The Father rends the heavens and declares that He loves the Son. His very words require us to infer distinctions because He declares that the Son is His beloved Son, defining the love He has for the incarnate God as the love of the Father for a Son. In the nature of the case, that must be different from the love the Son has for the Father. The Spirit, who is, as we have seen, the gift of love, expresses love differently. Instead of making a declaration, He gently descends onto the Son in loving submission to the Father who sent Him. The Son's love for the Father is also expressed in that His baptism by John is the first step of obedience on the way to the cross.

This picture of love expressed in distinct forms is paralleled by other passages in the Gospels. A few examples from the Gospel of John suffice for illustration, but there are many more verses testifying to the fatherly love of God and the filial affection of the Son:

> The Father loveth the Son, and hath given all things into his hand. (John 3:35)
>
> For the Father loveth the Son, and showeth him all things that himself doeth: and greater works than these will he show him, that ye may marvel. (John 5:20)
>
> Therefore doth the Father love me, because I lay down my life that I may take it again. (John 10:17)
>
> But that the world may know that I love the Father, and as the Father gave me commandment, even so I do. (John 14:31)
>
> If ye keep my commandments, ye shall abide in my love; even as I have kept my Father's commandments, and abide in his love. (John 15:10)

Note that in these passages, the Father's love is described in terms of self-giving and revelation, just as the Father's love for the Son at the baptism of Jesus is expressed in a revelatory declaration and the gift of the Spirit. To reveal, to teach and to give are essential to the distinctive character of fatherly love. Thus, just as the Father expresses His love for the Son by revelation and gift, so too He shows His love for the wayward world: "God so loved the world, that he gave his only begotten Son" (John 3:16).

We must also note that the Son's love for the Father is described differently and distinctly from the Father's love for the Son. Of course, the differences are not absolute, for we must also say that because the Son loves the Father, He reveals Himself and gives Himself. But the distinction is nevertheless real, because one could not say of the Father that He loves the Son and therefore obeys Him. Jesus' love for the Father expressed in His baptism is seen in His identification with sinners and His willingness to become one with them to die for them. It is to the beauty of Jesus' humble submission that the Father responds from heaven, declaring that He is well pleased with the Son. The Father loves the Son because the Son lovingly obeys His will and seeks His glory. Just as it is a special expression of the Father's distinct love for the Son to reveal and give, so it is special to the Son that He loves the Father and therefore obeys the Father's commands, laying down His life for the sheep. The Gospels depict the love of Father, Son, and Spirit in distinct terms peculiar to the particular persons and their relationships.

At least in the case of intratrinitarian love, the distinct manner in which the attributes of God come to expression in Father, Son, and Spirit is a subject of explicit biblical revelation. What does that mean for the rest of God's attributes? Since all the attributes of God are related, distinct expressions of love necessarily imply that all the attributes have some sort of Trinitarian dimension. For the Father to be faithful to the Son seems obviously to have a meaning distinct from what it means for the Son to be faithful to the Father. The same can even be said about righteousness, for the righteousness of the Father includes being righteous in His relationship to the Son, which includes carrying out His fatherly responsibilities. Likewise, the Son's righteousness includes His loving obedience to the Father, something distinct from the Father's righteousness. Similar considerations pertain to all of what are called God's "communicable" or "moral" attributes. Other attributes, such as infinity, eternity, and omnipresence, do not obviously require a personal aspect.

Why is this important? To neglect the features of love that pertain to each of the persons would be to reduce the biblical picture of the fullness of Trinitarian life to a bland oneness. Apart from missing the richness of the life of God, we would not be faithful to biblical testimony. The lack of an understanding of God's attributes in Trinitarian perspective may well be one cause for situation Letham complains of when he says that most Christians are "practical modalists." Both the East and the West have neglected certain aspects of the doctrine of the Trinity, matters that need to be explored and expounded for the edification of God's people. The story of Jesus' baptism may be the very place to start in order to correct the tendency toward modalism as Christians learn to understand that the God of the Bible is three persons who share a rich fellowship of love.

I hasten to add that nothing in the above is intended to deny the orthodox doctrine of God or the relationship of attributes to God's essence. I am not suggesting we reject the traditional view and adopt something new. Certainly God is one love, just as He is—to use the language Van Til adapted from Hodge—one person. In addition to this, however, we need to include the biblical picture of Father loving as a father and the Son responding as a son, with the Spirit expressing love in His own distinct manner. Perhaps we should say that God is one love and also that God is three loves. If this is not the right language to express the diversity of loves seen in the baptismal narrative, then other language should be found. What is important is that we do justice to the biblical portrayal of God. And that requires that we understand the relationship between the persons as the beginning of the expression of all of God's attributes, especially attributes such as love, wisdom, faithfulness, kindness, goodness, righteousness, and holiness.

Ritual Fellowship

Another neglected feature of the story of Jesus' baptism is the rituality of the Father and the Spirit. Though commentators and theologians have struggled with the question of why the sinless Messiah ought to be baptized, they have seldom, if ever, asked the question, Why do God the Father and the Spirit relate to the Son in so ceremonial a manner? Once we ask the question, we realize how profound the implications are. Once we take cognizance of the Father and the Spirit's participation in the ritual of the baptism of Jesus, we are compelled to consider the relationship between the Trinity and ritual. We are led into a whole new area of Trinitarianism: the ritual life of God.

A good place to begin our inquiry is with an article by Peter Leithart. Writing of the Trinitarian "frame" for Christian sacraments, Leithart challenges "the modern tendency to disrupt symbol and reality and to collapse the Trinity into unity," finding insight in Aquinas. He concludes his argument as follows:

> Sacraments are necessary for salvation, Aquinas argues, because, given the nature of God and of man, it is fitting that God makes use of sacramental signs and rites in redemption. In developing his argument, Thomas first quotes Augustine's statement (from *Contra Faustum* 19.11) that it is impossible to unite men in a religious association without the use of symbols or sacraments. Since it is necessary for salvation for men to be bound in one true religion, Thomas argues, sacraments are essential to the achievement of salvation. While the Reformers rightly rejected many aspects of the mechanistic medieval sacramental system, Thomas's insight is compatible with a Reformed anthropology and soteriology, and points toward the best of Reformed sacramental theology.[66]

It is "necessary for salvation for men to be bound in one true religion" because ecclesiology is inseparable from soteriology. God is not

---

66. Leithart, "'Framing' Sacramental Theology," 16.

saving unrelated, independent individuals; He is saving the Church, the Bride over which Christ is the Head. Ceremonies are important, then, because they define people and unite them into covenantal or quasi-covenantal groups. Leithart begins by discussing possible historical roots for the modern disdain of ceremonies, without concluding on a particular explanation. He goes on to discuss the theology of the sacraments, arguing that ceremonies like baptism and the Lord's Supper have their roots in the nature of the Trinity.

> The argument that follows is this: God's Trinitarian character is the "very foundation of the possibility," or the "foundation of the inescapability," of sacraments. Sacraments are not "exceptions" to God's typically "non-symbolic" means of communicating and communing with creatures. Rather, the Creator, because he is Trinity in Unity and Unity in Trinity, draws his people into fellowship with himself through symbols, of which the sacraments are a particular kind.[67]

The baptism of Jesus, though not specifically referred to in Leithart's article, puts the truth of God's rituality into sharp focus. That is, the story of the baptism of Jesus shows us that God is a ritual God, a notion so contrary to much of modern evangelical and Reformed thought that the very statement of it will sound absurd to some. However, in stark contrast to much of evangelical Christianity, the Bible has a high view of ritual, and the story of Jesus' baptism shows us that the reason for that high view begins in God Himself.

Consider just the baptismal accounts. We have argued that God the Father and the Spirit here are completing the baptismal anointing begun by John the Baptizer. The baptism of Jesus with water, like the ceremonial washing of Aaron for his priestly consecration, was only one part of a larger and more complex rite. Moses, after he has washed Aaron with water, finishes the rite by anointing Aaron with oil. But the Melchizedekian priesthood into which Jesus was inaugurated is greater and the ritual includes the whole Trinity. When the prophet has done his part, Jesus comes out of the water addressing the Father in prayer, and the Father and Spirit finish the ceremony. The Melchizedekian anointing is not with oil, but with the Messianic Spirit of God (Isa 42:1). The Father rends the heavens open to solemnly quote Scripture, while the

---

67. Ibid., 5. To demonstrate his thesis, Leithart gleans insights from Karl Rahner and John Zizioulas, while criticizing fundamental aspects of their approach.

Spirit descends in the form of a sacrificial animal. A more ceremonial format could hardly be imagined. And, as we pointed out above, nothing here in the relationship of Father, Son, and Spirit can be utterly new or unique. The Son is the eternal Son and the Father relates to Him in a manner consistent with their eternal fellowship in the Spirit. Thus, the baptism and consecration of Jesus to His Messianic ministry concretely reveals ceremonial fellowship among the Trinitarian persons, suggesting the ultimate source of the ceremonial nature of the created world and God's covenantal relationship with mankind.

Even if one took Dunn's approach to the baptismal accounts and saw the baptism by John as basically distinct from what followed, the purportedly separate event of the Father sending the Spirit and announcing His love for Jesus would remain profoundly ceremonial. The actions of the Father and Spirit occur, on anyone's account, in a ceremonial context, as Jesus is coming up from the waters of baptism. God the Father rips open the heavens and the Spirit, in the form of a sacrificial dove, descends upon Jesus. The fact that the Spirit descends in the form of a sacrificial animal places His coming in another ceremonial context, without which it does not make sense. Also, the Father speaks to the Son, not in spontaneous fashion or casually, but in the ritually weighty language of Scriptural quotation, adding resonance and deep background to each word. Thus, on Dunn's view, too, the Father and the Spirit "conduct" a ceremony, a rite of inauguration.

The rituality of God seen in the baptism of Jesus accords with what the Bible as a whole reveals about the nature of God, though again the broader witness of Scripture to the ceremonial nature of God is hardly noticed, indeed almost systematically overlooked. Modern Christians quote Isaiah and other prophets who complain of Israel's abuse of the sacrificial system as if that were the most important thing the Bible has to say about ritual. We are led to wonder who invented the sacrificial system to begin with.

Instead of taking our starting point with the prophets' complaints about abuse, we should begin, perhaps, with the observation that the God who inspired the book of Leviticus is a God who delights in ceremonies. This is not to deny that the old-covenant ceremonial law no longer applies, or that animal sacrifices, food and clothing laws, and other aspects of the law were given to Israel because Israel was a child and needed to be led as a child. Rather, we are emphatically affirming that if He so willed, God could have done things otherwise; He is not constrained by man's nature or history. Moreover, we need to note that ceremonies neither begin nor end with the law given to Israel.

The first manifestation of the ceremonial nature of God is in the creation, not only before the fall, but even before the creation of man. God takes six days to create the world and does it by a slow, careful process that involves verbal interaction with inanimate things such as light. If we were not so accustomed to the story, it would strike us as odd that God commands light which does not exist to come into existence. How can the non-existent light hear? Why this form of creation? The slow, dignified, command/response form of creation corresponds to covenant making ceremonies, as Meredith Kline argues at length.[68] The creation sequence—command, obedience, blessing—is covenantal to the core, for the world comes to exist only in covenantal obedience to God. Accordingly, we may describe the six-day story of creation as a six-day covenantal ceremony. To repeat this in different words, God did not make a covenant with the world He created; He created the world by a covenantal ceremony, so that the world by its very nature exists in covenant.

Moreover, the rituality of God is not confined to this material world below. We also find in Scripture that the highest heavens themselves reveal the ceremonial nature of God. For example, when Isaiah sees a vision of heaven, he sees Yahweh seated on a throne and the seraphim crying out, "Holy, Holy, Holy!" (Isa 6:3). Ezekiel's vision of heavenly glory corresponds (Ezek 1:4–28). If ritual were not fundamental to God's nature, why would He create the angels to be leaders in a never-ending ritual of praise?

We must not answer that this is simply old covenant revelation, couched in ceremonial forms for revelation to the ancient Jews. In the book of Revelation, the apostle John sees a heavenly worship service (Rev 4–5). In John's vision, Jesus and the Father participate in a ceremony in which the Lion of the Tribe of Judah, appearing in the form of a slain Lamb, receives the book of dominion from the Father. In the context of Revelation 4–5, there is no cause in the weakness or immaturity of ancient Israel for the Father to bring the Son before the angels and redeemed humanity in such a ceremonial fashion. Rather, we have to

---

68. Kline, *Kingdom Prologue*, 14–21.

conclude that the Father relates to the Son in this way because ceremony is essential to God's nature.

If this is not enough, there is still more. The Bible tells us that, when we reach the end of human history and Christ returns to the earth to judge and save, the climactic event is the marriage supper of the Lamb. The history of the world ends with the full coming of the new covenant and the resurrection of Christ's Church. Clothed in resurrection glory and saved from all sin and the limitations of the flesh, surely the Church now has no weakness or immaturity requiring another ceremony! But a ceremony is precisely what John's vision reveals. And his description of the city and life in the city is filled with ritual implications—bride descending (21:2), tabernacle (21:3), temple (21:22), water of life (21:6), unclean (21:27), a river proceeding from the throne (22:1), and the tree of life (22:2), to name only the most obvious features.

In the context, then, of a Book that begins and ends with ritual and that always includes ritual in man's relationship with God—whether in the Garden, after the flood, in the law of Moses, or in Jesus' last hours with His disciples—it is profoundly significant to observe that in the baptism of Jesus, the Father and the Spirit relate to the Son ritually. It is not merely that God delights in ritual. We have to say more. If the economic Trinity reveals the ontological Trinity, *ritual is fundamental to the nature of God.*

Think now again of the eternal generation of the Son and the eternal spiration of the Spirit. The Father eternally begets the Son, an act that constitutes and defines each of them. Unless He generated the Son, the Father could not be Father. Unless the Father generated Him, the Son could not be Son. The Father breathes the Spirit to the Son, constituting the Spirit as Spirit and the Son breathes the Spirit back to the Father, in some way defining Father, Son, and Spirit—all three—as the living God.

This movement in God is essential to the Christian understanding of the Trinity, for without it, God would be a static unity, unchangeable as a frozen, inert thing, a comatose god, lifeless and unable to give life. Certainly God is unchangeable, but in the Bible God's immutability is fundamentally different from the notion of static or frozen invariability. God's nature does not change, but immutable does not mean unmoving. God is dynamic, eternal motion apart from and before the creation of the world, as witnessed by the eternal generation of the Son and spiration of the Spirit.

Note that this eternal motion is regular. The Father is eternally generating the Son and breathing the Spirit to the Son. The Son is eternally proceeding from the Father and breathing the Spirit back to the Father. The Spirit is eternally proceeding from the Father to the Son and from the Son back to the Father. Although we cannot comprehend what this "motion" means or even begin to imagine it in concrete terms, in the human context a solemn, profound, regular, repetitious motion is inescapably ceremonial. There is no other form for such a motion to take. Must it be so with God? The ritual character of biblical revelation certainly suggests something analogous and within the whole context of that revelation, the narrative of the baptism of Jesus strongly suggests such a conclusion. We must say, then, that in the economy of Trinitarian relationships seen in Jesus' baptism, we catch a glimpse of the ritual ontology of God.

Covenantal Fellowship

It should be superfluous here to speak of covenantal fellowship, except that the point needs emphasis, because the covenant underlies much more of the Bible's teaching and stories than is often recognized. When in the Bible, we find personal, loving, verbal fellowship, ceremonially expressed, we are without doubt viewing a covenant initiation or renewal, a covenantal form of some sort, even if the word "covenant" does not appear in the passage.

Of course, not all interpersonal interaction in the Bible is covenantal in the narrow sense—buying and selling between Jews and Gentiles, for instance, can hardly be called covenantal. But even here, there is a larger covenantal context—no buying or selling on the Sabbath, laws about honest weights and measures, and so on.

Whatever may be said about very temporary and superficial relationships, the most fundamental personal relationships are distinctly covenantal. Marriage is entered by an oath and is a covenantal relationship. The Church is entered through baptism, a covenant oath ceremony that is renewed in the new-covenant Supper of the Lord. The authority of the civil government is given by God, so that civil authorities, too, may rightly demand oaths of their officers. More significantly, all men, whether they are conscious of it or not, are in covenant before God, either in Adam or in Christ. We are all either covenant keepers or covenant breakers. Human personhood is tied to covenant.

So is love. Of course, the word "love" in the Bible, as in our everyday speech, has different meanings in different contexts. To take an extreme example, we read that Amnon "loved" Tamar (2 Sam 13:1, 4),[69] but we know it was base lust, for as soon as he had forced her, he hated her more than he had loved her (13:15). The word "love," then, even in the Bible can mean mere physical desire. But when the word "love" is used in its most proper and exalted sense, it implies a total commitment of the self to the other sealed by a covenant oath. Such love is the very core of the covenant relationship: "Thou shalt love the LORD thy God with all thy heart, with all thy soul and with all thy mind" (Deut 6:5). This love is expressed, sealed, and confirmed through oath-taking covenant ceremonies, like Jesus' baptism. The Father's expression of love for Jesus on that occasion is part of the covenantal ceremony of Jesus' ordination to ministry as Messiah.

Righteous ceremonies in the Bible are exclusively covenantal. But of course, not all ceremonies are righteous. The Bible also refers to perverse ceremonies, such as oaths to idols, magical incantations and invocations of demonic powers, and consultations with the dead—sinful distortions of man's image and the revelation of true religion, which are actually debased forms of covenantal ceremonies.

The ceremonies God gave to Israel are fundamentally different. Though God gave Israel a rich catalog of ceremonies that spanned the time frame of a fifty-year Jubilee cycle, all of Israel's ceremonies—circumcision, the daily, weekly, and monthly rituals, seven year sabbaths, and the festivals—were either covenant initiation ceremonies or covenant renewal ceremonies. The covenant was central to everything. Baptism and the Lord's Supper fit into the same sort of covenantal framework. By baptism we take a covenant oath to Christ as our Lord. In the Lord's Supper, we renew that oath.

In the same way, when the Spirit descends as a covenantal sacrificial animal, He is revealing that Jesus is the final sacrifice, the one to establish a greater and everlasting covenant. To Jesus, as the Messiah and king of the new covenant, is first given the blessing of the new covenant, the Holy Spirit, whose full blessing makes Jesus a new sort of man, a Spirit-

---

69. The Hebrew verb used here is used for covenantal love in passages such as Deuteronomy 6:5. While the familiar Greek noun αγάπη (*agape*) is sometimes said to refer exclusively to divine or covenantal love, the Septuagint uses the related verb not only in Deuteronomy 6:5 but also for Amnon's love for Tamar in 2 Samuel 13.

man, though this is not fulfilled until the resurrection when Jesus takes on a new body. When God the Father quotes Scripture about Jesus as being the Messianic Lord, He is announcing Jesus' status as covenant Lord of the new world. As the new Adam, Jesus takes the place of the first covenant head and initiates a new humanity. It would be too repetitious here to review the verses we have looked at. We only need to be reminded of the emphatically covenantal context of the Scriptures quoted by the Father.

What this means, then, is that in the economy of salvation, the triune God reveals Himself to us as the covenantal God, not only in His relationship with His creation, but even in the intratrinitarian fellowship of Father, Son, and Spirit at Jesus' baptism. The economic Trinity relates in covenant, therefore the ontological Trinity is covenantal. Covenant, like love, must be seen as essential to the ontology of God.

CONCLUSION

The baptism of Jesus reveals Father, Son, and Spirit sharing the personal, loving, ritual fellowship of the covenant. In the passages that record our Lord's baptism, we see that Father, Son, and Spirit each loves the other in a distinct manner, expressing that love according to the order of Trinitarian personhood. The same can be said for the divine expression of rituality. The one God is three personal subjects who perfectly indwell one another, yet without erasing distinctions. The three persons are the one God. They are each coterminous with the one essence of God and share all that the one God is.

The revelation of the fellowship of the triune persons at the baptism of Jesus conveys clearly that each of the persons knows Himself in distinction from the others and relates to the others self-consciously. Though there is a deep mystery in the idea of the one omniscient God sharing something analogous to verbal fellowship in the personal relations of Father, Son, and Spirit, the story of the baptism of Jesus demands that we view God as an eternally communicative fellowship of love. More broadly, it demands that we view all the attributes of God as qualified by their expression in the Father, Son, and Spirit. Although Augustine did not intend exactly what I am trying to say, I believe that what he wrote still comports with my argument:

The Trinitarian Dimension

The purpose of all the Catholic commentators I have been able to read on the divine books of both testaments, who have written before me on the trinity which God is, has been to teach that according to the scriptures Father and Son and Holy Spirit in the inseparable equality of one substance present a divine unity; and therefore there are not three gods, but one God; although indeed the Father has begotten the Son, and therefore he who is the Father is not the Son; and the Son is begotten by the Father, and therefore he who is the Son is not the Father; and the Holy Spirit is neither the Father nor the Son, but only the Spirit of the Father and of the Son, himself co-equal to the Father and the Son, and belonging to the threefold unity.

It was not however this same three (their teaching continues) that was born of the Virgin Mary, crucified and buried under Pontius Pilate, rose again on the third day and ascended into heaven, but the Son alone. Nor was it this same three that came down upon Jesus in the form of a dove at his baptism, or came down on the day of Pentecost after the Lord's ascension, with a roaring sound from heaven as though a violent gust were rushing down, and in divided tongues as of fire, but the Holy Spirit alone. Nor was it this same three that spoke from heaven, *You are my Son,* either at his baptism by John (Mk 1:11), or on the mountain when the three disciples were with him (Mt 17:5), nor when the resounding voice was heard, *I have both glorified it* (my name) *and will glorify it again* (Jn 12:28), but it was the Father's voice alone addressing the Son; although just as Father and Son and Holy Spirit are inseparable, so do they work inseparably. This is also my faith inasmuch as it is the Catholic faith.[70]

---

70. Augustine, *The Trinity*, 69–70.

5

The Christian Dimension

THE BAPTISM OF JESUS is the most concrete New Testament picture of Christian baptism, the paradigm for the new covenant rite. This claim does not deny or diminish the unique cosmic and historical redemptive significance of Jesus' baptism; rather it is based upon the broader meaning of Jesus' baptism and ties Christian baptism to that cosmic significance. In a previous chapter I have made the case for the following two presuppositions, which are essential to this view: (1) Jesus' baptism in water by John the Baptizer is one event with the declaration of the Father and the gift of the Spirit, and (2) Jesus' baptism is His inauguration into the Melchizedekian priesthood.[1] It is time now to show how all of this relates to Christian baptism. Before doing so, however, a brief review of the history of the understanding of Jesus' baptism may be helpful.

THE HISTORICAL CONNECTION

As we have seen in chapter 1, John Calvin argued that since Christians are united with Christ, we also participate in the baptism of Jesus in some sense. We have baptism "in common" with Christ, and therefore we too are "sons of God." Our baptism, Calvin says, is fulfilled in Christ, so that He is "the proper object of baptism":

---

1. The baptism of Jesus is entirely neglected in Robert Letham's otherwise helpful book on the work of Christ, *The Work of Christ*. In spite of an extended discussion of Jesus' priesthood, focusing especially on Melchizedek, Letham says nothing about either the event of Jesus' baptism or its theological significance. Similarly, G. C. Berkouwer (*Sacraments*, 90–109), though well informed about the history of the discussion, somehow quite neglects the distinction between the baptism of Jews by John the Baptizer and the baptism of Jesus Himself. It seems to me quite remarkable that a theologian like Berkouwer should neglect the baptism of Jesus as he does, especially given Calvin's view.

> Lastly, our faith receives from baptism the advantage of its sure testimony to us that we are not only engrafted into the death and life of Christ, but so united to Christ himself that we become sharers in all his blessings. For he dedicated and sanctified baptism in his own body [Matt. 3:13] in order that he might have it in common with us as the firmest bond of the union and fellowship which he has deigned to form with us. Hence, Paul proves that we are children of God from the fact that we put on Christ in baptism [Gal. 3:26–27]. Thus we see that the fulfillment of baptism is in Christ, whom also for this reason we call the proper object of baptism.[2]

Calvin's view of baptism, as set forth his *Institutes of the Christian Religion*, begins with the following statement:

> Baptism is the sign of the initiation by which we are received into the society of the church, in order that, engrafted in Christ, we may be reckoned among God's children.[3] Now baptism was given to us by God for these ends (which I have taught to be common to all sacraments): first, to serve our faith before him; secondly, to serve our confession before men. We shall treat in order the reasons for each aspect of its institution. Baptism brings three things to our faith which we must deal with individually. The first thing that the Lord sets out for us is that baptism should be a token and proof of our cleansing; or (the better to explain what I mean) it is like a sealed document to confirm to us that all our sins are so abolished, remitted, and effaced that they can never come to his sight, be recalled, or charged against us. For he wills that all who believe be baptized for the remission of sins [Matt. 28:19; Acts 2:38].
>
> Accordingly, they who regarded baptism as nothing but a token and mark by which we confess our religion before men, as soldiers bear the insignia of their commander as a mark of their profession, have not weighed what was the chief point of baptism. It is to receive baptism with this promise: "He who believes and is baptized will be saved" [Mark 16:16].[4]

---

2. Calvin, *Institutes*, IV.15.6.

3. Wilhelm Niesel offers another translation of this sentence: "Baptism is the sign of our adoption, of our reception into the communion of the church, so that incorporated into the body of Christ we may be numbered among the children of God" (*Theology of Calvin*, 220).

4. Calvin, *Institutes*, IV.15.1

Clearly in Calvin's statement the ecclesiological and the soteriological dimensions meld into one.[5] Baptism is initiation into the society of the Church, and the chief point of baptism is the promise that "He who believes and is baptized will be saved." Calvin says, baptism is a proof of our cleansing from sin.

It is doubtful that Calvin would have allowed for the separation between soteriology and ecclesiology so common in systematic theologies today—soteriology as the doctrine of salvation for the individual and ecclesiology as the doctrine of the Church, treated almost as if the two were unrelated. For Calvin, as for the early fathers, the Church is our "mother." He can even say, "there is no other way to enter into life unless this mother conceive us in her womb, give us birth, nourish us at her breast, and lastly unless she keep us under her care and guidance until, putting off mortal flesh, we become like the angels [Matt. 22:30]."[6] In Calvin's view, soteriology can never be the doctrine of how unrelated individuals go to heaven, nor can the doctrine of the Church be the doctrine of a "voluntary association," entered by adult baptism.[7]

In this opening paragraph, Calvin writes that "Baptism brings three things to our faith." The three are discussed in the following paragraphs: (1) baptism is the "token and proof of our cleansing" (IV.15.1–4); (2) baptism "shows us our mortification in Christ, and new life in him" (IV.15.5); and (3) baptism unites us to Christ (IV.15.6).[8] It is in the exposition of the third point that Calvin mentions John the Baptizer baptizing Jesus so that "he dedicated and sanctified baptism in his own body [Matt. 3:13] in order that he might have it in common with us as the firmest bond of the union and fellowship which he has deigned to form with us."

---

5. Niesel writes, "Calvin certainly regarded the sacraments as occupying a paramount position in Church life" (*Theology of Calvin*, 40). I. John Hesselink agrees: "Calvin, in any case, had a high view of the sacraments, as high a view in many respects as Luther. (The same cannot be said of many modern Reformed/Presbyterian Christians, in contrast to their Lutheran counterparts)" (*Calvin's First Catechism*, 141).

6. Calvin, *Institutes*, IV.1.4.

7. John Bunyan's *The Pilgrim's Progress* (1678) is the perfect picture of the radical separation of soteriology and ecclesiology. The good pilgrim on his way to heaven never once attends a worship service and has no part in a local ecclesial body. In Bunyan's story, the Church as "the mother" of believers—to use Calvin's language—has no *essential* place in the life of the individual Christian. Indeed, it goes without mention.

8. Battles's translation of the *Institutes* makes clear what the three points are. Niesel uses different language but identifies the same three points (*Theology of Calvin*, 220).

Thus, baptism as union with Christ is one of the three main issues in his exposition of the doctrine of baptism, but in order to make that point, Calvin treats Jesus' baptism as the paradigm of Christian baptism. Actually, Calvin's formula is even more emphatic: "Thus we see that the fulfillment of baptism is in Christ, whom also for this reason we call the proper object of baptism."[9]

In Calvin's doctrine of baptism, the baptism of Jesus is the essential baptism that renders all other baptism meaningful. Jesus Himself is the "proper object" of baptism. In Calvin's theology, this means that because Jesus united Himself with us through the ceremony of baptism, baptism as a ceremony has—not by water nor merely by the Church, but by the Holy Spirit—the power to unite us to Him.[10] Calvin regards the topic of John's baptism and its relation to Christian baptism as so important that he devotes the next three sections (IV.15.7–9) to defending and expounding the subject.[11] Wallace summarizes Calvin's view well:

> In Baptism the baptised individual, as a member of Christ, is uprooted and separated from every corrupt source of life and introduced into a new sphere of common life which the members of Christ share with their exalted Head. Indeed, for Calvin each individual Christian's baptism is merely the sharing of one common Baptism, which the whole Church shares in common with Christ, Himself baptised in the Jordan, a common Baptism in which the whole Church is made one body and soul in union with Christ.[12]

---

9. Calvin, *Institutes*, IV.15.6

10. "The administration of the sacraments is not simply placed in the hands of the pastors as something ancillary to preaching (despite the fact that Calvin regards them alone as having the authority to administer the same) but they are stressed as something of particular importance. The focus of church life, that upon which the act of worship depends, is not simply the word of God proceeding from human lips, but also and above all the sacrament in its objective reality independent of man.... By the Spirit our hearts are opened to the penetrating power of Word and Sacrament. The Spirit links and unites us with Jesus Christ, so that in body, mind, and soul, we become his very own" (Niesel, *Theology of Calvin*, 211–12, 223).

11. Remarkably, Niesel's exposition of Calvin's view of baptism leaves this topic out entirely. Pierre Ch. Marcel's *Biblical Doctrine of Infant Baptism* is not specifically an exposition of Calvin's theology of baptism, but Calvin's view of Jesus' baptism is conspicuous for its absence.

12. Wallace, *Calvin's Doctrine of Word and Sacrament*, 175.

Calvin's view goes beyond what I am suggesting in this chapter. I am only arguing that Christ's baptism is the paradigm of Christian baptism, the example that defines the meaning of baptism for all those in Christ. But I believe that Calvin's profounder perspective includes and presupposes what I am arguing for. In other words, if all Christians share in the baptism of Jesus, then the baptism of Jesus is the defining baptism. Since all other baptisms derive their meaning from Jesus' baptism, we must regard it as the paradigm of Christian baptism. My own argument and Calvin's are not exactly the same, though nothing in my approach conflicts with his and the results overlap.

It must be emphasized, however, that Calvin's view—or something very like it—was not unique to him. Aquinas, for example, one of the scholastics whom Calvin respected and the best representative of the scholarship of his age, held a view rather similar to Calvin's. In his *Catena Aurea*, a commentary on the Gospels, consisting of a collection of quotations from the Fathers on each passage, Aquinas quotes Ambrose in connection with Matthew 3:16:

> For, as we have said, when the Saviour was washed, then the water was cleansed for our baptism, that a laver might be ministered to the people who were to come. Moreover, it behooved that in Christ's baptism should be signified those things which the faithful obtain by baptism.[13]

He follows this quotation with one from Rabanus:

> As by the immersion of His body He dedicated the laver of baptism, He has shewn that to us also, after baptism received, the entrance to heaven is open and the Holy Spirit is given, as it follows, *and the heavens were opened.*[14]

Earlier in the *Catena*, Aquinas quotes Augustine:

> The Saviour willed to be baptized not that He might Himself be cleansed, but to cleanse the water for us. From the time that Himself was dipped in the water, from that time has He washed away all our sins in water. And let none wonder that water, itself corporeal substance, is said to be effectual to the purification of the soul; it is so effectual, reaching to and searching out the hidden recesses of the conscience. Subtle and penetrating in its

---

13. Aquinas, *Catena Aurea*, 111.
14. Ibid., 111.

own nature, made yet more so by Christ's blessing, it touches the hidden springs of life, the secret places of the soul, by virtue of its all-pervading dew. The course of blessing is even yet more penetrating than the flow of waters. Thus the blessing which like a spiritual river flows on from the Saviour's baptism, hath filled the basins of all pools, and the courses of all fountains.[15]

Though the rhetoric is more devotional than theological, the similarity to Calvin's view is obvious enough. The baptism of Jesus is *the* baptism that makes all other baptisms meaningful.

Calvin and Aquinas both rely heavily on Augustine, but so far as I can tell, in the doctrine of baptism, Augustine's perspective, compared to that of Calvin or Aquinas, is rather minimalist. From repeated statements in his refutation of the Donatists, it seems that Augustine views the baptism of Jesus primarily as exemplary:

> And as our Lord was presently to enter on this way with all humility, and to lead those who humbly followed Him to perfection, as He washed the feet of His servants, so was He willing to be baptized with the baptism of a servant. For as He set Himself to minister to the feet of those whose guide He was Himself, so He submitted Himself to the gift of John which He Himself had given, that all might understand what sacrilegious arrogance they would show in despising the baptism which they ought each of them to receive from the Lord, when the Lord Himself accepted what He Himself had bestowed upon a servant, that he might give it as his own; and that when John, than whom no greater had arisen among them that are born of women, bore such testimony to Christ, as to confess that he was not worthy to unloose the latchet of His shoe, Christ might both, by receiving his baptism, be found to be the humblest among men, and, by taking away the place for the baptism of John, believed to be the most high God, at once the teacher of humility and the giver of exaltation.[16]

---

15. Ibid., 108–09. In his *Summa Theologica* (Part III, Q. 66, Art. 3), Aquinas says, "As stated above (Q. 62, A.1), sacraments derive from their institution the power of conferring grace. Wherefore it seems that a sacrament is then instituted, when it receives the power of producing its effect. Now Baptism received this power when Christ was baptized. Consequently Baptism was truly instituted then, if we consider it as a sacrament" (*Summa Theologica*, 2375). This statement clearly identifies Christian baptism and the baptism of Christ, though from a perspective somewhat different from Calvin's.

16. Augustine, "On Baptism, Against the Donatists" (V.9.10), 467. Augustine repeats this view in a number of places. However, he clearly differs from Calvin in his view of the re-baptism of John's disciples in Acts 19.

All the same, this does indicate that there is a relationship between Christ's baptism and ours, even if this view is not as theologically profound as the one expressed by Calvin.

But Calvin did not rely exclusively on Augustine. As Hughes Oliphant Old suggests, there were more remote sources for Calvin's view: "Christ's baptism in the Jordan as a consecration of all baptismal water is not an idea so clearly attested in Scripture, but it was certainly popular enough in the ancient Church."[17]

Chrysostom, for example, has a view of baptism much richer than what I have been able to discover in Augustine, clearly presupposing a theology of the baptism of Christ very similar to what I am arguing for:

> Wherefore were the heavens opened? To inform thee that at thy baptism also this is done, God calling thee to thy country on high, and persuading thee to have nothing to do with earth. And if thou see not, yet never doubt it. For so evermore at the beginnings of all wonderful and spiritual transactions, sensible visions appear, and such-like signs, for the sake of them that are somewhat dull in disposition, and who have need of outward sight, and who cannot at all conceive an incorporeal nature, but are excited only by the things that are seen: that so, though afterward no such thing occur, what hath been declared by them once for all at the first may be received by thy faith.
>
> For in the case of the apostles too, there was a *"sound of a mighty wind,"* and visions of fiery tongues appeared, but not for the apostles' sake, but because of the Jews who were then present. Nevertheless, even though no sensible signs take place, we receive the things that have been once manifested by them. Since the dove itself at that time therefore appeared, that as in place of a finger (so to say) it might point out to them that were present, and to John, the Son of God. Not however merely on this account, but to teach thee also, that upon thee no less at thy baptism the Spirit

---

17. Old, *Shaping of the Baptismal Rite*, 39. Old's remarks on Bucer show his view to be similar to Calvin's: "Bucer complains that many people attach too little attention to the inner baptism performed by Christ who baptizes us with the Holy Spirit. What is important about baptism is, according to Bucer, the inner cleansing from sin, the new birth, and the renewal of spirit. Much of what Bucer says grows out of his interpretation of the saying of John the Baptist, '"I baptize you with water for repentance, but he who comes after me . . . will baptize you with the Holy Spirit and with fire' (Matt. 3:11). For Bucer as for many Reformed theologians who will follow him, the water baptism of both John and the apostles was a sign of that baptism performed by the ascended Christ, who pours out his Holy Spirit upon the elect (Acts 1:5)" (*Shaping of the Baptismal Rite*, 54–55).

comes. But since then we have no need of sensible vision, faith sufficing instead of all. For signs are "not for them that believe, but for them that believe not."[18]

Athanasius likewise holds a view of baptism similar to Calvin's:

> Therefore "Jesus Christ is the same yesterday, to-day, and for ever," remaining unalterable, and at once gives and receives, giving as God's Word, receiving as man. It is not the Word then, viewed as the Word, that is promoted; for He had all things and has them always; but men, who have in Him and through Him their origin of receiving them. For, when He is now said to be anointed in a human respect, we it is who in Him are anointed; since also when He is baptized, we it is who in Him are baptized. But on all these things the Savior throws much light, when He says to the Father, "And the glory which Thou gavest Me, I have given to them, that they may be one, even as We are one." Because of us then He asked for glory, and the words occur, "took" and "gave" and "highly exalted," that we might take, and to us might be given, and we might be exalted in Him; as also for us He sanctifies Himself, that we might be sanctified in Him.[19]

Again, Gregory of Nyssa expounds baptism in language that suggests a view quite similar to Calvin's:

> But Christ, the repairer of his evil-doing, assumes manhood in its fullness, and saves man, and becomes the type and figure of us all, to sanctify the first-fruits of every action, and leave to His servants no doubt in their zeal for the tradition. Baptism, then, is a purification from sins, a remission of trespasses, a cause of renovation and regeneration.[20]

> Most manifestly also does Zechariah prophesy of Joshua, who was clothed with the filthy garment (to wit, the flesh of a servant, even ours), and stripping him of his ill-favored raiment adorns him with the clean and fair apparel; teaching us by the figurative illustration that verily in the Baptism of Jesus all we, putting off our sins like some poor and patched garment, are clothed in the holy and most fair garment of regeneration.[21]

---

18. Chrysostom, *Homilies on the Gospel of Saint Matthew*, 179–80.
19. Athanasius, "Four Discourses Against the Arians" (I.12.48), 334–35.
20. Gregory of Nyssa, "On the Baptism of Christ," 519.
21. Ibid., 522–23.

Tertullian, writing in the early third century, links Christian baptism not only with the baptism of Christ, but also with the ordination of Aaron to the priesthood. In Tertullian, it seems that Christ's baptism and Christian baptism are both seen as complex events with multiple elements. The Spirit hovering over the waters of creation and the Spirit coming on Christ as a dove are both part of the theology of Christian baptism. But in addition to water, Christian baptism includes an anointing with oil and the laying on of hands in order to receive the Spirit.

He explains the unction as follows in his treatise on baptism:

> After this, when we have issued from the font, we are thoroughly anointed with a blessed unction,—(a practice derived) from the old discipline, wherein on entering the priesthood, *men* were wont to be anointed with oil from a horn, ever since Aaron was anointed by Moses. Whence Aaron is called "Christ," from the "chrism," which is "the unction;" which, when made spiritual, furnished an appropriate name to the Lord, because He was "anointed" with the Spirit by God the Father; as *written* in the Acts: "For truly they were gathered together in this city against Thy Holy Son whom Thou hast anointed." Thus, too, in *our* case, the unction runs carnally, (*i.e.* on the body,) but profits spiritually; in the same way as the *act* of baptism itself too is carnal, in that we are plunged in water, *but* the *effect* spiritual, in that we are freed from sins.[22]

Similarly, he relates the laying on of hands to the baptism of Jesus, as well as the flood and the creation:

> Then, over our cleansed and blessed bodies willingly descends from the Father that Holiest Spirit. Over the waters of baptism, recognizing as it were His primeval seat, He reposes: (He who) glided down on the Lord "in the shape of a dove," in order that the nature of the Holy Spirit might be declared by means of the creature (the emblem) of simplicity and innocence, because even in her bodily structure the dove is without literal gall. And accordingly He says, "Be ye simple as doves." Even this is not without the supporting evidence of a preceding figure. For just as, after the waters of the deluge, by which the old iniquity was purged—after the baptism, so to say, of the world—a *dove* was the herald which announced to the earth the assuagement of celestial wrath, when she had been sent her way out of the ark, and had returned with the olive-branch, a sign which even among the na-

---

22. Tertullian, "On Baptism" (ch. 7), 672.

tions is the fore-token of *peace; so* by the selfsame law of heavenly effect, to earth—that is, to our flesh—as it emerges from the font, after its old sins, flies the *dove* of the Holy Spirit, bringing us the peace of God, sent out from the heavens where is the Church, the typified ark.[23]

Although this survey is very incomplete, enough evidence has been cited to demonstrate that it was common in the ancient Church to regard the baptism of Christ as an example for Christians and even as a picture of what happens in Christian baptism. There are differences of detail among the Church Fathers, as well as Calvin and Aquinas, which introduce complexities that I cannot deal with in this essay. The important point for this chapter is that viewing the baptism of Jesus as in some sense connected to Christian baptism is common from ancient times to Calvin and the reformers. Though variously understood, the fact of a link between Jesus' baptism and ours is presupposed so widely that it may be called the common view: "The primitive Christian tradition thus viewed Jesus' baptism already as the model of Christian baptism, especially as regards the link between baptism and the reception of the Spirit."[24] Geoffrey W. Bromiley expresses the traditional Reformed view when he writes, "The clue to the meaning of baptism is to be found in the baptism of Jesus Himself at the hands of John."[25]

THE BIBLICAL-THEOLOGICAL ARGUMENT

What we need to demonstrate in this chapter, at least by way of outline, is that Christian baptism, like the baptism of Jesus, is inauguration into the Melechizedekian priesthood. We are priests in Christ and are constituted as such in baptism. In arguing for baptism as inauguration into priesthood, I briefly repeat the in-depth study of the biblical theology of water baptism done by Peter Leithart. After this has been reviewed, I offer a

---

23. Ibid., 672–73.
24. Pannenberg, *Systematic Theology*, 279.
25. Bromiley, *Sacramental Teaching and Practice*, 21. Note that Bromiley struggles to explain the problems that have arisen concerning baptism. Although his discussion contains insights, he analyzes the errors of Roman Catholicism and the Anabaptists as the results of subjectivism, thereby missing the most basic issue—the Semi-Marcionite tendency in Catholic, Reformed, and Anabaptist theology. Leithart's analysis of the problems that have arisen in the theology of baptism is not only more penetrating, but it also points the way to a biblical solution (cf. Leithart, *Priesthood*, 1–47).

biblical argument for the connection between Christian baptism and Jesus' baptism, extending Leithart's discussion of this particular point.[26]

Reviewing Leithart's Argument

Leithart's argument can be summarized in the following points:

1. Rather than viewing new covenant ceremonies as fundamentally different from those of the old covenant, Leithart, borrowing from Augustine, describes new covenant rites as "conjugations" of the rites of ancient Israel.[27]

2. Priestly ordination in the law of Moses constituted the recipient as an "attendant to Yahweh in His house." Viewing priests as servants of Yahweh who took care of all the duties of the house offers us a broader understanding of the nature of the priesthood than does the view that emphasizes sacrifice and prayer. As a servant in Yahweh's house, the priest has duties both to God and to His people, duties in God's physical house, the temple, and His covenant house, the people of God. The ritual of ordination sets the priest apart for his various duties.

3. Christians are regarded as a priests in the new covenant, and baptism is seen as the rite that constitutes them as such. Leithart argues at length that baptism does for a member of the new covenant what the ordination rite did for a priest in the old covenant. Hence, baptism is the rite that constitutes new covenant members as priests.

4. By way of summary, Leithart says, "From Hebrews 10:19–22 and 1 Corinthians 6:11, I argued that since B [baptism] now does what O [ordination] did in Israel, B [baptism] fulfills and

---

26. Leithart has already demonstrated this connection, since he shows that Jesus was baptized as a priest and that our baptism ordains us as priests. I am clarifying and adding details to one aspect of his argument.

27. Leithart uses Augustine's grammatical analogy to describe differences between the rites of the old covenant and the new. He writes, "I draw on various texts from Augustine that characterize the transition from Old to New as a 'tense shift' in a 'root word,' the Logos, and this leads to the conclusion that New Testament sacraments are 'conjugations' of the sacraments of the Old" (*Priesthood*, xxi; for a fuller explanation, cf. 32–47). A shift in tense is not a change in the root word. For the ceremonies of the new to be conjugations of the old means that there is an underlying unity, despite the change in form.

replaces O [ordination]. The other texts support the weaker thesis that B [baptism] is described in terms reminiscent of O [ordination]. Overall, the combination of evidence is sufficient to establish that the New Testament practice and theology of baptism were founded, *inter alia*, on priestly ordination."[28]

The first point in this summary—new covenant ceremonies are fundamentally similar to old covenant ceremonies—fits with what we saw in chapter four about the rituality of God. Ritual is not an ornamental extra, a sort of window dressing for the covenant. Rather, as the baptism of Jesus reveals, ritual is essential to Trinitarian ontology. That being the case, we should expect old covenant and new covenant ritual to be related, for both systems are established by the same covenant Lord for the same covenantal purposes. Ritual in the old covenant either introduces one into the covenant or renews the covenant relationship. Circumcision of the eight-day-old son was the normal way for joining the covenant from Abraham onward. All the other ceremonies of the Mosaic law were designed as covenant memorials, reminding Yahweh of the covenant and renewing the covenant with Him. In the new covenant, baptism is the covenant initiation ceremony and the Lord's Supper is the covenant renewal ceremony.

The connection between baptism and circumcision, therefore, is relatively straight-forward, in spite of complexities.[29] However, the connection with priestly ordination is not so obvious. To begin with, priestly ordination seems like an exception to the basic rule I set forth in the previous paragraph. It appears to be neither "covenant initiation" nor "covenant renewal." Rather, it is a ceremony that confers a special status on the recipient, one that goes beyond the status conferred in circumcision. By circumcision, every child of Israel was made a member of the priestly nation. But priestly ordination set apart some of the children of Israel for special privilege and responsibilities. They were priests in

28. Leithart, *Priesthood*, 131–32. The summaries in the first three points above are based on Leithart's own summary of his argument (249–51).

29. In the old covenant, circumcision was initiation into the priestly people; it was not necessarily tied to salvation. Uncircumcised Gentiles who believed in the true God were saved without circumcision. However, in the new covenant, the rite of initiation into the priestly people also identifies those who are saved. The norm is that only those who are baptized into Christ can be saved. Exceptions similar to the thief on the cross are possible, but these exceptions have more to do with practice than with theology and they do not define or determine our theology.

narrow sense. In fact, the Mosaic system was even more complex, for the priestly nation had a hierarchical system of priestly privilege: high priest, priests, Levites, and Israelites. Gentiles were outside and did not have the privilege or responsibility of the members of the priestly nation, but they were included in Israel's prayers and could participate to a degree in the ceremonies, for the Temple was to be a house of prayer for all nations.[30]

In the context of the complex hierarchy of the Mosaic system, then, ordination functioned like "super-circumcision." It was initiation into a narrower priestly covenant, conferring even higher status than circumcision did. But insofar as it was a ceremony that conferred status, it was essentially similar to circumcision. Circumcision gave the Israelite access to God's house, the privilege of sharing a meal with Yahweh, and the responsibilities of prayer and witness to the nations. Priestly ordination brought essentially the same sort of blessings and responsibilities, but at a higher level. Since circumcision and priestly ordination were the two ceremonies that conferred priestly status in the old covenant and since there is no hierarchy in the new covenant priesthood, apart from the distinction between the high priest—Jesus—and the priesthood, it seems obvious that the ceremony that fulfills circumcision also fulfills priestly ordination. It is not surprising, therefore, that from ancient times, Christians have understood baptism as the fulfillment of priestly ordination.

However, the Bible itself does not give us the kind of statements that *explicitly* connect what seem to be links in a theological chain. As Leithart points out, there is no direct statement in the New Testament that baptism fulfills Aaronic ordination. Neither is there an explicit affirmation that baptism confers priestly status. What, then, is the biblical justification for the ancient Christian belief, apart from the kind of theological reasoning suggested above?

Leithart shows that though the New Testament does not specifically state that baptism fulfills the typology of Aaronic ordination or that it confers priestly status, it does quite clearly link baptism and priesthood

---

30. Deuteronomy 16:9ff. includes the alien in the Feast of Weeks and the Feast of Booths. Leviticus 17:8 and Numbers 15:14–16 speak of aliens offering sacrifices. Leviticus 19:10, 23:22, Deuteronomy 14:28–29; 24:19–21; and 26:11ff. include aliens among those who are permitted to glean and receive charity. The basic principle is given in Leviticus 19:34: "The stranger who resides with you shall be to you as the native among you, and you shall love him as yourself, for you were aliens in the land of Egypt; I am the LORD your God" (NASB). Cf. also Deuteronomy 10:19.

in another way. The New Testament shows that baptism *confers the tasks and privileges of a priest*. If one has priestly tasks and privileges, then one is a priest and the ceremony that confers those tasks and privileges is a priestly ordination ceremony. According to Leithart, Hebrews 10:19–22 "states precisely" that baptism confers priestly responsibility and privilege. He argues that 1 Corinthians 6:11 points in the same direction.

We have already seen in chapter two of this book that Jesus' baptism was His ordination into the Messianic office. The washing of water by the old covenant priest and prophet, John the Baptizer, together with the gift of the Spirit and the declaration of Messianic office from the heavenly Father was Jesus' ceremonial initiation into the priesthood at the age of thirty. For Aaron's ordination, he had to be washed by Moses and anointed with oil, as well as being invested with the robes of office and anointed with blood. For Jesus' ordination, He was washed by John the Baptizer, anointed with the Spirit of the new covenant, and publicly declared Messiah by the Father.

Like the baptism of other Jews of His day, Jesus' baptism was conducted in the context of the Mosaic system. By receiving it, He was associating Himself with the remnant who were faithful to God. But His baptism was fundamentally different from theirs, as we have seen. Their baptism was a restoration to priestly privilege for a nation that had strayed from God and needed a ceremonial expression of repentance. By baptism, they were reintroduced to the privilege of a covenant member, like the leper who must be washed before he can be restored to normal covenant status (Lev 14). Jesus' baptism was for the fulfillment of righteousness, an essentially distinct meaning. He was ordained to a different order of priestly privilege and responsibility, that of Melchizedek.

Extending Leithart's Argument

Leithart is concerned to prove that Christian baptism confers priestly status on the recipient. Proving a link between Jesus' baptism and Christian baptism is not part of his argument. Rather, he assumes the link between the two, noting that, "It is a commonplace of post-World War II discussions that the New Testament understanding of baptism grows out of the baptism of Jesus."[31] Of course, there are good reasons for this understanding to be commonplace; it may be profitable to set

---

31. Leithart, *Priesthood*, 111.

them forth. Here I offer an argument for the connection between Jesus' baptism and Christian baptism that is similar in form to Leithart's argument for baptism as the new covenant form of priestly ordination.

I have already shown that Jesus' baptism was distinct from the baptism of the Jews in His day, though not unrelated. In chapter two, I explained that Jesus was baptized as Messiah. His baptism was an inauguration into the Messianic office, fulfilling all righteousness in the sense of beginning to fulfill prophecies about the Messiah as a priest and king, as well as fulfilling the typology of the Aaronic priesthood. Assuming that is true, there is still no direct statement of a relationship between Jesus' baptism and ours, so the connection may be doubted.

How could such a relationship be demonstrated? The answer, I believe, is in an approach similar to Leithart's argument about the nature of baptism. If I can show that what baptism meant for Jesus is analogous to what baptism means for the Christian, then the link between the two would be established. To say the same thing in different words: the baptism of Jesus has such a prominent place in the New Testament—being recorded in all three Synoptics and referred to in John—that it is natural to assume it should have a large place in baptismal theology. And we have seen, it has been common in Church history to assume that Jesus' baptism is the paradigm for Christian baptism. What I intend to show now is that Jesus' baptism and Christian baptism bring about or result in very similar things happening. In this way, I believe the link between them can be established.

I argue for the relationship between Jesus' baptism and ours in six points.[32] Not all of these points have to be demonstrated as true to estab-

32. There is much similarity and overlap between my arguments and those of Allen Mawhinney in his excellent article "Baptism, Servanthood, and Sonship," 35–64. His main purpose is to establish that baptism is the sign and seal of sonship. He sums up his argument in the following words:

"The Reformed confessions give united witness to the conviction that one aspect of the significance of baptism is the signifying and sealing to the Christian of his sonship to God. This is the explicit affirmation of Paul in Gal 3:26–27: 'You are all sons of God through faith in Christ Jesus, for all of you who were baptized into Christ have clothed yourselves with Christ.' The Christian is a son of God, clothed with Christ through faith, being baptized into Christ.

This conclusion is buttressed by the recognition of the connection between Christ's Sonship and his baptism. The divine interpretation of the descent of the Holy Spirit is, 'You are my Son.' The Spirit is the endowment of the Son of God for his ministry as the Suffering Servant, assuring him of the good pleasure of the Father in his life of obedience and sacrifice.

lish the connection, though I believe they can all be shown to be valid. Even if only one or two could be demonstrated, we would be right to conclude that Jesus' baptism is the paradigm for Christian baptism, the defining baptism, because it is most natural to assume the connection.

Before I discuss each point, let me begin by stating them. First, Jesus' baptism initiated Him as a priest and Christian baptism initiates Christians as priests. Second, Jesus' baptism confers the privileges and responsibilities of a specifically Melchizedekian priesthood and Christian baptism also confers the privileges and responsibilities of a specifically Melchizedekian priesthood. Third, Jesus' baptism united Him with His people and Christian baptism unites Christians with Christ. Fourth, Jesus' baptism is baptism unto death and resurrection and Christian baptism is also baptism unto death and resurrection. Fifth, Jesus' baptism declares His priestly or royal status as a Son and Christian baptism confers priestly or royal status as sons. Sixth, Jesus' baptism brings the gift of the Spirit to Him and Christian baptism brings the Spirit to Christians.

A. Priestly Ordination

The first point has been argued in part in chapter two of this book, which shows that Jesus was baptized in a priestly ordination ceremony. The substance of the argument has been demonstrated in detail by Leithart's book on the theology of baptism, which shows that Christian baptism is priestly ordination. Thus, Jesus' baptism does for Him—priestly ordina-

---

That a similar relationship exists between the Christian's sonship and baptism is confirmed by three lines of evidence. First, the sonship of the Christian is always regarded as a derivative sonship. By nature, man is a child of wrath. It is by union with the Son of God that man becomes a son of God. The Christian's baptism is the sign and seal of that union with Christ. That union with Christ of which baptism is a sign and seal includes (but is not limited to) the Christian's sonship.

Second, the baptismal washing is described as a 'washing of regeneration' in Tit 3:5. Baptism is a sign of entrance into the family of God by being born again.

Third, the NT authors parallel Christ's baptism with the Christian's baptism and sonship. In Luke/Acts Luke presents Jesus' endowment with the Spirit for mission and assurance of sonship as parallel to the Pentecostal endowment of the Church for the continuation of the Messianic mission. Similarly the baptism of Christians in Acts is associated with the coming of the Spirit, the eschatological gift of the Father which makes men sons of God. Paul, in Ephesians, models his description of the adoptive sonship of Christians on the language which was used to describe Christ's baptism.

Baptism is, in part, a sign and seal of sonship. This is the teaching of the Reformed confessions. It is the teaching of the NT" (59–60).

tion—what Christian baptism does for Christians and should therefore be understood as the paradigm of Christian baptism.

B. The Melchizedekian Priesthood

The second point is actually included in the first, since the kind of priesthood into which Jesus was inaugurated was the Melchizedekian priesthood, but this point is worthy of separate emphasis, since Christian priesthood is not so clearly linked to Melchizedek. What Leithart proved was that Christian baptism is initiation into priesthood. The question now is, Can we show that to be a Melchizedekian priesthood? Even if the attempt to answer this were to fail, Jesus' baptism may still be the paradigm for Christian baptism. But if we can provide an adequate answer, we have further grounds for seeing Jesus' baptism as the foundation for understanding Christian baptism.

The first argument for this is theological and can be simply stated. There is no question about Christ's priesthood being Melchizedekian, and if His baptism was initiation into priesthood, then it was into the priesthood of Melchizedek that He was ordained. It follows, too, that if Christians are priests "in Christ" and His priesthood is of the order of Melchizedek, then theirs must be also, for the priesthood of the Christian cannot be independent of Christ Himself. Since there is no hint in the New Testament of another sort of priesthood for Christians, the Christian priesthood, like that of Christ, should be understood to be a Melchizedekian priesthood.

Besides the general theological argument, there is one passage in the New Testament that seems to call Christians both kings and priests, but it is not entirely clear and the Old Testament passage being quoted, Exodus 19:6, is not pointing to a Melchizedekian priesthood. All the same, 1 Peter 2:5 is significant for our study, since the notion of a royal priesthood fits exactly with the New Testament Melchizedekian typology. If the Christian priesthood joins king and priest, like the priesthood of Melchizedek, we are priests in the Melchizedekian order.

To begin with, the comment on the relevant words of Exodus 19:6 in Keil and Delitzsch is worthy of attention:

> The idea of the *segullah* is explained in ver. 6: "*Ye shall be unto Me a kingdom of priests.*" מַמְלָכָה signifies both *kingship,* as the embodiment of royal supremacy, exaltation, and dignity, and the

kingdom, or the union of both king and subjects, i.e., the land and nation, together with its king. In the passage before us, the word has been understood by most of the early commentators, both Jewish and Christian, and also in the ancient versions, in the first or active sense, so that the expression contains the idea, "Ye shall be all priests and kings" (*Luther*); *praeditos fore tam sacerdotali quam regio honore* (*Calvin*); *quod reges et sacerdotes sunt in republica, id vos eritis mihi* (*Drusius*). This explanation is required by both the passage itself and the context. For apart from the fact that kingship is the primary and most general meaning of the word מַמְלָכָה (cf. מַמְלֶכֶת דָּוִד, the kingship, or government of David), the other (passive) meaning would not be at all suitable here; for a kingdom of priests could never denote the fellowship existing in a kingdom between the king and the priests, but only a kingdom or commonwealth consisting of priests, i.e., a kingdom the members and citizens of which were priests, and as priests constituted the מַמְלָכָה, in other words, were possessed of royal dignity and power; for מַמְלָכָה, βασιλεία always includes the idea of מָלַךְ or ruling (βασιλεύειν). The LXX. have quite hit the meaning in their rendering: βασίλειον ἱεράτευμα. Israel was to be a regal body of priests to Jehovah, and not merely a nation of priests governed by Jehovah. The idea of the theocracy, or government of God, as founded by the establishment of the Sinaitic covenant institution in Israel, is not at all involved in the term "kingdom of priests." The theocracy established by the conclusion of the covenant (chap. xxiv.) was only the means adopted by Jehovah for making His chosen people a royal body of priests; and the maintenance of this covenant was the indispensable subjective condition, upon which their attainment of this divinely appointed destiny and glory depended. This promise of Jehovah expressed the design of the call of Israel, to which it was to be fully conducted by the covenant institution of the theocracy, if it maintained the covenant with Jehovah. The object of Israel's kingship and priesthood was to be found in the nations of the earth, out of which Jehovah had chosen Israel as a costly possession. This great and glorious promise, the fulfillment of which could not be attained till the completion of the kingdom of God, when the Israel of God, the Church of the Lord, which Jesus Christ, the first-begotten from the dead, and prince (ἄρχων, ruler) of the kings of the earth, has made a "kingdom," "priests unto God and His Father" (Rev. i. 6 and v. 10, where the reading should be βασιλεῖς καὶ ἱερεῖς), is exalted to glory with Christ as the first-born among many brethren, and sits upon His throne and reigns, has not been introduced abruptly here. On the contrary, the way was already prepared by the promises made to the patriarchs, of the blessing which Abraham would become to all the nations of the earth, and of the kings who were to spring from him and come out of the loins of Israel (Gen. xii. 3, xvii. 6, xxxv. 11), and still more distinctly by Jacob's prophecy of the sceptre of Judah, to whom, through *Shiloh,* the willing submission of the nations should be made (Gen. xlix. 10). But these promises and prophecies are outshone by the clearness, with which kingship and priesthood over and for the nations are foretold of Israel here.³³

This kingship, however, is not merely of a spiritual kind, consisting, as *Luther* supposes, in the fact, that believers "are lords over death, the devil, hell, and all evil," but culminates in the universal sway foretold by Balaam in Num. xxiv. 8 and 17sqq., by Moses in his last words (Deut. xxxiii. 29), and still more distinctly in Dan. vii. 27, to the people of the saints of the Most High, as the ultimate end of their calling from God. The spiritual attitude of Israel towards the nations was the result of its priestly character. As the priest is a mediator between God and man, so Israel was called to be the vehicle of the knowledge and salvation of God to the nations of the earth. By this it unquestionably acquired an intellectual and spiritual character; but this includes, rather than excludes, the government of the world. For spiritual and intellectual supremacy and rule must eventually ensure the government of the world, as certainly as spirit is the power that overcomes the world. And if the priesthood of Israel was the power which laid the foundation for its kingship,—in other words, if Israel obtained the מַמְלָכָה or government over the nations solely as a priestly nation,—the Apostle Peter, when taking up this promise (I.ii. 9), might without hesitation follow the Septuagint rendering (βασίλειον ἱεράτευμα), and substitute in the place of the "priestly kingdom," a "royal priesthood;" for there is no essential difference between the two, the kingship being founded upon the priesthood, and the priesthood completed by the kingship.³⁴

As Keil and Delitzsch point out, Daniel sees the people of the Most High God as receiving the dominion of all the kingdoms of the earth,

---

33. If Keil and Delitzsch are correct—and I think they are—it implies that the general priesthood of Israel as a nation was similar to the priesthood of Melchizedek. For Christian priesthood to be modeled after the priesthood of ancient Israel, means therefore that it is modeled after the Melchizedekian priesthood. The office of priest and king were clearly separated within Israel, but the nation as a whole had a priestly, kingly, and prophetic status with reference to the Gentile nations.

34. Keil and Delitzsch, *Pentateuch*, 2: 96–99.

their rule being under and with the rule of the Messiah (Dan 7:13–14, 27). The book of Revelation records a similar vision:

> And they sing a new song, saying, Worthy art thou to take the book, and to open the seals thereof: for thou was slain, and didst purchase unto God with thy blood men of every tribe, and tongue, and people, and nation, and madest them to be unto our God a kingdom and priests; and they reign upon earth. (Rev 5:9–10)

Here it is said both that the people of God will be a kingdom (βασιλείαν) and that they will reign (βασιλεύσουσιν). It is important to note that the word for reign implies "reign as king" and that the redeemed are said to be priests.

Since we know that baptism is ordination to priesthood and we know that the new covenant people of God are both kings and priests, or a royal priesthood, then it seems most natural to view them as priest-kings like Jesus, the Great High Priest, after the order of Melchizedek. Baptism is not merely ordination into priesthood; it is ordination into a royal priesthood like that of Christ. This means that Jesus' baptism by John is the paradigm baptism that reveals the profound meaning of Christian baptism.

C. Union with Christ

The third point concerns union. There is very little doubt that baptism unites the recipient with the body of Christ. By baptism one is marked out as a Christian. It is the defining rite of the Christian faith. So, we find in Paul that we were "baptized into Christ Jesus" (Rom 6:3), that we were "baptized into Christ" (Gal 3:27), and that "by one Spirit we were baptized into one body" (1 Cor 12:13). Our baptism, thus, brings us into union with Christ and His body, the Church.

With regard to Jesus' baptism, we saw that Luke emphasized that Jesus was baptized with the people: "Now it came to pass, when all the people were baptized, that, Jesus also having been baptized . . ." (Luke 3:21). Matthew clearly distinguishes the baptism of Jesus from the baptism of the people, but he also associates them in the sense that Matthew first introduces the ministry of John the Baptizer and defines his baptism and then tells us that Jesus came to John *in order to be* baptized (Matt 3:13). Jesus sought John out because He wanted to received the baptism that John was offering. Although there is no explicit statement that by baptism Jesus was uniting Himself with the people, that meaning must be inferred, since it was essential to John's baptizing that he was defining a remnant. Like Elijah, John stood against the rulers of his day and became a center for re-organizing the people of God. Those who rejected John's baptism rejected God's will (Luke 7:29–30). By receiving it, Jesus identified Himself with John's movement and the remnant people it defined, the people who became the core believers in Jesus and His leading disciples. The baptism of Jesus by John the Baptizer, therefore, united Jesus with the people of God, just as Christian baptism unites Christians to Him and to His Church. This also suggests that Jesus' baptism is the New Testament picture of baptism, the defining baptism for all subsequent baptisms.

D. Death and Resurrection

The fourth point concerns the relationship between baptism and death. Jesus' own baptism is linked to His death, as I argued in chapter 2, both by the words of the Father that associated Jesus with Isaac, the beloved son to be sacrificed, and by the descent of the dove, a sacrificial animal that pointed to the Spirit's anointing Jesus for the cross. Also, the words pronounced by the Father, alluding to Isaiah 42:1, mean that in His baptism Jesus was marked out as the Suffering Servant of Isaiah. This places a heavy emphasis on the cross, but the resurrection is implied as well.

In addition, Jesus Himself twice referred to the cross as a baptism:

> But I have a baptism to be baptized with; and how am I straitened till it be accomplished! (Luke 12:50)

> But Jesus said unto them, Ye know not what ye ask. Are ye able to drink the cup that I drink? or to be baptized with the baptism that I am baptized with? And they said unto him, We are able. And Jesus said unto them, The cup that I drink ye shall drink; and with the baptism that I am baptized withal shall ye be baptized. (Mark 10:38–39)

Finally, in the Gospel of Mark, Jesus' baptism and cross are linked through the literary device of *inclusio*, indicated by the parallel phrases and expressions in the narratives of the baptism at the beginning of the Gospel and of the cross near the end. A. B. Caneday expounds the connections and sets them forth in a table, demonstrating clearly that Jesus was baptized unto the death of the cross. In various ways, then, the Gospels emphasize that Jesus was baptized with a view to His crucifixion.

TABLE 1: Catchwords and Synonym Phrases that Form the Inclusio[35]

Mark 1:1–13		Mark 15:33–41	
1:1	Son of God	15:39	Son of God
1:2	a voice cries out	15:34	Jesus cried out with a loud voice
1:10	heavens torn open	15:38	temple curtain torn open in two
1:10	Spirit descending into him	15:37, 39	he yielded his spirit
1:10	descending	15:38	from top to bottom
1:11	a voice came from heaven	15:37	Jesus released a loud voice
1:11	a voice came from heaven	15:33	darkness came upon the earth
1:13	he was with the wild animals	15:39	[the centurion] who stood by in hostility to him
1:13	angels were ministering to him	15:40	[women] were ministering to him

Christian baptism is unquestionably linked with Jesus' cross and resurrection by the apostle Paul in Romans 6, one of the most famous New Testament passages about baptism. Baptism into Christ means baptism into His death (Rom 6:3). Paul goes on to say that in baptism Christians are united with Christ in death and in resurrection (6:4ff.). The analogy to the baptism of Christ is clear. Both Jesus and His people are baptized unto the death of the cross. For Jesus, baptism marked Him out as the one who must sacrifice Himself on the cross as a priest of the order of Melchizedek. For Christians, baptism defines them as united to the cross and resurrection of Christ, people who have died to sin and been made alive to righteousness in Christ. Again the correspondence of the two argues that Jesus' baptism is the paradigm for Christian baptism.

---

35. This table is copied from Caneday, "Christ's Baptism and Crucifixion," 72.

E. Sonship

The fifth point concerns baptism and sonship. When Jesus was baptized, God the Father declared from heaven, "Thou art My Son!" quoting the words of Psalm 2:7. The context is especially important for understanding the Messianic import of Jesus' baptism, as I argued in chapter 2. The Son in Psalm 2 is promised the nations for His inheritance. By quoting Psalm 2 at Jesus' baptism, the Father defined the baptism as a Messianic anointing, officially installing Jesus into the Messianic office—or at least *ordaining* Him for the Messianic task, since Jesus does not actually sit on the throne until after His resurrection. At any rate, the Father's declaration at Jesus' baptism associates sonship with *inheritance* (LXX κληρονομία) of the world, pointing to Jesus' rule as Melchizedekian priest-king.[36]

Paul makes the same sort of association when referring to Christian baptism in Galatians 3:26–29:

> For ye are all sons of God, through faith, in Christ Jesus. For as many of you as were baptized into Christ did put on Christ. There can be neither Jew nor Greek, there can be neither bond nor free, there can be no male and female; for ye all are one man in Christ Jesus. And if ye are Christ's, then are ye Abraham's seed, heirs according to promise.

Baptism here makes Christians sons of God in Christ. It is a ceremony of adoption that redefines who and what they are. And when Paul speaks of sonship here, he means that Christians have rights of inheritance as Abraham's descendants, a theme he also addresses in Romans first when he refers to "the promise to Abraham or to his descendants that he would be heir of the world" (Rom 4:13) and again when he speaks of Christians as heirs with Christ:

> For as many as are led by the Spirit of God, these are sons of God. For ye received not the spirit of bondage again unto fear; but ye received the spirit of adoption, whereby we cry, Abba, Father. The Spirit himself beareth witness with our spirit, that we are children of God: and if children, then heirs; heirs of God, and joint-heirs with Christ; if so be that we suffer with him, that we may be also glorified with him. (Rom 8:14–17)

---

36. Leithart argues for an association between sonship and priesthood, but the Messiah is a Melchizedekian priest, so both priesthood and royal authority are actually involved. Psalm 2 in particular emphasizes the royal aspect of the Messianic office.

For the Christian, then, baptism is an adoption ceremony, constituting him as a son and heir with Abraham, but more importantly as a fellow heir with Christ and heir of God, an inheritance infinitely greater than all the world. The association of baptism with sonship and inheritance here, therefore, is similar to the association in the baptism of Jesus, though Jesus' baptism is not adoption as a Son but the public declaration of His Messianic dignity as Son and the official beginning of His Messianic work.[37] The similarities demonstrate that Christian baptism is patterned after the baptism of Jesus.

The Spirit and Baptism

The final point deserves extended attention. It is perhaps the most important of the six points for our understanding of baptism and certainly the most controversial, for many Christians prefer to separate water and Spirit baptism entirely. As we saw in chapter 1, James D. G. Dunn, of course, is one of them.

The reasons for separating the two are usually more theological than exegetical. The reasoning is that if Spirit baptism and water baptism are concurrent and in some sense mutually related, then the highest blessing of salvation is being conveyed by a humanly administered rite, placing the Holy Spirit in the hands of men and binding God to a ceremony. But viewing water and Spirit baptism as an integrated whole need not imply that Spirit baptism is being subordinated to the whim of sinful man. We will return to the theological issue later.

What we have seen from Scripture is that when Jesus was baptized by John the Baptizer in water, the Father poured out His Spirit upon Jesus in the form of a dove, so that Jesus was the first man to be baptized by both water and the Spirit. Jesus Himself, early in His ministry, speaks of being anointed with the Spirit (Luke 4:18) and, in his sermon to the Gentiles, the apostle Peter refers to Jesus being anointed with the Spirit and power (Acts 10:38). Dunn avoids the obvious connection between water and Spirit baptism in the case of Jesus by claiming that the baptism

---

37. As Mawhinney demonstrates, the themes of union with Christ, regeneration, forgiveness, and sonship are all vitally related to each other and equally grounded in the parallel between the baptism of Jesus and the baptism of the Christian. In support of this thesis, he argues that Ephesians 1:3–14 is an adaptation of the baptismal narratives of the Gospels ("Baptism, Servanthood, and Sonship," 52–58).

in water by John and the gift of the Spirit are two entirely distinct events. As we saw in chapter 1, he even calls these events "antithetical."

I have already argued that it is highly artificial to make into two events Jesus' baptism by John and the immediately subsequent gift of the Spirit and commission by the Father. Even worse, this unnatural division of the narrative erases the real meaning of Jesus' baptism as priestly ordination. Ordination, as we saw, involves a complex set of ritual acts. Chapter 1 provides the exegetical and theological argument against Dunn's interpretation of the baptism narratives, but there is another matter that must be addressed here. Does Christian baptism in water really include, in some way, baptism by the Holy Spirit as well? This is the question I attempt to answer now.

First, it is hard to deny the *prima facie* evidence supplied by the use of the word "baptism." In other words, the very fact that the gift of the Spirit is regularly called a "baptism" (Matt 3:11; Mark 1:8; Luke 3:16; John 1:33; Acts 1:5; 1 Cor 12:13) already implies that water baptism and Spirit baptism belong together, especially considering Paul's emphasis that there is *one and only one* Christian baptism (Eph 4:5). On the common evangelical view, one would either have to say that the one baptism is Spirit baptism and that water baptism is really not important—a common position—or, contrary to Paul, that there are actually two baptisms, fundamentally distinct from one another, if not antithetical. Neither of these positions fits with the practice and teaching of the apostles.

Besides the use of the word "baptism" for both water and Spirit baptism, other expressions also suggest that, as in the baptism of Christ, the water and the Spirit are poured out together. For example, Paul speaks of "the washing of regeneration and renewing of the Holy Spirit" (Titus 3:5), and John records Jesus' words, "Truly, truly, I say to you, unless one is born of water and the Spirit he cannot enter into the kingdom of God" (John 3:5). Thus, the language of the New Testament referring to baptism, either directly or indirectly, brings the gift of the Spirit and the baptism with water together.

A very clear association of the gift of the Spirit and water baptism appears in the first sermon of the Christian era, in which Peter seems to imply that the Spirit is given as a consequence of, if not through, water baptism. The precise nature of the relationship between water baptism and the gift of the Spirit is not altogether transparent, but the connection itself is:

> And Peter said unto them, Repent ye, and be baptized every one of you in the name of Jesus Christ unto the remission of your sins; and ye shall receive the gift of the Holy Spirit. (Acts 2:38)

If this were all that was written in Acts about the Spirit and water baptism, no one would doubt they are joined. But there are passages in the book of Acts that have been used by Pentecostal Christians to prove that the baptism of the Spirit is something separate from conversion. Arguing against the Pentecostal view, Dunn treats the difficult passages in Acts in detail in his *Baptism in the Holy Spirit*, but, as we saw in chapter 1, his approach, too, presupposes that water and Spirit baptism are basically different, though related. As Dunn rightly notes, the relationship between the baptism of the Spirit and that of water in the book of Acts challenges the interpreter of Scripture:

> There are few problems so puzzling in NT theology as that posed by Acts in its treatment of conversion initiation. The relation between the gift of the Spirit and water-baptism is particularly confusing—sometimes sharply contrasted (1:5; 11:16), sometimes quite unconnected (2:4; 8:16f.; 18:25), sometimes in natural sequence (2:38; 19:5f.), sometimes the other way about (9:17f. (?); 10:44–48). The role and significance of both John's baptism and the laying on of hands are complicating factors.[38]

Dunn's own conclusion is that the conversion-initiation experience as a whole consists of faith/repentance expressed in water baptism to which God responds by pouring out the Holy Spirit. This means that water baptism is important only as an expression of faith, even though it is a necessary expression. The forgiveness of sins is given to the one who believes and so is the gift of the Spirit.

> To become a Christian, in short, is to receive the Spirit of Christ, the Holy Spirit. . . . Man's act in conversion is to repent, to turn and to believe; God's act is to give the Spirit to man on believing (Acts 2:38; 11:17; 15:9; 19:2; cf. John 7:39; Gal. 3:2). The two together are the essential components of conversion, but in the last analysis it is God's gift which alone counts.[39]

> Water-baptism is therefore to be regarded as the occasion by which the initiate called upon the Lord for mercy, and the means

---

38. Dunn, *Baptism in the Holy Spirit*, 90.
39. Ibid., 96.

> by which he committed himself to the one whose name was named over him.[40]
>
> At the same time, while recognizing that one cannot say "faith" without also saying "water-baptism," we must recognize that of the two it is the former which is the significant element. Baptism gives expression to faith, but without faith baptism is meaningless, an empty symbol. It is false to say that water-baptism conveys, confers or effects forgiveness of sins. It may symbolize cleansing, but it is the faith and repentance which receives the forgiveness, and the Holy Spirit who conveys, confers and effects it.[41]

Though Dunn himself is Methodist, the quotations above express the typical baptist view, which is also the common evangelical view. The problem with this view is at least threefold. After stating the problems briefly, I discuss them in the three subsections that follow.

First, this view approaches ceremonies of the new covenant as if the very rational for and philosophy of ceremony itself were radically disparate from that of the old covenant—an approach to new covenant ceremonies that Leithart labels as semi-Marcionism. As we have already seen, this approach to ceremony unnaturally divides the Bible, resulting in a new covenant *versus* old covenant approach to understanding the *nature* of biblical ceremonies. That is not only contrary to the fact that new covenant ceremonies are still covenantal rites, but also—and far more important—contrary to the consistent biblical presentation of God as a covenantal God, a God who creates through a covenantal ritual and saves through covenantal means. As we have seen, the triune God may be described as a God whose very ontology is covenantal and ceremonial.

The second problem is that it unnaturally separates matters that the Bible considers together. For Dunn, faith and its expression in water baptism are two very distinguishable things, even though he rightly notes that "one cannot say 'faith' without also saying "water-baptism." Dunn—like most evangelical interpreters—wants to separate various elements that the Bible keeps together, but in so doing, he creates his own theological problem. In the New Testament, there is not a category of "believers who are not baptized," nor is there a category of "baptized who are not believers," though there is a category of "baptized who have turned away from

---

40. Ibid., 97.
41. Ibid.

the faith and no longer believe." Contrary to the modern Baptist view, in the New Testament children are treated not as "potential believers," but as "ideal believers" (Luke 18:15–17; note that verse 15 speaks of infants; cf. also Luke 1:41, 44).

Third, in the previous discussion of the six points which associated Jesus' baptism and ours, we have seen that many passages in the New Testament do not lend themselves to Dunn's approach. Briefly stated, water baptism is ascribed power that cannot be applied to a mere expression of faith. The number of passages that do not fit well into Dunn's mold suggests that he has the wrong basic understanding of what Paul confesses as "one baptism" (Eph 4:5). But there are also problem passages for my view which must be discussed.

A. Covenant and rites

A biblical approach to ceremonies that interprets biblical rites in the context of the covenantal relationship between God and His people cannot reduce the ceremonial merely to man's expression of faith, nor can it regard any ceremony as "an empty symbol." In the ceremonies of ancient Israel—whether covenant initiation, covenant renewal, or ordination for covenant service—God is always present and active.

Especially significant as background for understanding baptism is the ordination of Aaron, a ceremony that can certainly not be interpreted as a mere expression of faith. God, through Moses, constitutes Aaron a priest—which means that when the ceremony is over, Aaron has a different status before God and man. And the fact that his sons Nadab and Abihu went through essentially the same ceremony *without faith* did not mean that the ceremony was without effect or that their status did not change. The rite was not nullified by their unbelief. In fact, they became priests and drew near to God. And precisely because they had been constituted as priests they were under God's severe scrutiny toward men who had been granted the right to enter His presence. When they approached God in their unbelief, they attracted special wrath (Lev 8:1—10:3).

Similarly, though baptism may also be called an expression of faith on the part of man, it is more important to stress that it is a gift and a promise from God. Luther's view of baptism is not covenantal, but he well expressed a vital aspect of the covenantal view:

Drawing from Matthew 28:19 and Mark 16:16, Luther meets the challenge that baptism is merely an "external thing" with the observation that God commands us to be baptized: "Baptism is no human plaything but is instituted by God himself ... We are not to regard it as an indifferent matter, then, like putting on a new red coat." When God commands something it is not our prerogative to question it. No matter what reason or the world may think, because God has instituted baptism it cannot be useless. Therefore, what is "mere water" to the outsider becomes "divine, heavenly, holy and blessed" when God's Word and commandment are added.[42]

If we view new covenant water baptism as a rite that follows the basic covenantal principles of old covenant rites, water baptism will be understood as a ceremony in which a representative for God, the one who administers baptism, applies the covenant oath to a recipient, who is made a covenant member by the action of the rite. Just as in circumcision, the recipient of the rite, though only an infant of eight days, has been given covenant promises and placed under covenant obligations, so also in water baptism the recipient both gives and receives promises. If water baptism is at all like the covenantal ceremonies of the law of Moses, God is present and active in water baptism. It is primarily His rite.

In taking a covenant oath, the recipient is newly defined. At eight days of age, the Israelite male is officially defined as "seed of Abraham." Nadab and Abihu took the oath of ordination and were defined as priests of Yahweh, servants in His house. When a man and woman take the marriage oath, they are re-defined and become "new persons," with new covenantal responsibilities. A covenant oath inescapably "takes." Baptism, as a covenant oath, redefines the baptized person and places him into the Church, the body of Christ.

That in no way places God and His blessings into the hands of men or under the control of ceremonies. Neither Moses or David, for example, could have ever imagined such a thing. They well knew God's absolute sovereignty over all and, therefore, would not have doubted His very real presence in the rites He ordained. In fact, they both experienced His presence—for blessing *and* for discipline.

---

42. Tranvik, "Luther on Baptism," 83.

From the history of Israel, too, it is clear that when men thought they could manipulate God because He had made promises to them, they learned the hard way that God could not be used for man's purposes.[43] Rites did not guarantee blessing. They guaranteed God's involvement, which was sometimes dangerous. The rites of the law were meaningful because of God's promise to be with His people to bless them. But when they abused His promises, He was with them to curse them. In either case, His presence is always presupposed. That was what made ceremonies meaningful. The presence of God with His people meant that covenantal rites always invited either blessing or cursing. No ceremony could ever be "an empty symbol."

In conclusion, then, the theological argument—or rather, bias—that suggests that a new covenant rite cannot possibly convey the positive blessings of the covenant misunderstands the very nature of biblical ceremonies, not seeing them as covenant oaths. The semi-Marcionite mentality of our modern world is so deeply ingrained in the hearts of modern Christians that questioning or denying it sounds like a denial of biblical faith. It is, however, our modern bias that is out of accord with the revelation of Scripture and a biblical understanding of covenantal ceremonies.

B. False Distinctions

In the Bible, covenantal relationships and covenantal ceremonies are multifaceted. We can distinguish the various elements, say, of Aaron's ordination ceremony and consider the meaning of each action. But if we separate the various parts to the point that they are virtually independent of one another, we no longer have an ordination oath at all. The whole is more than the sum of the parts.

To understand the problem of separating matters that the Bible keeps together, all we need to do is take one of Dunn's statements and push it a little further, as some actually do. Dunn says, "Baptism gives expression to faith, but without faith baptism is meaningless, an empty

---

43. One of the best examples of God's presence being real but not guaranteeing blessing is the story of the battle between Israel and the Philistines recorded in 1 Samuel 4:1–11. Israel brought the ark of God to the battle front because they assumed God's presence with the ark gave them something like magical power. They thought that if God was present in the ark, they would certainly win. As the outcome of the battle shows, they fundamentally misunderstood the meaning of God's presence with the ark.

symbol."[44] What if we said what some evangelicals today say: Since faith is what really counts, baptism as an expression of faith is not merely secondary, it is not even necessary? If baptism without faith is an empty symbol and utterly meaningless, how can baptism be very important at all? Obviously, faith is the thing that counts. Once people take Dunn's approach, a new problem appears. Why in the new covenant should Christians regard ceremonies as meaningful?[45]

This thinking, so common today, was not the thinking of the apostles. If it were, the book of Acts would not have been written as it was. Luke repeatedly depicts the apostles as administering baptism *immediately* after a profession of faith. There is no period of catechizing and very little in the way of explaining the implications of the gospel. The Philippian jailer, for example, almost certainly a pagan—he tried to commit suicide when he thought his prisoners were gone—was baptized with his entire family the very same night that he heard the gospel (Acts 16:25–34). If anyone in the book of Acts needed six months of instruction before being baptized, it was this man. But baptism followed profession without delay, even in places like Corinth, "many of the Corinthians hearing believed, and were baptized" (Acts 18:8).

It can be put with greater emphasis. In the context of the narrative of the early Church in Acts, there is little doubt that putting off baptism would have been regarded as a rejection of Christ or at least as continuing in unbelief. Though today people put off baptism, refuse baptism, and downplay infant baptism because they think that baptism is secondary and not very important, their view stands in profound contrast to what we find in the Bible.

For Dunn, faith, baptism, forgiveness, the gift of the Spirit, repentance, and regeneration are all so completely distinguishable that we can, in good scholastic fashion, not only define the order and logical relationship between each of these but also separate them and place them each in their own airtight box, as it were. Baptism may be defined as an act of applying water, but faith, the Spirit, or other elements may or may not be present, as if each one has to be considered on its own.

---

44. Dunn, *Baptism in the Holy Spirit*, 97.

45. For example, Thomas J. Nettles asserts, "Many contemporary Christian communities see little need for baptism because they reduce the entire process of salvation to justification by faith alone" ("Baptism as a Symbol," 152).

This is simply not the way the Bible speaks. The words "faith," "repentance," and "baptism" are used in ways that overlap. The whole "conversion-initiation" process is treated as a single event with various elements, a body with parts that should not be severed from one another. Dissecting the conversion-initiation process into its elements may be legitimate for certain purposes, but we have to remember that once we have dissected something, the most important aspects of the thing are gone, for it is then dead. Living things are harder to analyze, but they are the reality.

Conversion, repentance, faith, regeneration, baptism, adoption, the gift of the Spirit, and the forgiveness of sins are distinguishable elements of a single process that is initiated by God and depends entirely on His presence and action. That He chooses to work through means reflects His plan in creation and redemption. But it is His presence in and through those means that makes them living realities.

C. Problem Passages

There are difficult passages for any position. For Dunn's side, passages that associate baptism with the forgiveness of sins, the gift of the Spirit, and salvation present a problem because they seem to put together what he wants to separate.

But Dunn also points to a number of key passages that seem to separate what I am suggesting we should keep together. The complexity of the subject is well known and only a book length study, such as Peter Leithart's *The Priesthood of the Plebs*, can adequately address the larger concerns. I can only briefly suggest an approach here.

In an article directly addressing the relationship of repentance, baptism, and the gift of the Spirit, N. B. Stonehouse quotes the "solution" suggested by Jackson and Lake in their work on the beginnings of the Christian faith:

> The obvious meaning is—just as in Acts xix.1–7—that the gift of the Spirit is conditional on baptism; but this sudden introduction of baptism seems quite inconsistent with what was stated: the disciples had received the Spirit without having been baptized for that purpose, and the words of Jesus in Acts i.4 imply a baptism in Spirit as a substitute for baptism in water, not as a consequence of it. The redactor, however, like all his contemporaries in the Gentile Church, regarded baptism in the name of

Jesus as necessary for admission to the Christian society and its benefits, of which the gift of the Spirit was one of the chief; it is therefore not strange if he introduced the references to baptism in ii.38 and 41.[46]

Jackson and Lake concluded that the book of Acts gives us various contradictory views of baptism because the book was edited by a Gentile redactor who revised Peter's sermon to reflect his own views. It is an easy solution, but not at all satisfying—like amputating a leg to cure ingrown toenail. However, it does point to the difficulty of the material under consideration.

In response, I think that one of the most important presuppositions to stress in considering the book of Acts is that what happens in the earliest history of the Church in Acts is not normal. It is the history of the exceptional. Pentecost, for example, is unrepeatable. It is a once for all event, the results of which condition the history of the world ever since but which does not set a norm for Christian evangelism. We do not expect the same sort of phenomena whenever we gather in an upper room for prayer or even once a year on the day of Pentecost. Nothing exactly like Pentecost has ever happened again nor can it.

What seems to be forgotten by many evangelical interpreters is that the whole period from Pentecost to the destruction of the temple in AD 70 is an abnormal age, a transitional period during which the old covenant system and the new covenant system existed side by side. Paul and other Jewish Christians could still worship in the temple when they visited Jerusalem, because in some sense the old covenant temple was still a house of God. But the coming of the Spirit at Pentecost created a new temple, a new dwelling place of God. As a result, during the period from Pentecost to AD 70, the public status of God's covenant people was ambiguous. Which Israel is the true Israel, the circumcised Jews or the baptized Christians? Where is the true house of God?

AD 70 brought an final answer. The destruction of Jerusalem and the old covenant temple was Jesus' vindication as a true prophet and the end of the transitional era. As He had previously done in the days of Jeremiah, God made it resoundingly clear to the whole world that the temple in Jerusalem and its worship system was under His wrath and judgment. But between Pentecost and the public vindication of Jesus in

---

46. Stonehouse, "Repentance," 3–4. Stonehouse does not agree with Jackson and Lake, but I do not find his solution helpful either.

AD 70, there was a transitional period during which we encounter the anomalous and unusual.

With that in mind, let's consider three important events in the book of Acts, beyond Pentecost, which seem to contradict the view implied by Peter's promise in Acts 2:38: "Repent, and each of you be baptized in the name of Jesus Christ for the forgiveness of your sins; and you will receive the gift of the Holy Spirit." Peter's exhortation implies that forgiveness of sins and the gift of the Spirit are tied to baptism.[47] But in Acts 8, 10–11, and 19:1–7, there are three incidents that *appear* to be an ill fit for such a paradigm.

Acts 10–11 is the famous story of the conversion of the household of Cornelius. Almost from the beginning, the story is unquestionably depicting an exceptional situation. But before we consider that, we need to note that there is also a very important unexceptional part of the story—Cornelius is a Gentile believer in the true God (Acts 10:1–2). Contrary to what modern Christians often assume, there were many Gentile believers in the ancient world, especially from the time of the Babylonian captivity (cf. Acts 10:34–35). And Gentile believers were accepted by God. In other words, they would be saved.

However, in the old covenant, unless a man was circumcised, he would not be a member of the priestly nation. From the time of Abraham (Gen 17:9–14), *priestly status and salvation were distinguished.* In the new covenant, all of God's people—Jew and Gentile, slave and free, male and female, with no exception—are members of a new priesthood (Gal 3:26–29). But there was a transition era. In the earliest era of the Church, there was a period in which Gentile believers in the true God had not yet heard the story of Jesus. The story of Cornelius not only illustrates the situation of the true believing Gentile, there is something more. This incident is definitive, as if Cornelius is the representative Gentile believer. His inclusion opens the way for others like him.

The unusual part of the story begins with the appearance of an angel to Cornelius. Of course, this makes it clear that Cornelius is indeed a true believer. So his story is *not* a story of conversion from idols to

---

47. As Charles H. Talbert points out, "In Acts as a whole, Peter's speech functions as a frontispiece, just as Jesus' speech in Luke 4:16–27 does in the Third Gospel" (*Reading Acts*, 47). In that sense, Peter's speech should be seen as defining the paradigm for our basic understanding of baptism—an idea that seems to flow necessarily from Talbert's statement, though he himself goes on to deny it.

serve the living and true God. Rather, in this story about an old covenant Gentile believer being introduced to the new covenant—initiated by an angelic visitation no less—there is a larger event. When Peter, in describing his understanding of the coming of the Spirit on Cornelius and the rest, refers back to Pentecost, he confirms for us that what happened here was not part of the normal course of evangelism:

> And as I began to speak, the Holy Spirit fell on them, even as on us at the beginning. And I remembered the word of the Lord, how he said, John indeed baptized with water; but ye shall be baptized in the Holy Spirit. If then God gave unto them the like gift as he did also unto us, when we believed on the Lord Jesus Christ, who was I, that I could withstand God? (Acts 11:15–17)

The Holy Spirit fell on the Gentile believers just as He had fallen on the Jewish believers at Pentecost. The exceptional nature and historical significance of the event was not lost on Peter's hearers who concluded that God had granted repentance to the Gentiles also (Acts 11:18). The gift of the Holy Spirit here *preceded* baptism because, as the story itself witnesses, even Peter, who had heard the words of Great Commission directly from the mouth of the risen Lord, considered it unthinkable to cross the boundary separating Jew and Gentile. God had to show Peter and the Jewish church that Jew and Gentile were one in Christ. It was an extremely difficult lesson for the early Church to learn, and much of the New Testament is occupied with Jews and Gentiles becoming one in Christ. It is no wonder, then, that Peter would not have first baptized Cornelius, nor is it surprising that God gave this exceptional testimony to His saving plan and program. The event in Acts 10 and 11, therefore, is special, similar to Pentecost, a once-for-all transitional event—the acceptance of the first Gentiles on an equal par with Jews as members of the new priestly nation.

The next passage to consider, Acts 8, records the story of the conversion of the Samaritans and is similarly exceptional, though less so. In terms of the program outlined by Jesus in Acts 1, Samaria seems to be linked both to Jewish and to Gentile evangelism:

> But ye shall receive power, when the Holy Spirit is come upon you: and ye shall be my witnesses both in Jerusalem, and in all Judaea and Samaria, and unto the uttermost part of the earth. (Acts 1:8)

The disciples began to be witnesses in Jerusalem, which is what they did in Acts 1–7. Then they spread out to "all Judea and Samaria," which began in Acts 8. Finally their testimony extended to "the uttermost part of the earth," which began in Acts 10–11. Considered in the light of the introductory words of Acts 1:8, it seems clear that the two passages (Acts 8 and 10–11) which have been used to prove that water baptism and Holy Spirit baptism are not necessarily coincident are recording transitional events, similar to Pentecost itself—events that extend Pentecost to areas outside of Jerusalem, according to the geographical outline in the command of Jesus.

For the Jews, the conversion of Samaria was less of a problem than the conversion of Gentiles, because Samaritans were circumcised and considered in some sense God's covenant people. Philip therefore baptized them without hesitation, but apart from the coming of the apostles Peter and John, God did not allow them to enjoy the outward gifts of the Spirit that demonstrated His presence. The gift of the Spirit and baptism are separated in time. Why?

I think the answer is that the coming of the apostles to authenticate Philip's work and to be the channel of blessing for the Samaritan church secured the oneness of the Church under the apostles as the authoritative representatives of Christ. The general pattern in Acts and in the epistles, too, is that the gifts of the Spirit come with the laying on of the apostles' hands (2 Tim 1:6; Acts 9:17; 19:1–7). In the beginning at least, the baptism of the Spirit—the gift singular—was coincident with the miraculous manifestations of the Spirit—the gifts plural. Thus, Paul talks about the signs of an apostle (2 Cor 12:12) and imparting a spiritual gift to a church (Rom 1:11). The gift of the Spirit coming to the Samaritans through the apostles meant that the Samaritans were covenantally bound to the Jerusalem church and the authority of its apostolic representatives, preserving the unity of the early Church.

The third problem passage, Acts 19:1–7, also finds its solution in the approach I am suggesting. The gifts of the Spirit, which testify of His presence, were given through the laying on of an apostle's hands. The men Paul encountered had been baptized with John the Baptizer's baptism but, if we translate literally, had not "even heard if there be a Holy Spirit" (19:2). The passage raises a number of questions. Why are they called "disciples?" How could it be that followers of John the Baptizer would be ignorant of the Spirit? Why does Paul re-baptize them?

Given the way that Luke uses μαθητής in Acts (Acts 6:1–2, 7; 9:1, 10, 19, 25–26, 38; 11:26, 29; 13:52; 14:20, 22, 28; 15:10; 16:1; 18:23, 27; 19:1, 9, 30; 20:1, 30; 21:4, 16), it seems that he is speaking of these men as if they are followers of Christ. Luke may be speaking of them as disciples because they were baptized shortly after meeting Paul, "men who soon became disciples," or it may reflect the view that Paul had of them when he first met them. It seems most likely that these were men who believed the message of John the Baptizer and received his baptism. So they were disciples of the true way, even though immature and ignorant. Their immediate response to Paul's preaching indicates that they had faith, even if they were inadequately instructed.

If they were direct disciples of John, they should have known of the baptism of the Spirit through his message. Even if they had never met John and were baptized by one of his disciples, they should have known of the Spirit from the teaching of the Old Testament. Their statement is so odd that some translations, following the hint in John 7:39, suggest that what they did not know was the gift of the Spirit: "And they said unto him, Nay, we did not so much as hear whether the Holy Spirit was given" (ASV).[48] Even if this is not legitimate as a translation, it may capture the meaning. It is also possible to emphasize the word "heard" so that what they would be saying is not that they did not know of the existence of the Spirit as such, but that the message they heard said nothing about Him.

However we understand the reference to the Holy Spirit, these disciples seem to be Jewish believers in Ephesus who had been baptized by someone who preached John's message of the coming kingdom and Messiah and the need for national repentance—but either they did not know about the Spirit, perhaps because the one who preached to them had neglected to emphasize the Spirit, or they did not know that the Spirit had been poured out on Pentecost. Perhaps these Jewish believers had heard the message long after Pentecost. In any case, their baptism, like the baptism of others who came to John, was an old covenant Jewish rite, which is brought clearly to focus by the fact that it is *not* essentially linked with the gift of the Holy Spirit. As F. F. Bruce writes, "Paul's ques-

---

48. The Western text actually has "if any are receiving the Holy Spirit." Cf. Bruce, *Book of Acts*, 362.

tion about their baptism implies a connection between the receiving of the Spirit and baptism."[49]

They had been prepared for the gospel, but they had not yet understood the whole message of the Messiah. Apollos, too, though apparently better instructed than the twelve disciples mentioned in Acts 19, nevertheless had a deficient knowledge of the Gospel and Christian baptism (Acts 18:24–28). These two stories back to back remind us that the early years of the Church are a transitional era. By Acts 19, it had been about twenty-five years since John the Baptizer was put to death, but his ministry, mentioned often in Acts (Acts 1:5, 22; 10:37; 11:16; 13:24–25; 18:25; 19:3–4), is still relevant. It is also noteworthy that in the account of the transitional events that brought the blessing of the Holy Spirit on the Gentile believer Cornelius, John the Baptizer is mentioned both on the original occasion and when Peter retold the story to Jews who were disturbed that he had eaten with Gentiles (10:37; 11:16). Luke seems to be showing us that just as the Gentile Cornelius was a true believer in the one God who had not yet heard the Christian gospel, so there were Jews dispersed throughout the Roman Empire who believed in the true God but had not yet heard the story of Jesus. Like Gentile believers in the true God, former disciples of John the Baptizer needed to believe in Jesus, be baptized with Christian baptism, and receive the Holy Spirit.

Thus, all three of the events in the book of Acts that have been understood to demonstrate that Peter's exhortation in Acts 2:38 did not define a paradigmatic relationship between baptism and the gift of the Spirit turn out, on closer inspection, to be exceptional events relating to the transitional nature of the time between Pentecost and AD 70. They are just the kind of stories we would expect as the gospel slowly advances into the world of the Roman Empire and is introduced to people who were already believers in the true God, some Jews, some Samaritans, some Gentiles. These stories are not, therefore, descriptions of what we should normally expect, nor do they define our doctrine of baptism in the periods of Church history that follow AD 70, except that they remind us that there are transitional times during which God does unusual things.

---

49. Ibid., 363.

Conclusion

If we keep in mind that covenantal rites include both blessing and cursing, that they are essentially oath-making and oath-renewing rites, then our understanding of baptism and the Lord's Supper will be consistent with the nature of old covenant rites and with the larger biblical picture of God as *the Lord of ritual*. Baptism as a covenant-making ceremony introduces its recipient into the Church, the body of Christ, just as circumcision defined the covenant people from the time of Abraham. Like all oath-taking ceremonies, it brings with it objective changes in the definition of the individual. From the time of his baptism, the child or adult is defined as "Christian," and becomes heir both to promises and responsibilities.

In that sense, the baptismal ceremony always accomplishes what it is supposed to accomplish, in the same way that wedding vows make people married, regardless of the subjective state of the man or woman taking the vows. They may be joined for curse instead of blessing, but they are joined nonetheless. Thus, baptism also, as a covenant-oath ceremony, joins the recipient with Jesus and His Church. Whether it is a happy union or not, it is a true union with eternal consequences, for good or ill.

THE SIGNIFICANCE OF THE PARADIGM

The significance of the fact that Jesus' baptism is the paradigm for Christian baptism is broad and deep. I can only suggest a basic outline and then develop one aspect that is commonly ignored, the reign of Christ's Church as a body of Melchizedekian kings and priests in Christ.

First, if Jesus' baptism by John the Baptizer is the paradigm for Christian baptism, the following parallels, most of which have been pointed out in the argument above, illumine the nature of Christian baptism.

1. Jesus was baptized into union with His people; Christians are baptized into union with Christ and made members of His body (Rom 6:3; 1 Cor 12:13).

2. Jesus identified with the Jews' need of cleansing in His baptism; Christians are cleansed of sin in their baptism (Acts 22:16).

3. Jesus was declared Son at His baptism; Christians are adopted into sonship through baptism (Gal 3:26–29).

4. Jesus was anointed with the Spirit at His baptism; Christians are anointed with the Spirit in their baptism (1 Cor 12:13).

5. Jesus was declared the Father's beloved in His baptism; Christians are publicly declared to be loved and accepted by the Father in their baptism (Col 2:10–14).

6. Jesus was ordained into the priesthood in His baptism; Christians are ordained as priests in Christ at their baptism (Gal 3:27; 1 Pet 2:9–10).

These parallels confirm the view of the early Church and the Reformation that Jesus' baptism was the paradigm baptism for a Christian understanding of baptism and suggest many lines of meditation on the meaning of baptism. In the rest of this chapter, I would like to focus on an aspect of baptism that is almost completely ignored, baptism as ordination into the royal priesthood.

As we have seen, Jesus was baptized as Messiah, a new Adam, and a King-Priest after the order of Melchizedek. Our baptisms are similar. We are ordained into a priesthood. Specifically, we have been ordained as priests after the order of Melchizedek under the authority of the Great High Priest, Jesus the Messiah. Just as for Jesus, Sonship and the gift of the Spirit were part of His calling as the Melchizedekian King-Priest, so too, for us, sonship and the gift of the Spirit are part of what it means that we have been ordained into the new royal priesthood.

Emphasizing that our priesthood is of the order of Melchizedek is important because a royal priesthood must in some sense *reign*. But what does this mean for the Church? The question is complicated because the word "church" is ambiguous. We have to begin our answer by distinguishing different uses of the word "church."

First, there is a sense in which the institutional church is the central channel of Christ's rule as King-Priest. Usually, the word "church," when used of the institutional church, either is in the plural ("churches") or is qualified somehow (e.g., "St. John's Presbyterian Church of Columbus, Ohio").

Second, the Church is a body of believers in Christ composed of all baptized people from many nations, tribes, and tongues. Her influence as a body of believers may extend to all sorts of groups and institutions, but those institutions do not come under the authority of the local church. For example, Christian nations would be under Christ and the citizens of a Christian nation would belong to institutional churches, but the nation as such would not.

Third, the word "church" is used to refer to the whole body of Christ, all of Christ's elect, including those who have already gone to be with Him in heaven. This is a broader notion still but one that is relevant to the discussion.[50]

Since the very language of her royal priesthood comes from the Mosaic covenant, the model for the Church's rule over the nations must also come from the example of ancient Israel. As we have seen, the nation as a whole was the covenanted king-priest nation, a royal priesthood. To understand the meaning of the royal priesthood in the new covenant, we need to briefly consider first what it meant in the old covenant and then how things have been transformed by the coming of the new covenant.

The Old Covenant Background: Israel's Rule over the Nations

The Old Testament background for the notion of the Church as a Melchizedekian priesthood actually begins long before Melchizedek himself, with the creation of Adam and Eve. That is, Adam and Eve were created to rule the world (Gen 1:28), which implies their status as royalty under God. At the same time, they were also given, as their original residence, a Garden Sanctuary, in which to dwell with God, and their primary responsibilities are defined in priestly terms.[51] They are the guardians of the Garden Sanctuary. Thus, the human race in the first Adam was originally created to be a royal priesthood.[52] Melchizedek's

---

50. My description of the use of the word "church" here more or less parallels the helpful discussion in Leithart, *Kingdom and Power*, 143–45.

51. As James Jordan points out, the priestly responsibility came first. Adam and Eve in the Garden were not yet mature enough for kingly rule, but as they and their descendants matured, they would have inherited kingly rule, since it was part of the original purpose for their creation. The responsibility of the priest is obedience to the rules given by God. The king's responsibility is different, as the story of Solomon illustrates. The king must have wisdom to make difficult decisions. Adam's responsibility in the Garden was simple obedience, but through the discipline of simple obedience, he should have gained wisdom so that he could rule. Cf. Jordan, "Biblical Theology Basics 2002–2003," 12–23.

52. See also Jordan, *Through New Eyes*, 133–41.

own royal priesthood was grounded in Adam. So, for Christ to become the High Priest of the Melchizedekian order means that the new humanity has come to fulfill the task given to the first Adam and his seed.

It is in that larger context that we should understand that the nation of Israel was chosen as a royal priesthood (Exod 19:5–6). As we have seen in chapter 3, Israel was a new Adam, called by God to bring salvation to the world. That meant that she had a special responsibility to pray for the nations, to show by example what it meant to serve God, to teach the nations to know God. It also meant that she had a certain kind of rule over the nations, though not necessarily rule in a political sense. As we look at the law of Moses, in the light of the Abrahamic covenant, the history of Israel, the prayer book of ancient Israel (the Psalms), and the books of the prophets, we learn what it means that Israel was called to be a royal priesthood.

Israel's Spiritual Rule

Israel's spiritual rule had three important aspects. First, the law of Moses constitutes Israel as a priestly nation by giving her a tabernacle and worship system that establishes the true and only world center. The tabernacle as the dwelling place of the Creator God was the replacement of the original world center in the Garden of Eden. Though all ancient nations regarded themselves as the "true people" and saw their own temples as world centers, imitating the false world center of the tower of Babel,[53] only Israel was chosen by the Creator and only she had His dwelling place in her midst. Surrounded by nations that all claimed to possess the true priesthood and the gate to heaven, the ancient Israelites served the Creator God who had chosen the Mosaic tabernacle to be the new Eden and His dwelling place on earth.[54]

---

53. To see how important the notion of the center of the world was for ancient religion, see, e.g., Eliade, *Sacred and Profane*, as well as his *Patterns in Comparative Religion* and *Image and Symbols*.

54. The design of the tabernacle and the materials used suggested both its cosmic import and Israel's responsibility to the nations. The layers of the tabernacle tent correspond to various "layers" of society, as James Jordan points out: "Once we understand that the Tabernacle was a symbol of Israelite society, there are all kinds of correlations that can be made. The Inner Veil of the Most Holy has to do with God's angelic guardians. The Outer Veil of the Holy Place has to do with the priestly guardians. The goat's hair tent curtain over the Tabernacle has to do with the courtyard and the Levites. The red ramskin cover that was on top of the goat's hair tent curtain is to be associated with Passover, and thus with all Israel, who were claimed at Passover. The dolphin leather cover has to do with the Gentiles—dolphin being a *sea* creature" (*Through New Eyes*, 215).

Since Moses, trained in all the knowledge of Egypt, knew very well the significance of the tabernacle as the new Eden and the true center of the world, he and ancient Israelite priests and leaders also knew that the ceremonies performed in the tabernacle had cosmic significance. They were not merely sacrificing and offering for themselves. The ancient Levitical priests were chosen to serve God in praying for and sacrificing for the world. This was implicit in their calling as the children of Abraham, the man who was chosen to bring God's covenant blessing to all the families of the earth (Gen 12:1–3). Sacrificing for the world found more open expression in the yearly calendar, especially in the feast of tabernacles, when Israel offered seventy bulls for the seventy nations of the world (cf. Gen 10; Num 29:12–34).

Second, Israel was called by God to set an example of righteousness to the nations. At the individual level, a man or a woman setting a godly example often does more than we think, but at a national level, the impact can be tremendous. But if that righteous nation were to stand out in the world as a place of unique blessing, other nations would have to take note, whether they liked it or not. After all, the successful nation would gradually become more powerful and other nations would inevitably feel threatened, even if the successful nation were peaceful.

God's plan for ancient Israel included this aspect of international relations:

> Behold, I have taught you statutes and ordinances, even as Yahweh my God commanded me, that ye should do so in the midst of the land whither ye go in to possess it. Keep therefore and do them; for this is your wisdom and your understanding in the sight of the peoples, that shall hear all these statutes, and say, Surely this great nation is a wise and understanding people. For what great nation is there, that hath a god so nigh unto them, as Yahweh our God is whensoever we call upon him? And what great nation is there, that hath statutes and ordinances so righteous as all this law, which I set before you this day? (Deut 4:5–8)

> Yahweh will establish thee for a holy people unto himself, as he hath sworn unto thee; if thou shalt keep the commandments of Yahweh thy God, and walk in his ways. And all the peoples of the earth shall see that thou art called by the name of Yahweh; and they shall be afraid of thee. (Deut 28:9–10)

If Israel had kept God's law, the surrounding nations would have been impressed by her righteousness, peace, lack of disease, numerical growth, and prosperity. The nations might have responded in hatred and envy, or they might have responded, as some nations did in David's day, by turning to the Lord. In either case, leadership by example was an aspect of Israel's mission to the world. In Solomon's day, we see that at least one time in Israel's history, this aspect of her priestly rule over the nations was realized: "And there came of all peoples to hear the wisdom of Solomon, from all kings of the earth, who had heard of his wisdom" (1 Kgs 4:34; cf. 8:41–43).

Leading by Testimony

Third, Israel was called to be witnesses to the one true God in a world that worshiped idols. This is implicit in the Abrahamic covenant itself. In the Psalms, it is quite explicit, coming to expression in one of the important themes of the book. Israel, through praising God, witnessing of His goodness, and singing of His faithfulness, was to have a testimony to the nations of the world around her (Pss 9:11; 18:49; 22:27–28; 45:17; 47:1, 3; 48:1–8; 49:1–4; 57:9; 66:8; 67:1–7; 68:29; 72:8–19; 77:12–14; 86:9–10; 96:1–13; 97:6; 98; 99:1–2; 102:15; 105:1–4; 108:1–6; 117:1–2; 119:46; 126:1–3; 138:4–6; 148:11). The gods of the nations were tribal or local deities, at best—which is to say, demons with limited authority. Thus, the nations did not regard their gods as the one and only Creator of the world, nor did they love their gods. Israel's God was unique, the only national God who was also international, the God for the whole world.

Israel was to testify to the unique glory of the only true God and lead the nations to know and praise Him with her. As Yahweh's witness among the nations, Israel was to declare His greatness and glory (Isa 43:9–13; 44:6–20). This meant declaring to the nations that their gods were nothing, or worse than nothing—demons that infect the minds and ruin the lives of those who worship them. By testifying to the truth of the true God among the nations, Israel was to lead the world into the covenant blessings promised to Abraham and his seed (Gen 12:1–3).[55]

Israel's Political Rule

Israel was called by God to be a nation with political authority over the world, though not directly but indirectly. If she had obeyed God's

---

55. Though this is in fulfillment of the calling of the Abrahamic covenant, testimony through song and praise began especially with David's kingdom, as Peter Leithart demonstrates in detail in *From Silence to Song*.

commandments at all times, the kind of moral authority in the political realm that was seen in the days of David and Solomon would have been typical. During the height of the monarchy, other nations looked to Israel as an example and imitated her ways.

In addition to this moral authority, Israel also had a sort of political authority in that she was promised that if other nations attacked her, God would protect her. The victories of Joshua in Canaan were different from "normal" war, since the conquest was an act of special divine judgment against the Canaanites, dispossessing them and giving the land to Israel. Normally Israel was forbidden from engaging in wars of conquest. However, if nations outside of Canaan attacked Israel, she was promised God's help (Deut 28:7; Lev 26:6–8)—a promise that was realized most conspicuously in the days of Hezekiah when the king of Assyria sent his armies to attack Jerusalem and met annihilation by the hand of the Angel of God (2 Kgs 19:32–37).

Israel no doubt had a broader kind of social leadership as a function of the prosperity and peace she enjoyed through obedience to God's law. In other words, what the queen of Sheba did in visiting Solomon (1 Kgs 10:1ff.) was no doubt imitated on a smaller scale by common people who came to see the famed glory of Jerusalem and the great temple of Solomon. If Israel had consistently obeyed the law, other nations would have seen her success and been influenced by her in the course of trade and business, as well as by borrowing money from her and by visiting her cities to see the glory of her wealth and abundance.

Conclusion

A comprehensive discussion of Israel's relationship with the nations would have to include the historical dimension, for there is considerable change from the time of the twelve tribes to the monarchy and again to the post-captivity era. Still the broad outline suggested above gives a basic picture of the international implications of the Abrahamic covenant and Israel's calling as a new Adam. Of course, since Israel was called by God to be a political entity existing within defined boundaries and given a covenant constitution that defined her laws, we cannot apply her rules directly to the Church, whichever definition of "church" we are thinking of.

The Rule of the Church of Christ

As we turn now to consider what it means for the Church to rule, it must be emphasized to begin with that the rule of Christ's body, the Church, is the rule of Christ through the Church. Jesus rose from the dead and was seated as Messiah at the right hand of the Father. The man Jesus became Lord over all. The Church, therefore, rules under His authority and never as an independent authority. Moreover, the rule of Christ in the world is open. His covenant and law is available for all to read and understand, so that leaders in the institutional church, the Christian nation, or the Christian family have clearly specified limits on their authority.

The Rule of the Institutional Church

The authority of the institutional church is granted by God's covenant word and delineated through Christ's commandments. Broadly speaking, the rule of the institutional church can be described as authority that is exercised through covenantal evangelism and covenantal worship.

The command for covenantal evangelism is seen in Jesus' well-known commission to His Church, literally translated "disciple the nations" (Matt 28:19). The most common translation is something like "make disciples of all the nations," which in English can be, and is most commonly, read to mean "make some people from every nation to be disciples." In fact, Hal Lindsey offers this interpretation as exegesis of the Greek text:

> Go therefore and make disciples of [Greek = *out of*] all the nations. . . . We are told to make disciples from out of all the Gentiles. You don't disciple nations, you disciple individuals, so the Greek word translated *nations* should be understood in its most frequently used sense—*Gentiles*.[56]

Lindsey's exegesis here encounters a significant obstacle in the Greek text of the Gospel of Matthew. For unlike the text that Lindsey imagined, in the actual text, there is no Greek word "out of" in this verse. The words "make disciples of" are the translation of a single Greek verb, which

---

56. Lindsey, *Road to Holocaust*, 49. Virtually all translations render the Greek word ἔθνη in Matthew 28:19 as "nations." Though nothing essential would be changed by rendering the passage "all the Gentiles," the point in the passage is that Jesus has authority over all the world, and therefore all the nations must be brought into submission to Him. The preferred translation by all modern versions and almost all older ones, therefore, is "nations."

could be translated into English as a verb "disciple." Lindsey himself uses "disciple" as a verb in the quotation above. The words "the nations" represent the direct object of the verb "disciple," so Jesus' command is not to make some Gentiles to be disciples, but—exactly contrary to Lindsey's assertion that one does not disciple nations—to make *all the nations* into His disciples: "disciple the nations!"

The fact that this is to be done by baptizing and instructing them to obey the commandments of Jesus shows that it is the institutional church that is in view in this commission, for baptism and instruction in the word of God are the distinctive labor of the institutional church. In the context, discipling the nations through baptism and instruction is based upon Jesus having all authority in heaven and on earth. It is the means for His authority being realized in all the world.

When we remember that *baptism* brings one into the institutional church and makes one subject to her discipline, and that *teaching* aims at obedience to Jesus' commands, we see that the Great Commission aims at nothing less than changing the whole world by making it obedient to Christ. This is a distinctly covenantal commission, realized only through the oath of baptism and sincere submission to the authority of Jesus.

Similarly, the worship of the institutional church is also distinctly covenantal. We have already seen previously that there are two kinds of ceremonies in the Bible, covenant initiation and covenant renewal. Baptism is the initiatory rite in the new covenant and weekly worship centered in the Lord's Supper is covenant renewal. That modern Christians often cannot even imagine the relationship between covenant and worship evidences the widespread impact of the semi-Marcionite thinking that Leithart describes. However, just as baptism is best understood in the light of ceremonies of the old covenant, weekly worship in the new covenant should be understood as a new form of essentially the same kind of thing that was done in the old covenant. Thus, the apostle Paul refers to Christ as our Passover (1 Cor 5:7), to our praise as a sacrifice (Heb 13:15), and to the local church as a temple of God (1 Cor 3:16–17). This and related language points to old covenant roots for new covenant worship.[57]

There is even a relatively clear basic structure for weekly worship in the Old Testament law. Commentaries on Leviticus by Gordon Wenham

---

57. For a full discussion of new covenant worship and its old covenant background, see Meyers, *The Lord's Service*.

and R. K. Harrison both point to the sacrifices in Leviticus as providing an outline for Christian worship.[58] In particular, the sin offering corresponds to the confession of sin in Christian worship; the ascension offering (often called the whole burnt offering) to the reading of the word, prayer, and sermon; and the peace offering to the Lord's supper. Including the Lord's Supper in every worship service was clearly the custom in the New Testament era, as is evident in 1 Corinthians.[59]

Weekly worship is the heart of the institutional church's rule under Christ. When God's people gather together before His throne it is a "political" as well as a religious act. Christ exercises authority in His Church in and through every aspect of worship. Reading and teaching the Bible are vital because Jesus instructed His Church to train the nations to obey His commandments. Prayer calls upon Him to act in blessing and cursing. Songs of praise honor God and institute the kingdom, for where God's name is honored, there He is King. The Lord's Supper, central to the worship service in the New Testament, is a covenant meal with King Jesus, like the feasts of Israel in the Mosaic covenant.

When weekly worship is understood as covenant renewal, it is also understood as spiritual warfare. Paul reminded the Corinthians that Christ judged those who came to His supper, and Peter wrote that when judgment begins with the household of God, it embraces those who reject the Gospel also (1 Pet 4:17). In Revelation, the souls of the martyrs are under the altar in the place of worship, calling for God's vengeance to fall on those who murder His Church. Weekly worship in which God's people gather to pray the Lord's Prayer aggressively seeks the growth of His kingdom. The petition "Thy kingdom come," looks forward to the day that every enemy will be under Jesus' feet (1 Cor 15:25).

The Church's prayers, like Israel's, are to include rulers and men in authority at all levels, an indication of her priestly role in seeking God's

---

58. Cited in Meyers, *The Lord's Service*, 89.

59. In 1 Corinthians 11:20, Paul writes, "When, therefore, ye assemble yourselves together, it is not to eat the Lord's Supper." The word, "therefore" points back to verses 17 and 18, which also speak of the Corinthians assembling together (συνέρχομαι). The reference is clearly to weekly worship. The word "praise" in verse 17 and 22 define the beginning and end of the paragraph with an *inclusio*, so that the entire paragraph is about the Corinthians weekly gathering. In verse 22, then, the clear implication is that weekly worship is the time when Christians get together to take the Lord's Supper. The book of Acts gives us the same picture of frequent communion being the common custom of the early Church (Acts 20:7).

blessings and curses on men in authority (cf. 1 Tim 2:1–4; Rom 13:1–7). Her testimony and her example are powerful means for influencing those under her authority and outside it as well. Her teaching, too, comes with authority to those within her membership and influences non-Christians as they see the Church being blessed by God.

Through covenantal evangelism and covenantal worship, Christ uses the institutional church to build His body. As more and more nations are converted, local churches in untold multitudes of communities will take the lead in ministering the Word of God, leading the world through prayer and worship, and counseling leaders of families and of the nation at all levels so that they can apply God's law of God rightly to their labors His servants.

The Rule of the Church as Christ's Body on Earth

As the nations of the world are converted to Christ and taught by the institutional church to obey His commandments, the two other covenantal institutions spoken of in the Scriptures take up their role to represent the rule of Christ in the world also. I am speaking of the family and the nation. We will consider each briefly.

Remember that the assumption here is that the Gospel will conquer the nations of the world, so that the time will come when the vast majority of the people in every nation will be converted to Christ. When the nations are won to Christ, most individuals and families in any particular nation will be members of some institutional church. Also, the nation would be a Christian nation and therefore roughly coterminous with the body of Christ in that geographical area, though not necessarily coterminous with any particular institutional church.

First, consider political authority in such a nation. Paul teaches us that all political authority—whether Christian or non-Christian, whether in kings, presidents, governors, mayors, or parliaments—is essentially covenantal, for political authorities are given their authority by God (Rom 13:1–7). Therefore, magistrates in a Christian nation would have the right to demand an oath, for example, when a man is called to give evidence in a court of law or when someone is inducted into political office. Christian political leaders would have a responsibility as Christian men and women to obey the Bible and seek to govern in obedience to Christ, making laws that reflect God's righteousness. Note that their authority over the nation would not be an indirect expression of the authority of the institutional church, as if the leaders of the local church pull the strings behind the scenes. However, as servants of Christ instructed by their local churches, their exercise of authority would be an expression of the authority of Christ.

Second, consider the families in such a nation. Like the Church and civil government, the family is a covenantal institution because the Bible teaches that marriage is a covenantal relationship. Husband and wife are one in covenant. Children are under their parents' covenantal authority until they become adults and leave the home to begin another covenantal family.[60] When families are baptized and live in obedience to Christ, they apply the authority of Christ to their family situation, worshiping weekly in their local church, teaching their children the word of God, and solving family problems by recourse to the Scriptures.

When the nations are converted and the world is brought under the authority of Christ, the sum total of Christian individuals, nations, and families of the world will be the Church in the sense that they will be Christ's body on earth, but the political authorities of a nation and parents in the home have rights and responsibilities that the institutional church does not have. They exercise and manifest the authority of Christ in ways distinct from the institutional church and in spheres where it has no direct say. But whether in the Church as Christ's earthly body—the sum total of all living Christians—or in the Church as it is manifest in various institutional churches, authority is given by Christ to be exercised under Him by ministers of His grace.

The Rule of the Church as Christ's Body in Heaven

It might be assumed that the Church in heaven is no longer involved in the events of this world, but the book of Revelation gives us a very different picture:

> And when he opened the fifth seal, I saw underneath the altar the souls of them that had been slain for the word of God, and for the testimony which they held: and they cried with a great voice, saying, How long, O Master, the holy and true, dost thou not judge and avenge our blood on them that dwell on the earth? And there was given them to each one a white robe; and it was said unto them, that they should rest yet for a little time, until their fellow-

---

60. I am not suggesting that children must stay home until married. I am simply not addressing the matter of adult singles since it is not relevant to my purposes in this short outline.

servants also and their brethren, who should be killed even as they were, should have fulfilled their course. (Rev 6:9–11)

In John's vision, the saints in heaven are involved in the continuing warfare between the people of God and the servants of the devil. Though it is not possible to imagine the details, I assume that the vision here in Revelation depicts something that remains true and that saints in heaven are aware of the worldly battle for the gospel and that they make petition to God, just as the Church on earth does.

CONCLUSION

By baptism, Christians are adopted into the family of God, officially becoming God's children and sons, which means, too, that they become heirs (Gal 3:25–29). To be heirs in Christ means that Christians are heirs with Christ, heirs of the world with the Melchizedekian Priest-King (Rom 4:13; Ps 2:7–9; Heb 5:5–6). In baptism, the Spirit of God was poured out upon them to enable them to do the work of ministry (cf. Acts 1:8). His indwelling makes Christians temples as well as priests (John 7:37–39; 1 Cor 6:19–20). Thus, Christian baptism is priestly ordination in which God the Father declares Christians to be His beloved children, washes away their sins, and pours out His Spirit upon them. By this anointing they are made the younger brothers of Christ (cf. Rom 8:29), and as such they are led to walk in the way of the cross and resurrection as their High Priest Forerunner did (cf. Luke 14:25–27; Rom 6:1–11; Heb 6:19–20). All of the major themes associated with baptism come together when we see that just as Jesus' baptism was inauguration into His ministry as the Melchizedekian High Priest-King, Christian baptism is ordination into the Melchizedekian priesthood, in which Christians serve God and rule with Christ.

Appendix 1

Van Til, Shedd, and God's Self-Consciousness

In chapter 4 of this book, I briefly addressed the difficult question of God's self-consciousness. This appendix offers a fuller discussion of the issue based upon the writings of Cornelius Van Til and William G. T. Shedd. Van Til's view of the Trinity as both one person and three persons has been attacked as a novelty in spite of the fact that, as I have shown before, it is clearly grounded in Charles Hodge.[1] What I hope to show here is that Van Til's doctrine of God also has solid background in the theology of William G. T. Shedd. In particular, Shedd is important for understanding Van Til's view that in God there are three centers of self-consciousness, while at the same time, God's self-consciousness is coterminous with His being. Van Til's contribution was to provide an unusual expression of the doctrine that calls our attention to the unavoidable paradox of God. He was not an "innovator," nor was his theology out of line with Reformed orthodoxy.

VAN TIL'S VIEW OF GOD'S SELF-CONSCIOUSNESS

Although Van Til does not provide a systematic exposition of the subject of self-consciousness, he refers to it constantly, because for Van Til, the question of God's self-consciousness is vital for understanding Trinitarianism.

> For theism the nature of the self-consciousness of God is the thing of most fundamental importance, while for Webb this whole question may be relegated to the sphere of secondary matters.[2]

---

1. Smith, *Paradox and Truth*, 53ff.
2. Van Til, *Survey of Christian Epistemology*, 152.

Though he says that the subject of God's self-consciousness is "of most fundamental importance," it requires considerable searching in Van Til to be able to discover exactly what he believes on the topic and I have not found his view stated fully in any single place. That view seems to be that self-consciousness in God must be predicated both of the divine nature and also of the three persons. Remembering that Van Til refers to God as both one person and also as three persons, I believe it is accurate to say that for Van Til, self-consciousness is essential to personhood.

His most basic statement of his view is found in his work on systematic theology, where he is expounding the Trinity:

> Unity and plurality are equally ultimate in the Godhead. The persons of the Godhead are mutually exhaustive of one another, and therefore of the essence of the Godhead. God is a one-conscious being, and yet he is also a tri-conscious being.[3]

There is some ambiguity here. Does Van Til mean a single self-consciousness that is in some way threefold, which would make self-consciousness an attribute of God's being whether we think of the oneness or the threeness? Or does he mean three distinct self-consciousnesses, which would link self-consciousness to the three persons of the trinity as well as to the being of God? Van Til does not develop his view of God's self-consciousness in a context of explaining Trinitarianism, but in polemic writings where he sets the Reformed view over against his opponents, he repeatedly refers to the topic. So, for example, in arguing against Barth, where the question of the Trinity is central to his concern, Van Til states clearly that there are multiple centers of self-consciousness in God:

> But it is not the second person of the holy trinity who is, for Barth, the subject of the virgin birth. We have seen that Barth's christological principle requires the rejection of the idea of three centers of self-consciousness in God. Nor is his view that of Monarchianism or Patripassianism. His departure from the historic doctrine of the immanent or ontological trinity is much deeper than any found in the history of the ancient church. Barth's conception of the incarnation involves the complete immersion of divinity into pure contingency.[4]

---

3. Van Til, *Introduction to Systematic Theology*, 220.
4. Van Til, *New Modernism*, 277.

> For according to the classical Reformed doctrine of election *there are three centers of self-consciousness in God as he exists in himself.* And it is only one of these "persons," namely, the second person of this God in himself, who becomes incarnate.[5]

> On the other hand when the "second person of the trinity" is conceived of as a mode of divine being rather than as a center of self-consciousness it is possible to maintain the complete hiddenness and therewith the freedom of the revelation of God. Thus the orthodox doctrine of three persons in the ontological trinity would, according to Barth, lead to tritheism.[6]

These affirmations should not be understood as a denial that God is also and at the same time a "one-conscious being." As Van Til also points out in another place:

> We have therefore a two-layer theory of knowledge as we have a two-layer theory of reality. The two stand or fall together. God, we have contended, is self-determinative. He has no non-being over against himself in terms of which he needs or can to any extent interpret himself. He is *omniscient.* He is omniscient because of what he is as a self-sufficient Being. On the other hand we must add that the nature of God's being requires complete exhaustive self-consciousness. *God's Being is coterminous with his self-consciousness.*[7]

Obviously, if God's being is coterminous with His self-consciousness and He is only one being, then He is a single self-consciousness.

The conclusion of the matter, then, is that for Van Til, God is a single center of self-conscious Being and He is also three centers of self-conscious personhood. God's self-consciousness is to be understood along the same lines as His personhood. Just as Van Til can say that God is one person *and* He is three persons, he apparently could have also said—though I cannot find that he actually did say—God is a single center of self-consciousness *and* He is three centers of self-consciousness.

This creates a serious theological problem, however, because ascribing consciousness to the person rather than the nature seems to violate Chalcedon's definition of the relationship of the two natures of Christ. According to Chalcedon, Jesus has a truly divine nature and a truly hu-

---

5. Ibid., 274 (emphasis added).
6. Ibid., 275.
7. Van Til, *Defense of the Faith*, 52 (emphasis in original).

man nature. That means He has a divine consciousness and a human consciousness, for He has a rational human soul. Without a human consciousness, He would hardly be regarded as human. According to Chalcedon, then, consciousness seems to belong to nature rather than person. But in Van Til, consciousness seems to belong to the person rather than the nature, or to both.

Part of the problem in speaking of topics like personhood, personality, nature, being, consciousness, and self-consciousness is that these words—and similar ones—come in a wide variety of philosophical and theological packages. Though we should understand that the meaning of each word must change more or less according to the package it comes in, the history of the uses of these terms is so complex and contorted that even relatively sophisticated writers sometimes compound rather than relieve the confusion. The best one can do is try to define his own use of terms as clearly as he is able.

How the Greek and Latin fathers thought of personhood, nature, and being no doubt differs from how we think about these things. But the problem is not simply one of historical distance. Even in the days when the doctrines of the Trinity and the person of Christ were being debated, discussed, and formulated in dogmatic confessions, the confusion of language was a major obstacle in understanding, as John Frame reminds us:

> But the creedal tradition, too, fails to give a "precise" account of the relations between God's "essence" and his "persons." The Greek term *ousia*, which was used to designate God's essence, was not, in the Greek language, precisely differentiated from *hypostasis*, the term used for the three persons. The choice of these terms was to some extent arbitrary. The church fathers needed a term to designate God's unity, and they chose *ousia*. They needed a term for God's plurality, and they chose *hypostasis*. But there was nothing about either term that uniquely fitted it for its particular task, over against the other. Indeed, the church might have reversed them ("one *hypostasis*, three *ousia*") without loss. The Latin church in the West spoke of one *substantia*, but *substantia* is by etymology and use more interchangeable with *hypostasis* than *ousia*. In English, we can translate both *hypostasis* and *substantia* as "substance." On that account, we can see that in effect the Greeks spoke of God as "three substances" and the Latins of "one substance." Doubtless these choices of terms caused some

misunderstanding. But, from our vantage point, we cannot regard either formulation as unorthodox.[8]

Frame goes on to show that similar confusion applied to the term *prosopon*. Thus, even when the Church had some of its most gifted theologians struggling with the deepest truths of Scripture, the problem of language complicated every discussion. In our day as in theirs, what is important in all these discussions is not the terms being used so much as what is being designated by them.

CONSCIOUSNESS AND SELF-CONSCIOUSNESS DISTINGUISHED

With the difficulties of the subject in mind, I want to consider what seems to me to be a very helpful distinction, one that I have not discovered in Van Til's writings but that might help us to think Van Til's thoughts after him. I am referring to a distinction between *consciousness* and *self-consciousness*—language that appears often in Van Til in many connections. It may be that Van Til was selecting his words with a technical care that I have simply not recognized, but it seems to me that he uses "consciousness" and "self-consciousness" without necessarily making clear distinctions. Though Van Til speaks of God as being a "one-conscious being" and a "tri-conscious being" and also speaks of three centers of self-consciousness, he does not define the relationship of God's consciousness to self-consciousness or to His nature or to the persons. It is not entirely clear how he understands or distinguishes these notions.

In modern psychology and philosophy, debates about consciousness and self-consciousness abound. These debates are complex and often involve issues that Christian theology is not directly concerned with, such as whether or not lions consciously desire to eat deer and therefore have thoughts about their desires.[9] Some seemingly unrelated matters, however, may be more relevant than we appreciate. For example, Philippe Rochat, following Dan Zahavi, argues that a child has a primitive sort of self-consciousness, that is, awareness of the self as a self, from the first weeks after birth, a claim that goes against what is generally un-

---

8. Frame, *Cornelius Van Til*, 69–70.

9. Genaro, *Consciousness and Self-Consciousness*. See the online review by Drew McDermott at http://psyche.cs.monash.edu.au/v4/psyche-4-01-mcdermott.html.

derstood. The fact is that a child cannot pass a "mirror rouge test"[10] until eighteen months or later. Also, a few animals, chimpanzees for example, can pass the mirror test—which means that some regard them as having a "self-consciousness"—but most animals, including gorillas, cannot.

Thus, though some psychologists and philosophers may deny the distinction, drawing a line between consciousness and self-consciousness seems to fit empirical data as well as Christian theological reasoning. We would certainly say, for example, that dogs and cats are conscious, even if they cannot pass criteria for having self-consciousness. Lions are conscious, but it is highly doubtful that they think of themselves as desiring deer steak or as individually distinct from one another and having I-You relationships, even if a lion in captivity can be taught to respond to his name. It seems intuitively obvious that almost all animals that we regard as "conscious," in some sense of the word, lack the capacity for self-reflection and self-awareness that would be considered essential for the most minimal forms of self-consciousness. Small children, severely retarded people, and elderly people with Alzheimer's or similar diseases may lack what most people would recognize as true self-awareness, but we do not doubt that they may be conscious and we distinguish between their conscious and unconscious states.

In Christian theology, William G. T. Shedd argued that a distinction between consciousness and self-consciousness was important for our doctrine of Christ, but he also related it to the doctrine of man, explaining that a normal mature adult has a two-fold consciousness, one related to his physical nature, the other to his spiritual:

> Consciousness is very different from self-consciousness, and the two must be carefully discriminated. In consciousness, the object is another substance than the subject; but in self-consciousness the object is the same substance as the subject. When I am conscious of a tree, the object is a different entity from my mind; but when I am conscious of myself, the object is the same entity with

---

10. A mirror rouge test is a test in which an infant is placed before a mirror to look at himself. Then, a red spot is put on the child's nose and he is placed before the mirror again to see if the child can understand that the reflection in the mirror is himself. By eighteen or twenty-four months, babies recognize themselves in the mirror and will try to touch or wipe the red spot from their noses. It is an interesting example of growing self-awareness. However, psychologists rarely comment on the fact that by sixty many men no longer notice a red nose in the mirror and do very little to correct any other problems they may observe.

my mind. In consciousness, the duality required is in two things. In self-consciousness, the duality required is in one thing.

An animal has consciousness in the sense of sentiency, but not self-consciousness. It is impressed by external objects that are no part of its own substance, but it is never impressed *by itself*. It never duplicates its own unity, and contemplates itself. It is aware of heat and cold, of pleasure and pain, but it is never aware of the subject which experiences these sensations. It cannot refer any of its experiences back to itself as the *person* that experiences them. An animal is not a person, and cannot have the consciousness of a person; that is to say, it cannot have self-consciousness.[11]

A human person, again, is constituted of two natures: an immaterial soul and a material body. A man is not, like the unincarnate Son of God, purely and only spirit. He is composed of two substances or natures, as diverse as mind and matter. And yet there is only one self, only one self-consciousness, only one person. One and the same man is conscious of the spiritual feelings of his soul and of the physical sensations of his body. The former issue out of his immaterial nature, the latter out of his material; both are equally and alike the experience of one person. Having double natures, he has a double form of consciousness or experience, with only a single self-consciousness.[12]

A man can have two forms of consciousness, yet with only one self-consciousness. He can feel cold with his body, while he prays to God with his mind. These two forms of conscious experience are wholly diverse and distinct. He does not pray with his body, or feel cold with his mind. Yet this doubleness and distinctness in the consciousness, does not destroy the unity of his self-consciousness.[13]

This fluctuation of consciousness in the identity of a person is occurring continually in the sphere of human life. When a man says, "I am thirsty," the elements and form of his consciousness, at this particular instant, are furnished from his material and physical nature. When the same man says, with David, "I love the Lord, because he hath heard my voice and my supplications" (Psalm 116:1), the elements and form of his consciousness issue from his mental and spiritual nature. The difference between these two modes of consciousness, the sensuous and

11. Shedd, *Dogmatic Theology*, 169.
12. Ibid., 644.
13. Ibid., 641.

the spiritual, is as real and marked, though it is not as great, as between the divine and the human consciousness in the person of the God-man. And yet there is no schism in the person, or duplication of the person. It is the very same individual man who says, "I thirst," and "I love God."[14]

INCARNATION AND CHRIST'S HUMAN NATURE

Distinguishing between self-consciousness and consciousness is especially significant when we consider the doctrine of Christ. The Chalcedonian formula requires that we believe Christ is one person with two natures. That must mean that our Lord's human nature is different from that of every other child of Adam, for in the case of all of Adam's other descendants there is at least the possibility that each will develop to become a fully self-conscious person.[15]

How is Jesus' human nature different? He was born as a true man with a human nature, but one without the possibility of developing into a human person, for the divine person took upon Himself an impersonal human nature. Unlike every other descendent of Adam, Jesus was a person before He was born as a man. The human nature that He took upon Himself, therefore, was non-personal and could not develop into a person because it was already personalized through union with the divine person. In emphasizing the non-personal human nature, the Reformed view of the doctrine of Christ, following the ancient orthodox theology, is distinct from the Lutheran. However, there has been disagreement within the Reformed camp as well.

G. C. Berkouwer, for example, recounts the debate between Vollenhoven and Hepp. In the doctrine that Christ assumed a non-personal nature, Vollenhoven saw a danger to the true humanity of Christ. After all, if Christ is a true human, how could He not be a human person? From Vollenhoven's perspective, according to Berkouwer, the theologi-

---

14. Ibid., 652.

15. Infants dying at birth do not develop "normal personhood" before death. "Normal personhood" would have to be defined, I suppose, by the example of Adam, who was conscious of himself and his relationship with God. I believe infants dying at birth do become fully self-conscious persons after death. Severely retarded people, too, may never develop self-consciousness, though after death I believe they would. Children and adults who have suffered serious accidents or who contract diseases that cause major brain damage may suffer the loss of the normal self-consciousness that they previously possessed.

cal problem of Jesus having a fully personal human nature arises from the assumption that the human personhood of Jesus would somehow be equal to the divine personhood. That would be Nestorianism, the view that there are two persons who are united morally. Vollenhoven calls for a view in which Jesus' humanity is not non-personal. But he also regards the human personhood as subordinated to the divine, by which he believes he escapes Nestorianism.

Hepp—rightly it seems to me—critiques Vollenhoven's view as semi-Nestorian, for Vollenhoven's view seems to inevitably lead to the conclusion that there are two egos in Christ. But Berkouwer clearly believes that Vollenhoven has legitimate concerns. The problem is that the assertion that Christ assumed an "impersonal" human nature can be read to mean that His human nature was less than fully real, so that He only seemed to be human but was really divine. The danger of docetism, and perhaps also monophysitism, lurks in the formula or can be strained out of it by perverse minds. Berkouwer comes down in favor of Vollenhoven insofar as he believes that we can confess the Chalcedonian Creed without going further. The question of whether Jesus' human nature was impersonal or not can be set aside as speculation. We confront a mystery that we should no attempt to define too far.[16]

In contrast with Berkouwer, the American Reformed world of an earlier time required a clear recognition of the fact that Christ assumed an non-personal human nature as a point of Chalcedonian orthodoxy. Charles Hodge, for example, sets out the Orthodox position:

> The union of the two natures in Christ is a personal or hypostatic union. By this is meant, in the first place, that it is not a mere indwelling of the divine nature analogous to the indwelling of the Spirit of God in his people. Much less is it a mere moral or sympathetic union; or a temporary and mutable relation between the two. In the second place, it is intended to affirm that the union is such that Christ is but one person. As the union of the soul and body constitutes a man one person, so the union of the Son of God with our nature constitutes Him one person. And as in man the personality is in the soul and not in the body, so the personality of Christ is in the divine nature. Both of these points are abundantly evident from Scripture. The former, or the unity of Christ's person, has already been proved; and the latter is proved by the fact that the Logos, or Son, was from all eternity a distinct

---

16. Berkouwer, *Person of Christ*, 313–21.

person in the Godhead. It was a divine person, not merely a divine nature, that assumed humanity, or became incarnate. Hence it follows that the human nature of Christ, separately considered, is impersonal. To this, indeed, it is objected that intelligence and will constitute personality, and as these belong to Christ's human nature personality cannot be denied to it. A person, however, is a *suppositum intelligens*, but the human nature of Christ is not a *suppositum* or subsistence. To personality both rational substance and distinct subsistence are essential. The latter the human nature of Christ never possessed. The Son of God did not unite Himself with a human person, but with a human nature. The proof of this is that Christ is but one person. The possibility of such a union cannot rationally be denied. Realists believe that generic humanity, although intelligent and voluntary, is impersonal, existing personally only in individual men. Although realism may not be a correct philosophy, the fact of its wide and long continued prevalence may be taken as a proof that it does not involve any palpable contradiction. Human nature, therefore, although endowed with intelligence and will, may be, and in fact is, in the person of Christ impersonal. That it is so is the plain doctrine of Scripture, for the Son of God, a divine person, assumed a perfect human nature, and, nevertheless, remains one person.

The facts, therefore, revealed in Scripture concerning Christ constrain us to believe, (1.) That in his person two natures, the divine and the human, are inseparably united; and the word nature in this connection means substance. (2.) That these two natures or substances are not mixed or confounded so as to form a third, which is neither the one nor the other. Each nature retains all its own properties unchanged; so that in Christ there is a finite intelligence and infinite intelligence, a finite will or energy, and an infinite will. (3.) That no property of the divine nature is transferred to the human, and much less is any property of the human transferred to the divine. Humanity in Christ is not deified, nor is the divinity reduced to the limitations of humanity. (4.) The union of the natures is not mere contact or occupancy of the same portion of space. It is not an indwelling, or a simple control of the divine nature over the operations of the human, but a personal union; such a union that its result is that Christ is one person with two distinct natures forever; at once God and man.[17]

---

17. Hodge, *Systematic Theology*, 2:390–92.

The idea that the human nature assumed by the second person must be impersonal certainly expresses well the Chalcedonian doctrine that Christ is one person with two natures and provides obvious contrast to the Nestorian error, which claimed two persons in moral union. However, as we saw in Berkouwer, the idea that the human nature was impersonal may invite doubts about the reality of Jesus' humanity. An impersonal humanity is wholly unique. Can it be a true humanity?

SHEDD ON THE PERSON OF CHRIST

It is in answering such questions that Shedd's approach seems helpful. Shedd's aims to set forth an orthodox view of Christ in psychological detail, while at the same time distinguishing the Reformed view from the Lutheran view. Shedd explains that the human nature assumed by the second person was "not yet personalized."[18] He speaks of it as a "human nature unindividualized, not a distinct individual person."[19] To support his position, he cites John of Damascus, Richard Hooker, John Owen, Francis Turretin, Samuel Hopkins, Van Mastricht, and others.

The distinction between consciousness and self-consciousness helps us, I believe, to understand the notion of Christ as fully human and fully divine. Somewhat simplifying Shedd's view, I think we can say that, one the one hand, Jesus has a double consciousness. His human nature includes a human consciousness, just as it does a human will and mind. Also, Jesus shares the divine consciousness with Father and Spirit, for there is one divine consciousness shared by all three persons of the Trinity. On the other hand, Jesus has one self-consciousness, one ego because He is one eternal person, conscious of His own distinct identity among the persons.[20]

Shedd on the Incarnation

With regard to the incarnation and hypostatic union, Shedd explains at length, making use of the distinction between consciousness and self-consciousness. First, he reviews the hypostatic union of Christ, the union of His two natures in one personal subsistence. This implies the doctrine that Christ has two wills, for without a human will together

---

18. Shedd, *Dogmatic Theology*, 626.
19. Ibid., 627.
20. As will become clear later, Shedd's explanation is somewhat more complicated.

with His divine will, He would not have a real and full human nature. Before the incarnation, the Son of God could only think and feel as God, since "he had only one form of consciousness." Once incarnate, the Son could think and feel either like God or man, since "he has two modes of consciousness."[21]

By explaining the hypostatic union in this language, it seems that Shedd is associating consciousness with nature. Two natures mean two consciousnesses. He further explains the person of Christ and the notion of nature, saying that a Trinitarian person has just one nature, while a normal human has two: his bodily nature and his soul. It may be surprising to some readers to hear that according to Shedd, we may say that a "theanthropic person has three natures: namely, the divine essence, a human soul and a human body." He goes on to explain:

> By the incarnation, not a God, not a man, but a God-man is constituted. A theanthropic person is a trinitarian person *modified* by union with a human nature, similarly as a trinitarian person is the Divine essence *modified* by generation, or spiration. A theanthropic person is constituted, consequently, in the same general manner in which an ordinary human person is: namely, by the union of diverse natures. In the case of a human individual, it is the combination of one material nature and one immaterial that makes him a person.[22]

This might raise questions about God's immutability, but Shedd explains that there is an analogy between the inspiration of the Holy Spirit and the incarnation. Though the Spirit inspires prophets and indwells Christians, this in no way interferes with the intratrinitarian relationships the Spirit enjoys with Father and Son. Also, the Spirit works in our spirits so that we cry out to God, but in so doing, He does not erase or disrupt our self-consciousness. There are two distinct persons cooperating, but only one self-consciousness, that of the Christian, even though, in the case of inspiration, the Spirit dominates and guides the self-conscious prophet. When we consider Christ, there are two forms of consciousness, the divine and the human, but that does not, Shedd says, make two self-consciousnesses.

> The two different modes or forms of consciousness, the divine and the human, in the God-man, do not constitute two self-

21. Ibid., 640.
22. Ibid., 617.

consciousnesses, or two persons, any more than two or more different forms of consciousness in a man constitute two or more self-consciousnesses or persons. A man at one moment has a sensuous form of consciousness, and at another moment, a spiritual form; but he is one and the same person in both instances, and has but a single self-consciousness.[23]

In the quotations above, it is clear that Shedd associates self-consciousness with personhood. He speaks of the two notions as if they were synonymous when he says "two or more self-consciousnesses or persons." Shedd appears to link consciousness with nature and self-consciousness with person. Jesus has two natures and two consciousnesses, but one self-consciousness because He is one person.

Shedd on Nestorianism

Shedd makes the same sort of distinction in discussing Nestorianism. To distinguish orthodox faith from Nestorianism, it is important, Shedd shows, to understand Jesus as having both a divine and human consciousness but having only one self-consciousness. Human nature without a human self-consciousness consists in qualities "such as spirituality, rationality, and voluntariness."

By saying "such as," it seems that Shedd shies away from a definition and settles with a description that he recognizes may be partial. What is important is that the human nature can be unindividualized or nonindividualized. If we reject that possibility, we would have to say that in assuming a human nature, Jesus assumed a human personhood. That would make Christ two persons, subsisting side by side, two self-conscious egos. If and how they would be united becomes the question. The early Church rejected any such view when Nestorianism was pronounced heresy.

Shedd explains the matter at some length:

> Contemplating the mystery of the God-man in this way, as pointed out in Scripture, it is easier to see how only one person and one self-consciousness shall result. If we do not distinguish between nature and person—if we assume that there is no such reality as an unindividualized, or nonindividualized nature, and that we must think of a distinct individual or we must think of nothing—then we must say that the Logos united with a human

---

23. Ibid., 626.

person. This person must be a self-conscious ego, and when united with the second person of the Godhead, which is likewise a self-conscious ego, must still have its own distinct self-consciousness. The God-man, consequently, must be two persons with two *self*-consciousnesses.

But when it is said that the trinitarian person of the Logos assumes into union with himself a portion of human nature, which portion is not yet a distinct ego, but is capable by reason of its properties of becoming one, then the problem of the single self-consciousness of the God-man becomes much easier of solution. The human nature possessing, on the psychical side, all the properties requisite to personality, such as spirituality, rationality, and voluntariness, upon being assumed into union with the eternal Son is thereby personalized, that is to say, individualized. The properties of finite reason and finite will, potential in the human nature, now manifest themselves actively in the single self-consciousness of the God-man. He reasons like a man, thinks like a man, feels like a man, and wills like a man. These are truly personal acts and operations of Jesus Christ. But, unlike the case of an ordinary man, these are not the *whole* of his personal acts and operations. Over and besides these, there is in his complex theanthropic person another and higher series of acts and operations which spring from another and higher nature in his person. He thinks, and feels, and wills like God. And these are also, and equally with the others, the personal acts of Jesus Christ.

In the one person of Jesus Christ, consequently, there are two different kinds of consciousness or experience: one divine and one human. But these two kinds of consciousness do not constitute two persons, any more than the two kinds of experience or consciousness, the sensuous and the mental, in a man, constitute him two persons. There can be two general forms or modes of conscious experience in one and the same person, provided there enter into the constitution of the person two natures that are sufficiently different from each other to yield the materials of such a twofold variety. This was the case with the God-man. If he had had only one nature, as was the case previous to the incarnation, then he could have had only one general form of consciousness: the divine. But having two natures, he could have two corresponding forms of consciousness. He could experience either divine feeling, or human feeling; divine perception, or human perception. A God-man has a twofold variety of consciousness or experience, with only one self-consciousness. When he says "I thirst," and "I and my Father are one," it is one theanthropic ego with a finite human consciousness in the first instance, and an infinite divine consciousness in the second.[24]

In the distinctions that Shedd is making here, we see that Jesus as the second person of the Trinity united with a human nature has a single self-consciousness, a single and distinct ego, that is His as the second person of the Trinity. We also see that He has a divine consciousness because He has a divine nature and a human consciousness because He has a human nature.

Shedd on Monothelitism

This same distinction between consciousness and self-consciousness, that Shedd has so carefully drawn for us, also helps in avoiding the heresy of Monothelitism:

> In opposition to this error, the catholic theologians asserted two wills in order to the completeness of each nature, and met the objection of the Monothelites that there must then be two persons, by affirming that by reason of the intimate personal union of the two natures neither will works without the other's *participation* in the efficiency. If the human will acts, the divine will submits and co-acts. This is the humiliation of the divine. If the divine will acts, the human will submits and co-acts. This is the exaltation of the human. One and the same Christ, therefore, performs the divine or the human action, as the case may be, although each action is wrought in accordance with the distinctive qualities of the will that corresponds with it, and takes the lead in it. Moreover, as the human will in Christ was sinless, there was no antagonism between it and the will of the Logos. This is taught in the words, "Nevertheless, not my will, but thine be done," Luke 22:42. Thus, in any agency of the God-man, although there are two wills concerned in it, a divine and a human, there is but one resulting action. Two wills are not incompatible with a single self-consciousness, even when they are not hypostatically united in one person. The divine will works in the regenerate will "to will and to do," and yet there is not duality in the self-consciousness of the regenerate man.
>
> We have already observed, that the personalizing of the human nature by its union with the Logos is seen in the fact, that the activities of the human nature appear as factors in the single self-

---

24. Ibid., 640–41.

consciousness of the God-man. He is conscious of finite inclination, and finite volitions; this proves that there is voluntariness in the human nature that has been individualized. He is conscious also of finite and limited perceptions, judgments, and conclusions; this proves that there is rationality in the human nature that has been individualized. These two elements or properties of human nature, the rational and the voluntary, are no longer dormant, as they are in all non-individualized human nature, but are active and effective in the one self-conscious person Jesus Christ. And one of them is as necessary as the other, to the wholeness and completeness of the human nature. To omit the will from the humanity, is as truly an error as to omit the reason; and therefore the Monothelites deviated from the true doctrine as really as did the Apollinarians.[25]

Thus in his discussion of the incarnation and hypostatic union and the heresies of Nestorianism and Monothelitism, Shedd consistently views consciousness a property of a nature and self-consciousness a property of a person, enabling us to understand Christ as having two consciousnesses and one self-consciousness. In his exposition of the doctrine of Christ, the distinction between self-consciousness and consciousness is an aid for both understanding and defending the orthodox doctrine. We need to consider next what this means for our understanding of the Trinity.

SHEDD ON THE TRINITY

Now we turn to the doctrine of the Trinity in Shedd and consider the meaning of his distinction between consciousness and self-consciousness. If we apply simply and directly the notion that nature is associated with consciousness and person with self-consciousness, we would assume that Shedd would expound the doctrine of God as one consciousness belonging to the one nature and three self-consciousnesses belong to the three persons. In fact, his view is more complicated.

Shedd on Self-consciousness

To begin with, Shedd argues that the notion of self-consciousness itself, as an idea, is trinal, reflecting the fact that God is a Trinity:

> This analysis shows that self-consciousness is *trinal*, while mere consciousness is only *dual*. The former implies three distinctions;

25. Ibid., 657.

the latter only two. When I am conscious of a tree, there is first, a subject, namely, my mind; and secondly, an object, namely, the tree. This is all there is in the process of consciousness. But when I am conscious of myself, there is first, a subject, namely, my mind as a contemplating mind; there is, secondly, an object, namely, my mind as a contemplated mind; and, thirdly, there is still another subject, namely, my mind as perceiving that these two prior distinctions are one and the same mind. In this trinal process of self-consciousness, there is much more than in the dual process of simple consciousness.[26]

In Shedd's view, man is able to think in this trinal manner because he is the image of the God who is a Trinity:

In the Christian scheme of the trinity, the media to self-consciousness are all *within the divine essence*, and are wholly separate from, and independent of, the finite universe of mind and matter. The divine nature has all the requisites to personality in its own trinal constitution. God makes use of his own eternal and primary essence, and not of the secondary substance of the world, as the object from which to distinguish himself, and thereby be self-knowing, and self-communing. God distinguishes himself from *himself*, not from something that is not himself. This latter would yield consciousness merely, not self-consciousness....[27]

The self-consciousness of God has an analogue in the *self*-consciousness of man, in that the latter also seems to be constituted without the aid of any other substance, or object, than the mind itself.

Shedd on Trinitarian Self-consciousness

When Shedd explains the Trinity, his view sounds in places quite like Van Til. Together with Charles Hodge, he may have been one of the sources behind Van Til's formulation of the Trinity as "God is one person and God is three persons." The following quotations in particular offer insights that might be called "proto-Vantillian":

The personality of the Essence or Godhead, must be distinguished from that of a person in the Essence or Godhead. The existence of three divine persons in the divine essence results in the self-consciousness of the essence. This general self-consciousness of

26. Ibid., 175.
27. Ibid., 173.

the triune Godhead must not be confounded with the particular individual consciousness of the Father as Father, of the Son as Son, of the Spirit as Spirit. The personality of the trinity is not the same as that of one of its persons. The personality of a trinitarian person consists in the fatherhood, or the sonship, or the procession, as the case may be. But the personality of the trinity consists not in any one of these individual peculiarities, but in the *result* of all three. The three hypostatical consciousnesses make one self-consciousness, as the three persons constitute one essence.

The personality of one of the persons, the Greek trinitarians denominated *idiotēs* (individuality); that peculiarity which distinguishes him from the others. The personality of the Son, is his sonship; of the Father, his paternity; of the Spirit, his procession. In this reference, it is preferable to speak of the *personality* of the essence, rather than of the *person* of the essence; because the essence is not one person, but three persons. The personality of the Divine essence, or of God in the abstract, is his self-consciousness, which, as we have seen, results from the subsistence of three persons in the essence and the corresponding trinal consciousness. From this point of view, it is less liable to misconception, to say that God is personal, than to say that God is a person. The latter statement, unless explained, conflicts with the statement that God is three persons; the former does not.

The Divine essence cannot be at once three persons and one person, if "person" is employed in one signification; but it can be at once three persons and one personal Being. The Divine essence, by reason of the three distinctions in it, is self-contemplative, self-cognitive, and self-communing. If there were only a single subject, this would be impossible. Consequently, that personal characteristic by which the trinitarian persons differ from each other cannot be the personal characteristic of the essence, or the entire Godhead. The fatherhood of the first person is not the fatherhood of the Trinity. The sonship of the second person is not the sonship of the Trinity. The procession of the third person is not the procession of the Trinity. If, however, the distinction is marked between *a single* Trinitarian person, such as the Father, or the Son, or the Spirit, and *a triune* person such as the Godhead, it would not be self-contradictory to say that God is three persons and one person; because the term "person" is employed in two senses. In one instance, it denotes the hypostatical personality, in the other, the tripersonality; in one case, it denotes a consciousness that is single, in the other a consciousness that is trinal; in one case the consciousness is simple, in the other complex.[28]

Note that Shedd expresses the problem of speaking of God as one person and three persons very much the way that John Frame does when he explains why Van Til's view does not necessarily involve a contradiction.[29] In Van Til's view, Frame explains, the word "person" is not being used in exactly the same way in saying that God is one person and that He is three persons, so the two statements are not in logical tension. Also, since the equivocation in the use of the word "person" is not part of an argument, there is no violation of the laws of logic. Van Til himself did not provide that perspective, nor did he offer a fuller statement like Shedd's. Why not? Perhaps he assumed his students had already read Shedd and they didn't need it. Or perhaps he didn't think a fuller explanation really helps. It may also be that he disagreed with some of the details of Shedd's explanation here.[30]

Shedd on Sabellianism

Just as in the doctrine of Christ Shedd's view of consciousness and self-consciousness plays a role in refuting heresies, so, also, his understanding of the self-consciousness of the persons is used to set Christian Trinitarianism over against heresies like Sabellianism. In opposing Sabellianism, Shedd expounds his view of consciousness and self-consciousness more fully, leading to a deeper understanding of his view of the Trinity.

> In opposition to this [Sabellianism], the Scriptures teach that the Father, Son, and Holy Spirit are three persons independently and

---

28. Ibid., 177–78.
29. Frame, *Cornelius Van Til*, 68–69.
30. This is pure speculation based on a computer search of Van Til's books, but I find little reference to Shedd in Van Til. John Frame does not include Shedd at all in his book on Van Til, though there are many references to Hodge. Van Til does mention Shedd as one of the great reformed theologians that he consulted for his work on a Christian theory of knowledge, but he does not mention Shedd even once in his syllabus on systematic theology. Since he mentions Charles and A. A. Hodge a total of thirty-seven times, it is remarkable that a Reformed giant like Shedd is left out entirely. Shedd addresses pantheism and deism from a distinctly Trinitarian perspective, which is the kind of approach Van Til would endorse, but his views include philosophical perspectives with which Van Til disagreed, for the few times Van Til does address Shedd's views, it is to criticize his understanding of apologetics and common grace.

irrespective of creation, redemption, and sanctification. If God had never created the universe, but had existed alone from all eternity, he would be triune. And the three persons are so real and distinct from each other, that each possesses a *hypostatical* or trinitarian consciousness different from that of the others. The second person is conscious that he is the Son, and not the Father, when he says, "O Father, glorify thou me," John 17:5. The first person is conscious that he is the Father and not the Son, when he says, "Thou art my Son, this day have I begotten thee," Hebrews 1:5. The third person is conscious that he is the Spirit, and neither the Father nor the Son, when he says, "Separate Barnabas and Saul for the work whereunto I have called them," Acts 13:2. These three hypostatical consciousnesses constitute the one self-consciousness of the Divine essence. By reason of, and as the result of these three forms of consciousness, the Divine essence is self-contemplative, self-cognitive, and self-communing. Though there are three forms of consciousness, there are not three essences or three understandings or three wills in the Godhead; because, a consciousness is not an essence or an understanding or a will. There is only one essence, having one understanding and one will. But this unity of essence, understanding, and will, has three different forms of consciousness: namely, paternal, filial, and spiritual; because it has three different forms of subsistence: namely, the Father, the Son, and the Spirit. If it had only one form of subsistence, as in the Sabellian scheme, it would have only one form of consciousness. It would exist only as a single subject, and would have only a corresponding consciousness. But this would not be a full and true self-consciousness, because this requires the three distinctions of subject, object, and percipient-subject, which are not given in the Sabellian triad.

It must be noticed that the Divine self-consciousness is not a fourth consciousness additional to the three hypostatical consciousnesses, but is the resultant of these three. The three hypostatical consciousnesses are the one Divine self-consciousness, and the one Divine self-consciousness is the three hypostatical consciousnesses. The three hypostatical consciousnesses in their combination and unity constitute the one self-consciousness. The essence in being trinally conscious as Father, Son, and Holy Spirit, is self-conscious. As the one Divine essence is the same thing with the three persons, and not a fourth different thing by itself, so the one Divine self-consciousness is the same thing with the three hypostatical consciousnesses and not a fourth different thing by itself. In this way, it is evident that the three hypostatical consciousnesses are consistent with a single self-consciousness, as the three hypostases themselves are consistent with a single essence. There are three persons but only one essence; and three hypostatical consciousnesses but only one self-consciousness.[31]

When he shows how the doctrine of the Trinity differs from Sabellianism, Shedd offers a fuller statement of his view of God's self-consciousness. Reading his view of the person of Christ, one might have assumed that associating consciousness with nature and self-consciousness with person would lead to a Trinitarian formulation of one consciousness, three self-consciousnesses. Instead, Shedd says that God is one self-consciousness and three hypostatic consciousnesses. Though the notion of a hypostatic consciousness seems to be very much the same thing as a "self-consciousness," he offers a distinction and posits that the self-consciousness associated with the divine essence is the union of the three hypostatic consciousnesses. Or, following the orthodox view of the essence and the persons, we could say that just as the Father is all that God is, so also the Father is the self-consciousness of God. The Son and the Spirit in the same way are the divine essence. The essence of God is not a thing by itself that the three persons share. The three persons are the essence. But each person is wholly and truly God, so that each single person may be said to be identical to the essence of God. Shedd applies the same sort of paradoxical identity to the relationship of the hypostatical consciousnesses and the one self-consciousness of God.

CONCLUSION

For Shedd, the two essential characteristics of personality are self-consciousness and self-determination. This would seem to mean that if God is three persons, He must have three distinct self-consciousnesses. But Shedd's explanation is more complex than this. Since in God, each person is identical to the essence and the essence is the three persons, not a separate "thing," the one essence of God is the one self-consciousness of God, for the essence has no separate existence from the persons. The one self-consciousness of God is realized in the threefold form of the three hypostatical consciousnesses of the three persons.

Shedd is obviously concerned to prevent the influence of deism and pantheism in the doctrine of God. He seeks to show that only

---

31. Shedd, *Dogmatic Theology*, 239–40.

Trinitarianism offers a truly personal idea of God. With that in mind, it is clear that it would have been odd to formulate his doctrine of God's consciousness as "one nature, one consciousness" and "three persons, three self-consciousnesses," for it would invite the misunderstanding that God in His oneness is impersonal. Just as Jesus' human nature was an impersonal nature with a human consciousness, but without the ego or self-consciousness of a human person, God in His unity would be thought of as an impersonal nature. Self-consciousness and personhood would only belong to the three. But, then, who or what would the one God be?

Like Van Til, Shedd insists that God is an absolute personality. He even can accept the formula "God is one person and He is three persons," because the word "person" does not have the same meaning in each case. With regard to God's consciousness, Van Til does not offer a systematic treatment, but his statement that God is a one-conscious being and a tri-conscious being is close to his statement about God being one person and three persons. Shedd's way of stating the relationships between the consciousness and self-consciousness of God is helpful. But I have to admit it seems to me that the distinction between a hypostatic consciousness and a self-consciousness is hard to make. After all, Shedd himself speaks of each of the persons being conscious of Himself in distinction from the other two. Even if we call this "hypostatic consciousness," it is a consciousness of self in relation to others, which we usually call self-consciousness.

I would prefer to state the relation of God's self-consciousness as the one God and His self-consciousness as the three persons along the lines suggested by Van Til: God is one self-consciousness and God is three self-consciousnesses. With Shedd, I would see the single self-consciousness of God as essential to our understanding of God as one and an aspect of what Van Til means when he says God is an absolute person. And of course I agree with Shedd that because the three persons of the Trinity mutually indwell one another perfectly, their threefold self-consciousness *is* a single self-consciousness.

In addition, I believe that the traditional notion that God has one will and one understanding should be conceived along the same lines. We can say, if we wish, that God has one will that comes to a threefold expression, or something similar. In the same way, we must also say that God has one understanding that is common to the three persons. But I think we can express the truth more fully if we also add something like

Van Til's paradoxical formulation for the Trinity, because that allows us to more fully express one aspect of the Bible's teaching.

Consider just a few passages from John:

> Jesus saith unto them, My meat is to do the will of him that sent me, and to accomplish his work. (4:34)

> I can of myself do nothing: as I hear, I judge: and my judgment is righteous; because I seek not mine own will, but the will of him that sent me. (5:30)

> But the witness which I have is greater than that of John; for the works which the Father hath given me to accomplish, the very works that I do, bear witness of me, that the Father hath sent me. (5:36)

> For I am come down from heaven, not to do mine own will, but the will of him that sent me. (6:38)

> And he that sent me is with me; he hath not left me alone; for I do always the things that are pleasing to him. (8:29)

Now it is true that all of these passages could be said to show that the human will of Christ is in conformity to the one divine will of God. But since the incarnation cannot fundamentally change the relationship between the Father and the Son and since the economy reveals the ontology, we would still have to assume that the relationship among the persons of the ontological Trinity was such that the Son in eternity related to the Father in a manner analogous to the relationship of the human Messiah to the Father.

However, the context of the Father sending the Son to accomplish a specific work in this world suggests more. It implies that the Father and the Son had counsel together before the foundation of the world and that the Son cheerfully acquiesced in the will of the Father. If there were no distinction whatsoever between the will of the Father and the will of the Son, it would be more than difficult to imagine the meaning of John's picture of the Father sending the Son into the world to accomplish a specific task and the Son rejoicing to do what the Father commanded.

At least two other well-known verses in John's Gospel make this even more explicit:

> For as the Father raiseth the dead and giveth them life, even so the Son also giveth life to whom he will. (5:21)

> I can of myself do nothing: as I hear, I judge: and my judgment is righteous; because I seek not mine own will, but the will of him that sent me. (5:30)

In both cases here the Greek noun or verb for "will" is used. The Son gives life to whom He wills to give life. He is the final judge of the world who does not seek His own will but the will of the Father. Now these are certainly the actions of Jesus as God. It is His will as the Son that determines who receives life. He seeks the Father's will in judging the world. By the same token, the constant emphasis in John is that the Father sent the Son. The Father's will is repeatedly referred to and we are not to think of that as some "general will of the three persons," but specifically the will of the Father.

Van Til's remarks on the covenantal nature of God are relevant here:

> On the other hand the reality and vitality of the personal and therefore covenant relation within the Trinity, however unharmonizable it is for our logic, with the Oneness of the divine essence also forms the basis for a real freedom of the finite person. God can thus also enter into historical covenant relation with man, and have this relation be real and vital, giving to man a genuine free finite covenant personality. The covenant relation is therefore the only relation in which the finite stands to the infinite, because the eternal persons of the divine Trinity stand to one another in covenant relation. Nor is it a valid objection to say that you cannot speak of a covenant relation within the Trinity because there is only one will in God. The same argument would also destroy genuine personality. There is, to be sure, one will only in the Godhead but here exactly lies the mystery of the relation of the divine persons to the divine substance. So also there is only one will of God with relation to the creature, and yet also there is a threefold relation. The Father is always represented as the ultimate origin of all acts in the temporal world, whether it be in creation or redemption, as he within the divine essence eternally generates the Son, the Son is the second and the Spirit the finisher. God creates the world but he creates through the Logos, and the Spirit broods upon the void to give perfect shape to creation. So in the history of redemption the Father is the architect of the Covenant of Peace, and the Son as the second person of the

Trinity fittingly becomes the son of man, God incarnate, and the Holy Spirit applies salvation to the heart.[32]

For some, it may be preferable to speak of one will in a threefold relation, or something similar, but whatever expression we use, the fact remains that the Father, Son, and Spirit each make choices that are distinct to their persons. The Bible gives us a picture of real persons with real relationships. The Father sends the Son into the world. The Son freely cooperates with the Father's plan. The Spirit, sent by both Father and Son, joyfully submits and obeys.

A similar argument can be made for the understanding of the Father, Son, and Spirit. The Father understands the Son as Father. The Son understands the Father as Son. There is an obvious distinction in their viewpoints and understanding. To deny the distinctions would be to deny the full personality of Father or Son.

Rather than force the biblical teaching into a mold that attempts to explain the paradox away, or at least to reduce it, it seems to me better to say that God has one understanding and that He has three understandings, that He has one will and that He has three wills. We would also have to say that the one understanding *is* the three understandings and that the three are one because the persons mutually and wholly indwell one another. It seems to me better to say that God's will is one and three than to say the one will of God has a threefold expression or something similar, because the one and the many in God are equally ultimate. The one and three sort of formula is just our way of confessing the equal ultimacy of the one and the many without pretending to understand the mystery.

Thus, in speaking of will, understanding, and self-consciousness as one and three, we are simply repeating in different forms the basic doctrine that God is one and three. The main difference between Van Til's paradoxical expression and the traditional expressions—which Van Til does not deny, but only intends to supplement—is that Van Til's way of speaking about God brings into greater emphasis the fact that the one and the three are equally ultimate. This is indeed the paradox of God. We confess the paradox because we have to believe the testimony of Scripture. We have to believe it because the Spirit testifies to us in our hearts that it is true and we have ourselves experienced its truth in our

---

32. Van Til, *Will*, 49.

lives, for Jesus has saved us by His grace and through the work of His Spirit has brought us to the Father.

The paradoxical formula confronts us with the reality that God is incomprehensible. It prevents us from reducing God to rationally digestible formulas that either tend to reduce the three to the one—the general tendency of the Western tradition—or that overemphasize the three—the tendency of the social theories of the Trinity. Worship is the only response we can make to a God who stands before us in such awesome glory and incomprehensible greatness.

> We argue that unless we may hold to the presupposition of the self-contained ontological trinity, human rationality itself is a mirage. But to hold to this position requires us to say that while we shun as poison the idea of the really contradictory we embrace with passion the idea of the apparently contradictory. It is through the latter alone that we can reject the former. It is the self-contained ontological trinity that we need for the rationality of our interpretation of life. It is this same ontological Trinity that requires us to hold to the apparently contradictory. This ontological trinity is, as the larger Catechism of the Westminster Standards puts it, "incomprehensible." God dwells in light that no man can approach unto. This holds of His rationality as well as of His being inasmuch as His being and His self-consciousness are coterminous. It follows that in everything with which we deal we are, in the last analysis, dealing with this infinite God, this God who hideth Himself, this mysterious God. In everything that we handle we deal finally with the incomprehensible God. Everything that we handle depends for what it is upon the counsel of the infinitely inexhaustible God. At every point we run into mystery. All our ingenuity will not aid us in seeking to avoid this mystery. All our ingenuity cannot exhaust the humanly inexhaustible rationality of God.[33]

---

33. Van Til, *Reformed Apologetics*, 885.

Bibliography

Alter, Robert. *The Art of Biblical Narrative*. New York: Basic Books, 1981.
———. *The Art of Biblical Poetry*. New York: Basic Books, 1985.
———. *The World of Biblical Literature*. New York: Basic Books, 1992.
Anderson, James N. *Paradox in Christian Theology: An Analysis of Its Presence, Character, and Epistemic Status*. London: Paternoster, 2007.
Aquinas, Thomas. *Catena Aurea*. Vol. 1, pt. 1, *Gospel of Matthew*. Translated by John Henry Newman. London: J. G. F. & J. Rivington, 1845. Reprint, New York: Cosimo, 2007. Online: http://www.ccel.org/ccel/aquinas/catena1.ii.iii.html.
———. *Summa Theologica*. Translated by the Fathers of the English Dominican Province. 5 vols. Reprint, New York: Cosimo, 2007.
Athanasius. "Four Discourses Against the Arians," trans. John Henry Newman. In Athanasius. *Select Works and Letters*, 303–447. Vol. 4 of *A Select Library of the Nicene and Post-Nicene Fathers of the Christian Church*. Series 2. Edited by Philip Schaff and Henry Wace. Reprint, Grand Rapids: Eerdmans, 1991.
Atkinson, Nigel. "Richard Hooker—Evangelical Theologian of the English Church." *Cross Way* 61 (Summer 1996). Online: http://www.churchsociety.org/crossway/documents/Cway_061_AtkinsonHooker2.pdf.
Augustine. "On Baptism, Against the Donatists," translated by J. R. King. In Augustin. *The Writings Against the Manichaeans and Against the Donatists*, 411–514. Vol. 4 of *A Select Library of the Nicene and Post-Nicene Fathers of the Christian Church*. Series 1. Edited by Philip Schaff. Reprint, Grand Rapids: Eerdmans, 1996.
———. *The Trinity*. Translated by Edmund Hill. Brooklyn, NY: New City, 1991.
Ayres, Lewis. *Nicea and its Legacy: An Approach to Fourth-Century Trinitarian Theology*. New York: Oxford University Press, 2004.
Balentine, Samuel E. *Leviticus*. New York: Westminster/John Knox, 2003.
Barnes, Michel René. "Augustine in Contemporary Trinitarian Theology." *Theological Studies* 56, no. 2 (June 1995): 237–50.
———. "The Fourth Century as Trinitarian Canon." In *Christian Origins: Theology, Rhetoric and Community*, ed. Lewis Ayres and Gareth Jones, 47–67. New York: Routledge, 1998.
———. "The Visible Christ and the Invisible Trinity: Mt. 5:8 in Augustine's Trinitarian Theology of 400." *Modern Theology* 19 (Summer 2003): 329–55. Online: http://www.marquette.edu/maqom/augustine.pdf.
Bavinck, Herman. *Reformed Dogmatics*. Vol. 2, *God and Creation*. Edited by John Bolt. Translated by John Vriend. Grand Rapids: Baker, 2004.
Beardslee, John W., III, ed. and trans. *Reformed Dogmatics: Seventeenth Century Reformed Theology through the Writings of Wollebius, Voetius, and Turretin*. Grand Rapids: Baker, 1965.
Beasley-Murray, G. R. *Baptism in the New Testament*. Grand Rapids: Eerdmans, 1973.

Beiser, Frederick C. *The Sovereignty of Reason: The Defense of Rationality in the Early English Enlightenment*. Princeton, NJ: Princeton University Press, 1996.

Berkhof, Louis. *Systematic Theology*. Grand Rapids: Eerdmans, 1996.

Berkouwer, G. C. *The Person of Christ*. Translated by John Vriend. Studies in Dogmatics. Grand Rapids: Eerdmans, 1954

———. *The Sacraments*. Translated by Hugo Bekker. Studies in Dogmatics. Grand Rapids: Eerdmans, 1969.

Bernard, David K. *The Oneness of God*. Online: Online: http://ourworld.compuserve.com/homepages/pentecostal/One-Top.htm.

Bock, Darrell L. *Luke 1:1—9:50*. Baker Exegetical Commentary on the New Testament. Grand Rapids: Baker, 1994.

Bromiley, Geoffrey W. *Sacramental Teaching and Practice in the Reformation Churches*. Grand Rapids: Eerdmans, 1957.

Bruce, A. B. *Matthew*. In *The Expositor's Greek Testament*, ed. W. Robertson Nichols. 5 vols. Grand Rapids: Eerdmans, 1960.

Bruce, F. F. *The Book of Acts*. 2nd ed. New International Commentary on the New Testament. Grand Rapids: Eerdmans, 1988.

Calvin, John. *Commentary on a Harmony of the Evangelists: Matthew, Mark, and Luke*. Translated by William Pringle. Calvin's Commentaries 16. Grand Rapids: Baker, 1984.

———. *The Institutes of the Christian Religion*. Edited by John T. McNeill. Translated by Ford Lewis Battles. 2 vols. Philadelphia: Westminster, 1960.

Campbell, R. Alastair. "Jesus and His Baptism." *Tyndale Bulletin* 47, no. 2 (Nov. 1996): 191–214.

Caneday, A. B. "Christ's Baptism and Crucifixion: The Anointing and Enthronement of God's Son." *Southern Baptist Journal of Theology* 8, no. 3 (Fall 2004): 70–85. Online: http://www.beginningwithmoses.org/articles/christbaptismcrucifixion.pdf.

Capes, David B. "Intertexual Echoes in the Matthean Baptismal Narrative." *Bulletin for Biblical Research* 9 (1999): 37–49.

Catechism of the Catholic Church. Liguori, MO: Liguori Publications, 1994.

Dabney, Robert Louis. *Lectures in Systematic Theology*. Grand Rapids: Zondervan, 1972.

Dumbrell, William J. *The End of the Beginning: Revelation 21-22 and the Old Testament*. Grand Rapids: Baker, 1985.

Dunn, James D. G. *Baptism in the Holy Spirit*. Philadelphia: Westminster, 1970.

———. *Christology in the Making: A New Testament Inquiry into the Origins of the Doctrine of the Incarnation*. 2nd ed. London: SCM Press, 1989.

Edwards, Jonathan. *An Unpublished Essay on the Trinity: With Remarks on Edwards and His Theology* by George Fisher. New York: Scribner's, 1903.

Eliade, Mircia. *Image and Symbols: Studies in Religious Symbolism*. New York: Sheed and Ward, 1969.

———. *Patterns in Comparative Religion*. New York: Sheed and Ward, 1958.

———. *The Sacred and the Profane: The Nature of Religion*. Orlando, FL: Harcourt, 1987.

Emory, Gilles. *The Trinitarian Theology of St. Thomas Aquinas*. Oxford: Oxford University Press, 2007.

"Esaias." Translated by Moisés Silva. In *A New English Translation of the Septuagint*, eds. Albert Pietersma and Benjamin Wright, 823–75. Oxford: Oxford University Press, 2007.

Fanning, William. "Baptism." In *The Catholic Encyclopedia*. Vol. 2. New York: Robert Appleton, 1907. Online: http://www.newadvent.org/cathen/02258b.htm.
Fee, Gordon. *Pauline Christology: An Exegetical Theological Study*. Peabody, MA: Hendrickson, 2007.
Frame, John. *Cornelius Van Til: An Analysis of His Thought*. Phillipsburg, NJ: P & R, 1995.
France, R. T. *The Gospel of Mark: A Commentary on the Greek Text*. New International Greek Testament Commentary. Grand Rapids: Eerdmans, 2002.
Frye, Northrop. *The Great Code: The Bible and Literature*. London: Routledge & Kegan, 1982.
Gaffin, Richard. *Resurrection and Redemption: A Study in Paul's Soteriology*. Grand Rapids: Baker, 1978. Reprint, Phillipsburg, NJ: Presbyterian & Reformed, 1987.
Gage, Warren. "St. John's Vision of the Heavenly City." PhD diss., University of Dallas, 2001.
Genaro, Rocco. *Consciousness and Self-Consciousness: A Defense of the Higher-Order Thought Theory of Consciousness*. Philadelphia: John Benjamins, 2004.
Gregory of Nyssa. "On the Baptism of Christ: A Sermon," translated by H. A. Wilson. In Gregory of Nyssa. *Dogmatic Treatises, Etc.*, 518–24. Vol. 5 of *A Select Library of the Nicene and Post-Nicene Fathers of the Christian Church*. Series 2. Edited by Philip Schaff and Henry Wace. Reprint, Grand Rapids: Eerdmans, 1991.
Guelich, Robert A. *Mark 1—8:26*. Word Biblical Commentary 34a. Dallas: Word, 1989.
Hart, David Bentley. *The Beauty of the Infinite: The Aesthetics of Christian Faith*. Grand Rapids: Eerdmans, 2003.
Hasel, Gerhard F. *Old Testament Theology: Basic Issues in the Current Debate*. Grand Rapids: Eerdmans, 1991.
Hays, Richard. *The Conversion of the Imagination: Paul as Interpreter of Israel's Scripture*. Grand Rapids: Eerdmans, 2005.
———. *Echoes of Scripture in the Letters of Paul*. New Haven: Yale University Press, 1989.
Hengstenberg, E. W. *Commentary on the Psalms*. Translaged by John Thomson and Patrick Fairbairn. 3 vols. Edinburgh: T. & T. Clark, 1864.
Hesselink, I. John. *Calvin's First Catechism: A Commentary*. Columbia Series in Reformed Theology. Louisville, KY: Westminster/John Knox, 1997.
Hill, William J. *Three-Personed God: The Trinity as a Mystery of Salvation*. Washington, DC: Catholic University of America Press, 1982.
Hodge, A. A. *Outlines of Theology*. Reprint, Grand Rapids: Zondervan, 1973.
Hodge, Charles. *Systematic Theology*. 3 vols. Reprint, Grand Rapids: Eerdmans, 1973.
House, Paul R. *Old Testament Theology*. Downers Grove, IL: InterVarsity Press, 1998.
John Chrysostom. *Homilies on the Gospel of Saint Matthew*. Translated by George Prevost. Vol. 10 of *A Select Library of the Nicene and Post-Nicene Fathers of the Christian Church*. Series 1. Edited by Philip Schaff. Reprint, Grand Rapids: Eerdmans, 1991.
Jordan, James B. "Biblical Theology Basics 2002–2003." Niceville, FL: Biblical Horizons, 2003.
———. "Cosmos Constructors: An Investigation of the Tabernacle-Building Labors of Merari, Gershon, and Kohath as Recapitulations of Genesis One." *Biblical Horizons Occasional Paper* 24 (January 1996).
———. "An Introduction to the Seven-Fold Covenant Model, With Notes on the Five-Fold Covenant Model." *Biblical Horizons Occasional Paper* 29 (June 2002).

———. "King Saul: A New Adam and a New Fall." *Geneva Papers* 2, no.9 and no. 11 (July 1987 and July 1988).

———. "The Production of the New Testament Canon: A Revised Suggestion." *Biblical Horizons* 56 (Dec. 1993).

———. "The Sequence of Events in the Creation Week, Part 1." *Biblical Chronology* 9.10 (October 1997). Online: http://www.biblicalhorizons.com/biblical-chronology/9-10-the-sequence-of-events-in-the-creation-week-part-1/.

———. "The Tabernacle: A New Creation." *Biblical Horizons Occasional Paper* 5 (December 1988; revised June 1993).

———. *Through New Eyes: Developing a Biblical View of the World*. Brentwood, TN: Wolgemuth & Hyatt, 1988. Reprint, Eugene, OR: Wipf & Stock, 1999.

Kavanagh, Aiden. *The Shape of Baptism: The Rite of Christian Initiation*. New York: Pueblo Publishing, 1978.

Keil, C. F., and Delitzsch, F. *The Pentateuch*. Translated by James Martin. 3 vols. in one. Commentary on the Old Testament. Grand Rapids: Eerdmans, 1986. Reprint, Peabody, MS: Hendrickson, 1989.

Kelly, J. N. D. *Early Christian Doctrines*. 5th ed. London: A&C Black, 1977.

Kline, Meredith G. *Kingdom Prologue*. Overland Park, KS: Two Age Press, 2000.

Koehler, Ludwig and Baumgartner, Walter. *The Hebrew and Aramaic Lexicon of the Old Testament*. Revised by Walter Baumgartner and Johann Jakob Stamm. 5 vols. Leiden: Brill, 1996.

LaCugna, Catherine M. *God for Us: The Trinity and Christian Life*. New York: Harper-Collins, 1991.

Leithart, Peter J. *Deep Comedy: Trinity, Tragedy, and Hope in Western Literature*. Moscow, ID: Canon, 2006.

———. *Deep Exegesis: The Mystery of Reading Scripture*. Waco, TX: Baylor University Press, 2009.

———. "'Framing' Sacramental Theology: Trinity And Symbol." *Westminster Theological Journal* 62 (Spring 2000): 1–16.

———. *From Silence to Song: The Davidic Liturgical Revolution*. Moscow, ID: Canon, 2003.

———. *A House for My Name: A Survey of the Old Testament*. Moscow, ID: Canon, 2000.

———. *The Kingdom and the Power: Rediscovering the Centrality of the Church*. Phillipsburg, NJ: P & R, 1993.

———. *The Priesthood of the Plebs: A Theology of Baptism*. Eugene, OR: Wipf & Stock, 2003.

Letham, Robert. *The Holy Trinity: In Scripture, History, Theology, and Worship*. Phillipsburg, NJ: P & R, 2004.

———. *The Work of Christ*. Contours of Christian Theology. Downers Grove, IL: InterVarsity Press, 1993.

Lindsey, Hal. *The Road to Holocaust*. New York: Bantam Books, 1989.

Marcel, Pierre Ch. *The Biblical Doctrine of Infant Baptism*. Translated by Philip Edgcumbe Hughes. Cambridge: James Clarke, 1953.

Mawhinney, Allen. "Baptism, Servanthood, and Sonship." *Westminster Theological Journal* 49 (Spring 1987): 35–64.

McDermott, Drew. *Review of Consciousness and Self-Consciousness: A Defense of the Higher-Order Thought Theory of Consciousness*, by Rocco Genaro. Online: http://psyche.cs.monash.edu.au/v4/psyche-4-01-mcdermott.html

McDonnell, Kilian. *The Baptism of Jesus in the Jordan: The Trinitarian and Cosmic Order of Salvation*. Collegeville, MN: Liturgical Press, 1996.

Meyers, Jeffrey J. *The Lord's Service: The Grace of Covenant Renewal Worship*. Moscow, ID: Canon, 2003.

Moltmann, Jürgen. *The Trinity and the Kingdom*. Minneapolis: Fortress, 1993.

Moo, Douglas. *The Epistle to the Romans*. New International Commentary on the New Testament. Grand Rapids: Eerdmans, 1996.

Moyise, Steve. "Intertextuality and the Study of the Old Testament in the New." In *The Old Testament in the New Testament: Essays in Honour of J. L. North*, ed. Steve Moyise. JSNTSup 189. Sheffield: Sheffield Academic Press, 2000. Online: http://www.chiuni.ac.uk/theology/documents/JSNT.pdf.

Murray, John. *Christian Baptism*. Phillipsburg, NJ: Presbyterian & Reformed, 1980.

Navas, Patrick. *Divine Truth or Human Tradition? A Reconsideration of the Roman Catholic-Protestant Doctrine of the Trinity in Light of the Hebrew and Christian Scriptures*. Bloomington, IN: AuthorHouse, 2007.

Nettles, Thomas J. "Baptism as a Symbol of Christ's Saving Work." In *Understanding Four Views on Baptism*, ed. John H. Armstrong, 25–41. Grand Rapids: Zondervan, 2007.

Neuser, Jacob. *Judaism's Story of Creation: Scripture, Halakhah, Aggadah*. Leiden: Brill, 2000.

Niesel, Wilhelm. *The Theology of Calvin*. Grand Rapids: Baker, 1980.

Nolland, John. *The Gospel of Matthew: A Commentary on the Greek Text*. New International Greek Testament Commentary. Grand Rapids: Eerdmans, 2005.

———. *Luke 1—9:20*. Word Biblical Commentary 35a. Dallas: Word, 1989.

Norton, David. *A History of the Bible as Literature*. 2 vols. Cambridge: Cambridge University Press, 1993.

O'Carroll, Michael. *Trinitas: A Theological Encyclopedia of the Holy Trinity*. Collegeville, MN: Liturgical Press, 1987.

Old, Hughes Oliphant. *The Shaping of the Baptismal Rite in the Sixteenth Century*. Grand Rapids: Eerdmans, 1992.

Pannenberg, Wolfhart. *Systematic Theology*. Translated by Geoffrey W. Bromiley. Vol. 3. Grand Rapids: Eerdmans, 1993.

Pelikan, Jaroslav. *The Christian Tradition: A History of the Development of Doctrine*. Vol. 1, *The Emergence of the Catholic Tradition (100–600)*. Chicago: University of Chicago Press, 1971.

Powell, Samuel M. *The Trinity in German Thought*. Cambridge: Cambridge University Press, 2001.

Poythress, Vern S. "Course Materials on Biblical Hermeneutics." Online: http://campus.wts.edu/homepages/VPoythress/nt123/nt123.html.

———. *In the Beginning Was the Word: Language—A God-Centered Approach*. Wheaton, IL: Crossway, 2009. Online: http://www.frame-poythress.org/Poythress_books/In_The_Beginning/Poythress.IntheBeginning.pdf.

———. "Reforming Ontology and Logic in the Light of the Trinity: An Application of Van Til's Idea of Analogy." *Westminster Theological Journal* 57 (Spring 1995): 187–219. Online: http://www.frame-poythress.org/poythress_articles/1995Reforming.htm.

Rahner, Karl. *The Trinity*. Translated by Joseph Donceel. New York: Crossroad, 1997.
Rumrich, John R. "Milton's Arianism: Why it Matters." In *Milton and Heresy*, ed. Steven B. Dobranski and John R. Rumrich, 75–92. Cambridge: Cambridge University Press, 1998.
Ryle, J. C. *Expository Thoughts on the Gospels: John*. Vol. 1. Reprint, Cambridge: James Clarke, 1975.
Schaff, Philip, ed. *The Creeds of Christendom*. Revised by David Schaff. 3 vols. Reprint, Grand Rapids: Baker, 1983.
Shedd, William G. T. *Dogmatic Theology*. 3rd ed. Ed. Alan W. Gomes. Reprint, Phillipsburg, NJ: Presbyterian & Reformed, 2003.
Simonetti, Manlio, ed. *Matthew 1–13*. Ancient Christian Commentary on Scripture, New Testament Ia. Downers Grove, IL: InterVarsity, 2001.
Smith, Ralph Allan. "Against Karl Rahner's Rule." Online: http://www.berith.org/pdf/against-karl-rahner-s-rule.pdf.
———. *The Covenantal Structure of the Bible*. Tokyo: Covenant Worldview Institute, 2006. Online: http://www.berith.org/pdf/The-Covenantal-Structure-of-the-Bible.pdf.
———. *The Eternal Covenant: How the Trinity Reshapes Covenant Theology*. Moscow, ID: Canon, 2003.
———. *Paradox and Truth: Rethinking Van Til on the Trinity by Comparing Van Til, Plantinga, and Kuyper*. 2nd ed. Moscow, ID: Canon, 2002.
———. *Trinity and Reality: An Introduction to the Christian Faith*. Moscow, ID: Canon, 2004.
Steinmetz, David. *Calvin in Context*. New York: Oxford University Press, 1995.
Stonehouse, N. B. "Repentance, Baptism, and the Gift of the Holy Spirit." *Westminster Theological Journal* 13 (Nov. 1950): 1–19. Online: http://www.the-highway.com/articleNov98.html.
Strauss, Mark L. *The Davidic Messiah in Luke–Acts*. Sheffield: Sheffield Academic Press, 1995.
Talbert, Charles H. *Reading Acts: A Literary and Theological Commentary on the Acts of the Apostles*. New York: Crossroad Publishing, 1997.
Tertullian. "On Baptism," translated by S. Thelwall. In *Latin Christianity: Its Founder, Tertullian*, 669–79. Vol. 3 of *The Ante-Nicene Fathers*. Eds. Alexander Roberts and James Donaldson. Reprint, Grand Rapids: Eerdmans, 1993.
Tranvik, Mark D. "Luther on Baptism." *Lutheran Quarterly* 13 (1999): 75–90. Online: http://www.lutheranquarterly.com/Articles/1999/1-Spring/lut131_05.75_90.pdf.
Tuggy, Dale. "Trinity." Online: http://plato.stanford.edu/entries/trinity/.
———. "The Unfinished Business of Trinitarian Theorizing." *Religious Studies* 39 (June 2003): 165–83.
Turretin, Francis. *Institutes of Elenctic Theology*. Edited by James T. Dennison Jr. Translated by George Musgrave Giger. 3 vols. Phillipsburg, NJ: Presbyterian & Reformed, 1997.
Van Groningen, Gerard. *Messianic Revelation in the Old Testament*. Grand Rapids: Baker, 1990.
Van Til, Cornelius. *The Defense of the Faith*. Phillipsburg, NJ: Presbyterian & Reformed, 1955.
———. *An Introduction to Systematic Theology*. Phillipsburg, NJ: Presbyterian & Reformed, 1974.

Bibliography

———. *The New Modernism: An Appraisal of the Theology of Barth and Brunner*. 3rd ed. Bellingham, WA: Logos Library System, 1997.

———. *Reformed Apologetics*. In *Mimeographed Studies*, 822–967. Bellingham, WA: Logos Library System, 1997.

———. *A Survey of Christian Epistemology*. Phillipsburg, NJ: Presbyterian & Reformed, n.d.

———. *The Will in its Theological Relations*. Bellingham, WA: Logos Library System, 1997.

Von Rad, Gerhard. *Old Testament Theology*. 2 vols. Louisville: Westminster/John Knox, 1962, 1965.

Vos, Geerhardus. *The Pauline Eschatology*. Grand Rapids: Eerdmans, 1966.

Wallace, Ronald S. *Calvin's Doctrine of Word and Sacrament*. Grand Rapids: Eerdmans, 1957.

Waltke, Bruce. *An Old Testament Theology: An Exegetical, Canonical, and Thematic Approach*. Grand Rapids: Zondervan, 2007.

Warfield, Benjamin B. "God's Immeasurable Love." In *The Saviour of the World: Sermons Preached in the Chapel of Princeton Theological Seminary*, 69–87. Cherry Hill, NJ: Mack, 1972.

Webb, Robert L. "Jesus' Baptism: Its Historicity and Implications." *Bulletin for Biblical Research* 10, no.2 (2000): 261–309..

Weinandy, Thomas G. *Athanasius: A Theological Introduction*. Hampshire: Ashgate Publishing, 2007.

Wenham, John. *Redating Matthew, Mark and Luke*. Downers Grove, IL: InterVarsity, 1992.

Wright, N. T. *The Climax of the Covenant: Christ and the Law in Pauline Theology*. Minneapolis: Fortress, 1992.

———. *Jesus and the Victory of God*. Christian Origins and the Questions of God 2. Minneapolis, MN: Fortress, 1996.

Young, John M. L. *By Foot to China: Mission of the Church of the East, to 1400*. Lookout Mountain, GA: Grey Pilgrim Publications, 1991. Online: http://www.aina.org/books/bftc/bftc.htm.